SÖZLER PUBLICATIONS
NURUOSMANIYE CAD. 28/2 CAĞALOĞLU. ISTANBUL TURKEY. TEL. (1) 527 76 07

The Nineteenth Letter
from the Risale-i Nur Collection

THE MIRACLES OF MUHAMMAD

Bediuzzaman SAID NURSI

ISBN 975-432-005-5

The miracles of Muhammed

Translated from the Turkish *Mu'cizat-ı Ahmediye (A.S.M.)*
by The Risale-i Nur Institute of America (1976).
Revised by Şükran Vahide (1994)

New (revised) editions 1995, 1998, 2001

Esenşehir Mah. Natoyolu Cad. Filiz Sok. No:86
34775 Y.Dudullu / İstanbul
Tel: +90 216 540 33 66 Pbx
Fax: +90 216 313 57 31

Printed at: Reyhan Ofset
İstanbul - 2004

www.sozler.com.tr

Contents

Who was Bediuzzaman Said Nursi and what is the Risale-i Nur?

Bediuzzaman Said Nursi was born in eastern Turkey in 1877 and died in 1960 at the age of eighty-three after a life of exemplary struggle and self-sacrifice in the cause of Islam. He was a scholar of the highest standing having studied not only all the traditional religious sciences but also modern science and had earned the name Bediuzzaman, Wonder of the Age, in his youth as a result of his outstanding ability and learning.

Bediuzzaman's life-time spanned the final decades of the Caliphate and Ottoman Empire, its collapse and dismemberment after the First World War, and, after its formation in 1923, the first thirty-seven years of the Republic, of which the years up to 1950 are famous for the Government's repressive anti-Islamic and anti-religious policies.

Until the years following the First World War, Bediuzzaman's struggles in the cause of Islam had been active and in the public domain. He had not only taught many students and had engaged in debate and discussion with leading scholars from all over the Islamic world, but he had also commanded and led in person a volunteer regiment against the invading Russians in eastern Turkey in 1914 for nearly two years until taken prisoner. Furthermore, up to that time he had sought to further the interests of Islam by actively engaging in public life. However, the years that saw the transition from empire to republic also saw the transition from the 'Old Said' to the 'New Said'. The 'New Said' was characterized by his withdrawal from public life and concentration on study, prayer and thought for what was required now was a struggle of a different sort.

After a period of some two years, in 1925, Bediuzzaman was sent into exile in western Anatolia and for the next twenty-five years, and to a lesser extent for the last ten years of his life, he suffered nothing but exile, imprisonment, harassment and persecution by the authorities. But these years of exile and isolation saw the writing of the Risale-i Nur, the Treatise of Light, and its dissemination throughout Turkey. To quote Bediuzzaman himself, "Now I see clearly that most of my life has been directed in such a way, outside my own free-will, ability, comprehension and foresight, that it might produce these treatises to serve the cause of the Qur'an. It is as if all my life as a scholar has been spent in preliminaries to these writings, which demonstrate the miraculousness of the Qur'an."

Bediuzzaman understood an essential cause of the decline of the Islamic world to be the weakening of the very foundations of belief. This weakening, together with the unprecedented attacks on those foundations in the 19th and 20th centuries carried out by materialists, atheists and others in the name of science and progress, led him to realize that the urgent and over-riding need was to strengthen, and even to save, belief. What was needed was to expend all efforts to reconstruct the edifice of Islam from its foundations, belief, and to answer at that level those attacks with a '*manevi jihad*' or '*jihad of the word*.'

Thus, in his exile, Bediuzzaman wrote a body of work, the Risale-i Nur, that would explain and expound the basic tenets of belief, the truths of the Qur'an, to modern man. His method was to analyse both belief and unbelief and to demonstrate through clearly reasoned arguments that not only is it possible, by following the method of the Qur'an, to prove rationally all the truths of belief, such as God's existence and unity, prophethood, and bodily resurrection, but also that these truths are the only rational explanation of existence, man and the universe.

Bediuzzaman thus demonstrated in the form of easily understood stories, comparisons, explanations, and reasoned proofs that, rather than the truths of religion being incompatible with the findings of modern science, the materialist interpretation of those findings is irrational and absurd. Indeed, Bediuzzaman proved in the Risale-i Nur that science's breathtaking discoveries of the universe's functioning corroborate and reinforce the truths of religion.

The importance of the Risale-i Nur cannot be overestimated, for through it Bediuzzaman Said Nursi played a major role in preserving and revitalizing the Islamic faith in Turkey in the very darkest days of her history. And indeed its role has continued to increase in importance to the present day. But further to this, the Risale-i Nur is uniquely fitted to address not only all Muslims but indeed all mankind for several reasons. Firstly it is written in accordance with modern man's mentality, a mentality that, whether Muslim or not, has been deeply imbued by materialist philosophy: it specifically answers all the questions, doubts and confusions that this causes. It answers too all the 'why's' that mark the questioning mind of modern man.

Also, it explains the most profound matters of belief, which formerly only advanced scholars studied in detail, in such a way that everyone, even those to whom the subject is new, may understand and gain something without it causing any difficulties or harm.

A further reason is that in explaining the true nature and purpose of man and the universe, the Risale-i Nur shows that true happiness is only to be found in belief and knowledge of God, both in this world and the hereafter. And it also points out the grievous pain and unhappiness that unbelief causes man's spirit and conscience, which generally the misguided attempt to block out through heedlessness and escapism, so that anyone with any sense may take refuge in belief.

TO CONCLUDE:

The Holy Qur'an addresses the intellect as well as man's other inner faculties. It directs man to consider the universe and its functioning in order to learn its true nature and purposes as the creation and thus to learn the attributes of its Single Creator and his own duties as a creature. This, then, is the method that Bediuzzaman employed in the Risale-i Nur. He explained the true nature of the universe as signs of its Creator and demonstrated through clear arguments that when it is read as such all the fundamentals of belief may be proved rationally.

When this method is followed, a person attains a true belief that will be sound and firm enough to withstand any doubts that may arise in the face of the subtle attacks of Materialism, Naturalism and atheism, or the materialist approach to scientific advances. For all scientific and technological advances are merely the uncovering of the workings of the cosmos. When the cosmos is seen to be a vast and infinitely complex and meaningful unified book describing its Single Author, rather than causing doubt and bewilderment, all these discoveries and advances reinforce belief, they deepen and expand it.

Man's most fundamental need is the need for religion, the need to recognize and worship Almighty God with all His Most Beautiful Names and attributes, and to obey His laws; those manifest in the universe and those revealed through His prophets. In explaining the message of the Qur'an, Almighty God's final Revealed Book, brought and perfectly expounded by His final Prophet, Muhammad (Upon whom be blessings and peace), and Islam, the complete and perfected religion for mankind, Bediuzzaman Said Nursi demonstrated in the Risale-i Nur that there is no contradiction or dichotomy between science and religion; rather, true progress and happiness for mankind can, and will, only be achieved in this way, the way of the Qur'an.

Sözler Publications

* * *

Translator's Note

Since this work addresses non-Muslims as well as Muslims, the word 'God' has been used throughout in preference to 'Allah'. In addition, 'Messenger' denotes 'Resûl'—Turkish. (Arabic: *Rasūl*)

Messengership, 'risâlet'—Turk. (Ar., *risāla*).

Prophet, 'Nebî' (Ar., *nabī*).

Prophethod, 'nübüvvet' (Ar., *nubūwwa*).

Miracle(s), 'mu'cize, mu'cizat' (Ar., *mu'jiza,-āt*). The translators have endeavoured to remain as faithful to the original as possible.

The Nineteenth Letter

This treatise describes more than three hundred miracles. And as it describes the messengership of Muhammad (PBUH), itself a miracle, so is it itself a wonder in three or four respects, proceeding from the miracle of his messengership.

The First: Although it is more than a hundred pages in length and is based on traditions and narrations, it was written in an unusual fashion—in the mountains and countryside, completely from memory, and without referring to any book. It was completed, moreover, in a few days by working two to three hours every day, for a total of twelve hours.

The Second: Despite its length, this work did not cause tedium to its writer, nor does it lack pleasantness for its reader. In fact, it aroused such ardour and enthusiasm in even my apathetic scribes that in these hard and distressing times, as many as seventy copies were handwritten in this neighbourhood within a single year. Those aware of this property of the treatise concluded that this must be a wonder proceeding from the miracle of his messengership (Blessings and peace be upon him.)

The Third: In the copies handwritten by nine different scribes who did not communicate with one another, including one very inexperienced and unaware of 'coincidence'[1]—it was also before we were aware of the phenomenon— the words referring to the Noble Messenger 'coincided' to such a degree throughout the whole of the treatise, and in the fifth part for the words referring to the Qur'an, that any one who is fair to the slightest degree would not consider this to be the result of chance. In fact, whoever observed it definitely concluded that it was a mystery of the Unseen and a marvel proceeding from the miracle of Muhammad (Upon whom be blessings and peace).

The Principles explained at the beginning of this treatise have extreme importance. As for the prophetic Hadiths related, they are accepted as authentic by the authorities on Hadith, and they report the most established phenomena concerning the messengership of Muhammad. Now, to enumerate the merits of this treatise, another treatise of the same length would be needed; we therefore invite those who wish to read it, if only once.

Said Nursi

A REMINDER: In this work, I have related many Hadiths, despite having no books to refer to. Should there be any errors in the wording of the Hadiths, I request that they either be corrected, or be considered as paraphrases of Hadith. For, according to the prevailing opinion, "To relate the meanings of Hadiths is permissible," in which case the narrator puts the meaning of the Hadith into his own words. This being the case, Hadiths with possible errors of wording should be regarded as paraphrases.

1. 'Coincidence' (*tawāfuq*): the unintentional correspondence of letters or words in lines or patterns on one or several pages. (Tr.)

The Miracles of Muhammad (PBUH)

In His Name, be He glorified!
And there is nothing but it glorifies Him with praise.

In the Name of God, the Merciful, the Compassionate.
*He it is Who has sent His Messenger with guidance and the religion of truth to make it supreme over all religion: and sufficient is God as a Witness. * Muhammad is the Messenger of God...* [to the end of the verse][2]

[Since the Nineteenth and Thirty-First Words concerning the messengership of Muhammad (Upon whom be blessings and peace) prove it with decisive evidence, we assign the verification of that side of the subject to those Words. As a supplement to them we will merely show here, in Nineteen Signs, some of the flashes of that great truth.]

■ FIRST SIGN

The Possessor and Master of the universe surely does everything with knowledge, disposes every affair with wisdom,

2. Qur'ān, 48:28-9.

directs everything all-seeingly, treats everything all-knowingly, and arranges everything willing the instances of wisdom, purposes, benefits that are apparent in them. Since, then, the One Who creates knows, surely the One Who knows will speak. Since He will speak, surely He will speak to those who possess consciousness and thought, and those who will understand His speech. Since He will speak to those who possess thought, surely he will speak to mankind, whose nature and awareness are the most comprehensive of all conscious beings. Since He will speak to mankind, surely He will speak to the most perfect of mankind and those most worthy of address. Since He will speak to those who are most perfect, most worthy of address, highest in morality, and who will guide humanity; He will certainly speak to Muhammad, who, as friend and foe alike testify, is of the highest disposition and morality, who is obeyed by one fifth of humanity, to whose spiritual rule half of the globe has submitted, with the radiance of whose light the future of mankind has been illumined for thirteen centuries, to whom the believers, the luminous segment of humanity, renew five times daily the oath of allegiance, for whose happiness they pray, for whom they call down God's blessings and bear admiration and love in their hearts. Certainly, He will speak to Muhammad (Upon whom be blessings and peace) and indeed He has done; He will make him the Prophet, and indeed He has done; He will make him the guide for the rest of humanity, and indeed He has done.

■ SECOND SIGN

God's Most Noble Messenger (Upon whom be blessings and peace) declared his prophethood, and presented to humanity such a decree as the Qur'an of Mighty Stature and such manifest miracles as number, according to the scholars, one thousand.[3] The occurrence of those miracles in their entirety is as certain as

3. al-'Asqalānī, *Fatḥ al-Bārī* vi, 454; Muslim (*Sharḥ:* Nawawī) i, 2.

the fact that he declared himself prophet. In fact, as is shown by the words of the most obstinate unbelievers quoted in various places of the Wise Qur'an, even they could not deny the occurrence of his miracles, but only called them—God forbid!—sorcery, in order to satisfy themselves, or to deceive their followers.

The miracles of Muhammad (PBUH) have the certainty of confirmation by consensus to the hundredth degree. The miracle is the confirmation by the Creator of the cosmos of his declaration of prophethood; it has the effect of the words, "You have spoken truly!" Suppose that you said in the assembly of a ruler, while being observed by him, "The ruler has appointed me to such-and-such a position." At a time when you were asked for a proof of your claim, the word "Yes" uttered by the ruler would sufficiently support you. Or, if the ruler changed his usual practice and attitude at your request, this would confirm your claim even more soundly and more definitely than would the word "Yes."

In the same way, the Noble Messenger (Upon whom be blessings and peace) claimed: "I am the envoy of the Creator of the universe. My proof is that He will change His unbroken order at my request and my prayer. Now look at my fingers: He causes them to run like a fountain with five spigots. Look at the moon: by a gesture of my finger, He splits it in two. Look at that tree: to affirm me and to bear witness to me, it moves and comes near to me. Look at this food: although it is barely enough for two or three men, it satisfies two or three hundred." And he demonstrated too hundreds of similar miracles.

However, the evidences of the veracity of this being and the proofs of his prophethood are not restricted to his miracles. All his deeds and acts, his words and behaviour, his moral conduct and manners, his character and appearance prove to the attentive his truthfulness and seriousness. Indeed, many people such as 'Abd Allah b. Salam, the famous scholar of the Children of

Israel, came to believe merely by seeing him, and said, "No lie can hide in this face, nor fraud be found in it!"[4]

Although many scholars who have researched the matter have concluded that the proofs of the prophethood of Muhammad (PBUH) and his miracles number about one thousand, there are thousands, perhaps hundreds of thousands, of proofs of his prophethood. And hundreds of thousands of men with varying opinions have affirmed his prophethood in an equal number of ways. The Wise Qur'an alone demonstrates a thousand of the proofs of his prophethood, in addition to its own forty aspects of miraculousness.

Since prophethood is a phenomenon of humanity, and hundreds of thousands of individuals who claimed prophethood and performed miracles have lived and passed away,[5] of a certainty the prophethood of Muhammad is superior to all the others. For whatever evidences, qualities, and attributes made prophets such as Jesus and Moses (Upon whom be peace) be known as prophets and were the means of their messengership, they were all possessed in a more perfect and comprehensive fashion by Muhammad (Upon whom be blessings and peace). And since the causes and means of prophetic authority were more perfectly present in the person of Muhammad, this authority was to be found in him with more certainty than in all the others.

■ THIRD SIGN

The miracles of the Most Noble Messenger (Upon whom be blessings and peace) were extremely varied. Since his messengership was universal, he was distinguished by miracles that related to almost all species of creation. Just as the supreme lieutenant of a renowned ruler, arriving with many gifts in a city

4. *Tirmidhī*, Qiyāma 42; Ibn *Māja*, Iqāma 174; Aṭ'ima 1; *Dārimī*, Ṣalāt 156; Isti'dhān 4; *Musnad* v, 451.

5. *Musnad* v, 266; Valiyyuddīn Tabrīzī, *Mishkāt al-Maṣābīḥ* iii, 122; Ibn al-Qayyim al-Jawzī, *Zād al-Ma'ād* (*Taḥqīq*: al-Arnavūd) i, 43-44.

where various peoples live, will be welcomed by a representative of each people, who acclaims him and bids him welcome in his own language; so too when the supreme Lieutenant of the Monarch of Pre-Eternity and Post-Eternity honoured the universe by coming as an envoy to the inhabitants of the earth, and brought with him the light of truth and spiritual gifts sent by the Creator of the universe, which were connected to the truths of the whole universe, each species of creation —from water, rocks, trees, animals and human beings to the moon, the sun and the stars— each welcomed him and acclaimed his prophethood, each in its own language, and each bearing one of his miracles.

Now it would require a voluminous work to mention all his miracles. As punctilious, investigating scholars have written many volumes concerning the proofs of his prophethood, here we will briefly point out only the general categories into which fall the miracles that are definite and accepted as accurate reports.

The evidences of the prophethood of Muhammad (Upon whom be blessings and peace) fall into two main categories:

The First is called *irhasat* and includes the paranormal events that happened at the time of his birth, or before his prophetic mission.

The Second group pertains to all the remaining evidences of his prophethood, and contains two subdivisions:

The first are those wonders that were manifested after his departure from this world in order to confirm his prophethood, and **the second,** those that he exhibited during the era of his prophethood. The latter has also two parts:

The first, the evidences of his prophethood that became manifest in his own personality, his inner and outer being, his moral conduct and perfections, and **the second**, the miracles manifested in the outer world. The last part again has two branches:

One, those concerning the Qur'an and spirituality, and **the other,** those relating to materiality and the universe. This last branch is again divided into two categories:

The first involves the paranormal happenings that occurred during his mission either to break the stubbornness of the unbelievers, or to augment the faith of the believers. This category has twenty different sorts, such as the splitting of the moon, the flowing of water from his fingers, the satisfying of large numbers with a little food, and the speaking of trees, rocks and animals. Each of these sorts has also many instances, and thus has, in meaning, the strength of confirmation by consensus. As for **the second category**, this includes events lying in the future that occurred as he had predicted upon God's instructions. Now, starting from the last category, we will summarize a list of them.[6]

■ FOURTH SIGN

There is no limit to the reports God's Most Noble Messenger (Upon whom be blessings and peace) gave concerning the Unseen through the instruction of the One All-Knowing of the Unseen. As we have mentioned the types of these reports in the Twenty-Fifth Word, which is about the miraculousness of the Qur'an, and to a degree explained and proved them, we now refer to that Word the explanation of the information he gave concerning the Unseen about past times and prophets, as well as truths concerning Divinity, the universe, and the hereafter, and will point out a few of his many correct predictions concerning his Companions, his Family and his community. But first, for a complete understanding of the subject, we will state Six Principles by way of an introduction.

---

6. Unfortunately, I could not write as I had intended. Without choice, I wrote as my heart dictated, and I could not completely conform to the order of this classification.

FIRST PRINCIPLE

All the states and acts of the Noble Messenger (Upon whom be blessings and peace) testified to his veracity and prophethood, but not all of them had to be miraculous. For God Almighty sent him in the form of a human being so that he might be a guide and leader to human beings in their social affairs, and in the acts and deeds by means of which they attain happiness in both worlds; and so that he might disclose to human beings the wonders of Divine art and His disposive power that underlie all occurrences and are in appearance customary, but in reality are miracles of Divine power. If, then, he had abandoned the human state in his acts and become extraordinary in all aspects, he could not have been a leader, or have instructed human beings with his acts, states, and conduct. He was, indeed, honoured with paranormal phenomena in order to prove his prophethood to obstinate unbelievers, and from time to time performed miracles as the need arose. But his miracles never occurred in such an obvious fashion as would have compelled everyone to believe, whether willingly or unwillingly. For, in accordance with the purpose of the examinations and trials that man is to undergo, the way must be shown to him without depriving him of his free will: the door of the intelligence must remain open, and its freedom must not be snatched from its hand. But if miracles had occurred in so apparent a way, intelligence would have had no choice; Abu Jahl would have believed as did Abu Bakr, coal would have had the value of diamonds, and no purpose would have remained for testing and accountability.

It is a source of amazement that while thousands of men of different character came to believe through observing a single of his miracles, a single proof of his prophethood, or a word of his, or through merely seeing his face, some wretches are nowadays going astray, as if those thousands of proofs of his prophethood were not sufficient evidence, although they all have come down to us through authentic transmission and with certain proofs, and have caused many thousands of exacting scholars and thinkers and different men to accept faith.

SECOND PRINCIPLE

God's Most Noble Messenger (Upon whom be blessings and peace) was a human being; hence he acted like a human being. He was also a messenger and prophet, and with regard to his messengership, he was an interpreter and an envoy of Almighty God. His messengership was based upon Revelation, which is of two kinds:

The First is explicit Revelation. In this case, the Noble Messenger is merely an interpreter and announcer, with no share in the content. The Qur'an and some Sacred Hadith are included in this kind of Revelation.

The Second is implicit Revelation. The essence and summary of this is also based on Revelation or inspiration, but its explanation and description were left to the Messenger. When he explained and described such Revelation, sometimes he again relied on Revelation, or on inspiration, or sometimes he spoke in terms of his own insight. And, when he resorted to his own interpretation, he either relied on the perceptive power given him on account of his prophetic mission, or he spoke as a human being and conformably to usage, custom and the level of common comprehension.

Thus, all the details of every Hadith are not necessarily derived from pure revelation, nor should the lofty marks of messengership be sought in such thoughts and transactions of his as are required by his participation in the human state. Since some truths were revealed to him in a brief and abstract form, and he himself described them in the light of his insight and according to common comprehension, the metaphors and allusions in his descriptions sometimes may need explanation, or even interpretation. There are, indeed, some truths that the human mind can grasp only by way of comparison. For example, once in the presence of the Prophet, a loud noise was heard. The Prophet said, "This is the noise of a rock that has been rolling down for seventy years and has now reached the lowest depths of Hell."[7] An hour later the news came that a famous dissembler who had recently turned seventy years old had died and gone to Hell, thus explaining the event the Prophet had described by means of an eloquent comparison.

THIRD PRINCIPLE

If any related tradition is in the form of *tawatur*,[8] it is indisputable. There are two kinds of this sort of report: one is those reports about which there is 'explicit consensus,' the other is 'consensus in meaning.' The latter is also of two kinds: the first includes those concerning which the consensus is implied 'by silence.' For example, if a man in a community relates an incident in front of his people and the listeners do not contradict him, that is, they respond to him by keeping silent, this implies their acceptance of the report. In particular, if that community is such as will not acccept any error, as will consider any lie reprehensible, as is ready to criticize and, in addition, shows an interest in the reported incident, the silence of that community testifies strongly to the incident having occurred.

The second kind of 'consensus in meaning' is that which occurs when different people relate a particular incident, for example, one *okka*[9] of food fed two hundred people, in different versions—one person describes in one way, another in another way, and another in yet another way, but all are unanimously agreed on the occurrence of the incident. Thus, the occurrence of this certain incident is supported by 'consensus in meaning,'

7. *Muslim*, Janna 31; *Musnad* iii, 341, 346.

8. *Tawātur* is the kind of report that is transmitted by numerous authorities and about which there is no room for doubt, that is, a report concerning which there is a consensus of opinion. (Tr.)

9. One *okka* was the equivalent of 2.8 lbs. or 1,300 gr. (Tr.)

and is definite; its actual occurrence is not harmed by differences in detail. But apart from this, there are times when a report supplied by a single person expresses the certainty of consensus, under certain conditions. And it also sometimes happens that single report expresses certainity when supported by other, outside evidences.

Most of the reports concerning the miracles and the evidences of the prophethood of the Most Noble Messenger (Upon whom be blessings and peace) that have come down to us are either of the category of 'explicit consensus,' or 'consensus in meaning,' or 'consensus implied by silence.' As for the others, although they are the report of a single person, they also have the certainty of 'consensus' as they have received the acceptance of the meticulous authorities on Hadith. Of such meticulous authorities were those geniuses who were called *al-Hafiz*, who had committed to memory at least 100,000 Hadiths, who offered for fifty years their morning prayer with the ablution of the night prayer, and who produced the six accurate books of Hadith headed by those of Bukhari and Muslim. Without doubt, any report scrutinized and accepted by them cannot fall short of the certainty of 'consensus.' For they acquired such intimacy with the Hadiths of the Noble Prophet (Upon whom be blessings and peace) and became so familiar with his exalted style and manner that they could spot at first sight a single false Hadith among a hundred reports, and would reject it, saying, "This cannot be a prophetic tradition; it does not have his wording." Since they were able to recognize the precious quality of the Hadith, like an expert jeweller, there was no possibility of their confusing any other word with that of the Prophet. Some researchers, however, such as Ibn al-Jawzi, went to such excesses in their criticism as to regard many accurate traditions as false.[10] Nevertheless, this does not mean that the meaning of

10. 'Abd al-Ḥayy al-Laknawī, *al-Ajwibat al-Faḍīla* (*Taḥqīq*: Abū Ghuḍḍa) 80, 120, 163, 170.

every false wording is wrong; rather it means that the wording itself is not that of the Prophet.

Question: What is the benefit of citing the chain of transmission of a tradition so that even if it is not called for in the case of a well-known incident they say: "So-and-so informed so-and-so, etc."?

Answer: Its benefits are many, and one is that the citing of the chain shows the concurrence of the truthful, reliable and exacting scholars of Hadith and the unanimity of the discerning authorities whose names are included; each of the scholars and authorities signs, as it were, for the accuracy of the tradition, and places his seal on it.

Question: Why were the miraculous events not transmitted through numerous chains in the form of 'consensus' and with as great emphasis as the basic injunctions of the Sacred Shari'a?

Answer: Because the majority of the injunctions of the Shari'a are needed by most people at most times, for they all are applicable to each individual, like an obligation incumbent on all. But not everyone needs to know of every miracle; even if he does, it suffices him to hear it only once. It is, in fact, like the kind of obligation the observance of which by some will absolve the rest; it is quite enough for miracles to be known only to some. For this reason, even if the occurrence and reality of a miracle ten times more certain than that of an injunction of the Shari'a, it will still come to us through one or two narrators, whereas the injunction is narrated by ten or twenty persons.

FOURTH PRINCIPLE

The future events that the Most Noble Messenger (Upon whom be blessings and peace) predicted were not isolated incidents; he rather predicted general and recurring events in a particular way. That is, in each such report, he displayed a different aspect of one phenomenon out of several. This is why when the narrator combines these different aspects, they may seem at variance with reality. There are, for example, varying narrations concerning the Mahdi, each with different details and descriptions. However, as was explained in a section of the Twenty-Fourth Word, the Noble Messenger gave the tidings, relying on Revelation, of a Mahdi who would come in every century to preserve the morale of the believers, help them not to fall into despair in the face of disasters, and link the hearts of the believers with the people of the Prophet's Family, who constitute a luminous chain in the world of Islam. Similar to the Great Mahdi who is promised to come at the end of time, one Mahdi from the Prophet's Family, or more, has been found in every century. Indeed, one of them, found among the 'Abbasid Caliphs who were descendants of the Prophet's Family, was found to have many of the characteristics of the Great Mahdi. In this way the attributes of the Mahdi's deputies and of the spiritual poles who were Mahdis who were to precede the Great Mahdi and were samples and forerunners of him, were confused with the attributes of the Great Mahdi himself, and the narrations concerning him were seen to conflict with one another.

FIFTH PRINCIPLE

Since none other than God knows the Unseen, the Noble Messenger (Upon whom be blessings and peace) too could not know it himself. Instead, God Almighty communicated to him the tidings of the Unseen, and he made them known. And since God Almighty is All-Wise and Compassionate, His wisdom and mercy require that most of the matters of the Unseen be veiled or obscure. For in this world events disagreeable to human beings are numerous; prior knowledge of their happening would be painful. It is for this reason that death and the appointed hour of death are left obscure, and the calamities that are to befall human beings remain behind the veil of the Unseen.

Again, as a result of His wisdom and mercy, God Almighty did not entirely or in detail inform His Messenger about the dreadful events that would befall his Family and Companions after his demise, in order not to hurt his extremely tender compassion for his community and his firm affection for his Family.[11] For certain Divine purposes, He made some of these significant events known to him, but not in all their awesomeness. As for pleasant events, He communicated them to the Messenger sometimes in outline and sometimes in detail, and the Messenger in turn made them known to his Companions. Thus those tidings were accurately transmitted to us by the scholars of Hadith who were at the height of piety, justice, and truthfulness, and who feared very much the warning of the Hadith, *Whoever knowingly tells a lie concerning me should prepare for a seat in Hell,*[12] and that of the Qur'anic verse,

> *Who, then does more wrong than the one who utters lie concerning God?*[13]

SIXTH PRINCIPLE

Although some qualities and aspects of the Most Noble Messenger (Upon whom be blessings and peace) have been described in books of history and biography, most of those qualities relate to his humanness. But in reality, the spiritual personality and the sacred nature of this blessed being are so exalted and luminous that the qualities described in books fall short of his high stature. For according to the rule, "The cause is like the doer," everyday, even at this moment, the amount of the worship performed by all his community is being added to the

---

11. For example, he was not made to know about 'Ā'isha's taking part in the Battle of the Camel so that his deep love and affection toward her (May God be pleased with her) would not be hurt. He said, in fact, to his wives: "I wish I knew which one of you will be involved in that incident." Later he was apparently made aware of it to a slightly greater extent, as he once said to 'Alī (May God be pleased with him): "Some event will take place between you and 'Ā'isha."*

* *Musnad* vi, 393; Bayhaqī, *Dalā'il al-Nubūwwa* vi, 410; al-Haythamī, *Majma' al-Zawā'id* vii, 234.

12. *Bukhārī*, 'Ilm 38; Janā'iz 33; Anbiyā' 50; Adab 109; *Muslim*, Zuhd 72; *Abū Dā'ūd*, 'Ilm 4; *Tirmidhī*, Fitan 70; 'Ilm 8, 13; Tafsīr 1; Manāqib 19; *Ibn Māja*, Muqaddima 4; *Dārimī*, Muqaddima 25, 46; *Musnad* i, 70, 78; ii, 159, 171; iii, 13, 44; iv, 47, 100; v, 292.

13. Qur'ān, 39:32.

record of his perfections. He is also everyday the object of the countless supplications of his vast community, in addition to being the object of infinite Divine mercy in an infinite fashion and with an infinite capacity to receive. He is, indeed, the result and the most perfect fruit of the universe, the interpreter and the beloved of the Creator of the cosmos. Hence his true nature in its entirety, and the truth of all his perfections, cannot be contained in the human qualities recorded in books of history and biography. Certainly, the stature of a blessed being with the Archangels Gabriel and Michael as two aides-de-camp at his side in the Battle of Badr,[14] is not to be found in the form of a person bargaining with a beduin in the marketplace over the price of a horse, bringing forth Hudhayfa as his sole witness.[15]

In order not to proceed in error, one should raise his head beyond the ordinary qualities of the Prophet (PBUH) that pertain to his participation in the human state, and behold instead his true nature and luminous stature that pertain to the rank of messengership. Otherwise, one will either show him irreverence, or instil doubts in oneself. Heed the following comparison for an understanding of this mystery.

Suppose that a seed of the date-tree was planted under the earth, has sprouted and become a large, fertile tree, and is still continuing to grow taller and broader. Or that the egg of a peacock was incubated, a chick was hatched from it and became a beautifully adorned peacock gilded all over with the imprint of Power, and is still growing bigger and more beautiful. Now, there exist qualities, properties and precisely balanced elements that belong to the seed and the egg, but are not as great and significant as those of the tree and the bird that emerge from them. So, while describing the qualities of the tree and the bird together with those of the seed and the egg, one should turn one's attention from the seed to the tree, and from the egg to the

14. *Bukhārī*, Maghāzī 11; Aḥmad al-Bannā al-Sā'atī, *al-Fatḥ al-Rabbānī* xxi, 26.
15. *Abū Dā'ūd*, 'Aqdiyya 20; *Musnad* v, 215.

bird, so that one's reason may find the description acceptable. Otherwise, if you claim: "I have obtained thousands of dates from a seed," or, "This egg is the king of all birds," you will invite others to contradict and deny your words.

The humanness of God's Messenger may be likened to the seed or egg, and his essential nature, illumined with the function of messengership, to the Tuba-tree of Paradise, or to the birds of Paradise. His essential nature is, moreover, continually moving to greater perfection. That is why, when you think of the man who disputed in the market with a beduin, you should also turn the eye of imagination to that luminous being who, riding the *Rafraf*, leaving Gabriel behind, reached the *Distance of Two Bowstrings.*[16] Otherwise you will either be disrespectful toward him, or fail to convince the evil-commanding soul.

■ FIFTH SIGN

We will cite in this Sign a few examples of Hadiths concerning the matters of the Unseen.

It has come down to us through an authentic chain of transmission at the degree of 'consensus,' that the Noble Prophet declared from the pulpit in the presence of his Companions: "*This my grandson Hasan is a master of men by means of whom God will reconcile two great groups.*"[17]

Forty years later, when the two largest armies of Islam met each other, Hasan made peace with Mu'awiya, and thus proved the prophecy of his noble grandfather (Upon whom be blessings and peace).

According to another authentic narration, the Prophet said to 'Ali: "*You will fight the perfidious, the just, and the deviator,*"[18]

16. See: Qur'ān, 53:9.

17. *Bukhārī*, Fitan 20; Sulḥ 9; Faḍā'il Aṣḥāb al-Nabī 22; Manāqib 25; *Dārimī*, Sunna 12; *Tirmidhī*, Manāqib 25; *Nasā'ī*, Jum'a 27; *Musnad* v, 38, 44, 49, 51; 'Abd Allāh Kattānī, *Naẓm al-Mutanāthir* 125.

18. al-Ḥākim, *al-Mustadrak* iii, 139, 140; al-Haythamī, *Majma' al-Zawā'id* vii, 138; Bayhaqī, *Dalā'il al-Nubūwwa* vi, 414.

thus predicting the battles of the Camel and Siffin, and that fought against the Kharijites.

He again said to 'Ali, when he was displaying love for Zubayr: "*He will fight against you, but will be in the wrong.*"[19]

He also said to his wives: "*One among you will take charge of a rebellion; many around her will be killed;*"[20] "*and the dogs will bark all around her.*"[21]

All these certain and authentic traditions are the proven predictions of the struggles of 'Ali against 'A'isha, Zubayr and Talha during the Battle of the Camel, against Mu'awiya at Siffin, and against the Kharijites at Harawra and Nahrawan.

The Prophet (PBUH) also informed 'Ali about a man who would stain 'Ali's beard with the blood of his own head.[22] 'Ali knew the man; it was 'Abd al-Rahman b. Muljam the Kharijite.

He also mentioned a man marked with a peculiar sign, Dhu'l-Thudia. When the man was found among the dead of the Kharijites, 'Ali showed him as a proof of the rightness of his cause, declaring at the same time the miracle of the Prophet.[23]

According to another authentic tradition related by Umm Salama and others, the Noble Prophet also predicted that Husayn would be killed at Taff (Karbala).[24] Fifty years later the painful event took place as predicted.

He also repeatedly predicted that after his demise, his Family would face death, calamities, and exile, and gave some details.[25] What he had predicted later came true exactly.

---

19. Ibn Kathīr, *al-Bidāya wa'l-Nihāya* vi, 213; al-Ḥākim, *al-Mustadrak* iii, 366, 367; 'Alī al-Qārī, *Sharḥ al-Shifā'* i, 686, 687.

20. al-'Asqalānī, *Fatḥ al-Bārī* xiii, 45.

21. *Musnad* vi, 52, 97; Ibn Ḥibbān, *Ṣaḥīḥ* viii, 258 no: 6697; al-Ḥākim, *al-Mustadrak* iii, 120.

22. al-Ḥākim, *al-Mustadrak* iii, 113; *Musnad* i, 102, 103, 148, 156.

23. *Bukhārī*, Manāqib 25; Adab 95; Istitāba 7; *Muslim*, Zakāt 148, 156, 157; *Abū Dā'ūd*, Sunna 28; *Musnad* iii, 56, 65.

24. Imām Aḥmad, *Faḍā'il al-Ṣaḥāba* 1357; *Musnad* i, 85; iii, 242, 256; vi, 294; 'Alī al-Qārī, *Sharḥ al-Shifā'* i, 702.

25. *Ibn Māja*, Fitan 34.

In this connection, a question may be asked: although 'Ali, with his extraordinary bravery and profound knowledge in addition to his kinship to God's Messenger, greatly deserved to be Caliph, why did he not precede others in holding the Caliphate, and why did Islam experience such disorder during his Caliphate?

Answer: A great spiritual pole from the Prophet's Family is reported as saying: "The Noble Messenger (Upon whom be blessings and peace) had desired that 'Ali be Caliph, but it was made known to him from the Unseen that the will of God Almighty was different. He then abandoned his desire, submitting himself to God's will."

One of the reasons why God's will was different could have been that after the demise of the Prophet (PBUH), when the Companions were more than ever in need of alliance and unity, if 'Ali had taken the leadership, this would most probably have aroused in many persons and tribes a tendency to compete, because of his uncompromising nature, and fearless, ascetic, heroic, and independent character, and widely known courage —as was the case during his Caliphate— and divisions among the believers would have resulted.

Another reason for the delay of 'Ali's Caliphate is the following: at the time of his Caliphate, the Muslim community, which had rapidly developed through the intermingling of many tribes and peoples, possessed such traits as reflected the opinions of the seventy-three sects that the Noble Prophet (PBUH) had predicted would evolve in due time.[26] Therefore, in the face of such disturbances, someone was then needed with the wondrous strength, courage, respectability and sagacity of 'Ali, someone having the force of the respected Hashimites and the Prophet's Family, so that he could resist the sedition. And indeed he did so, in a fashion conformable to the prediction of

26. See, Page 40 fn. 60

the Prophet, who had said to him: "*I have fought for the revelation of the Qur'an; you will fight for its explanation.*"[27]

A further reason for this delay is that without 'Ali, worldly rule would most probably have caused the Umayyad kings to go completely astray. However, being confronted with 'Ali and the Prophet's Family, and having to appear equal to them and to preserve their prestige before the Muslims, all the leaders of the Umayyad dynasty, even if not they themselves, in any event due to their encouragement and recommendations, their followers and supporters, worked with all their strength to preserve and disseminate the truths of Islam and belief and the Qur'anic decrees. Thus, they produced thousands of punctilious interpreters of the Law, and authorities on Hadith, and saints and purified scholars. Had they not been faced by the strong religiosity, sainthood, and virtuousness of 'Ali and of the Prophet's Family, it is possible that the Umayyads would from the very beginning have gone completely astray, as happened at the end of their rule, and as did the 'Abbasids.

It might also be asked: "Why did the Islamic Caliphate not remain in the Prophet's Family, since they were the most deserving and fitted for it?"

The Answer: Worldly rule is deceptive, and the Prophet's Family had been appointed to preserve the decrees of the Qur'an and the truths of Islam. Not to be deceived by power, the one who was to hold it and the Caliphate had to be as sinless as a prophet, or as purehearted and unworldly as the Four Rightly Guided Caliphs, 'Umar b. 'Abd al-'Aziz and the Mahdi of the 'Abbasids. In fact, the Caliphate of the Fatimid state which was founded in the name of the Prophet's Family in Egypt, and the rule of the Almohads in Africa, and the Safavid state in Iran showed that worldly rule was not suitable for the

27. al-Haythamī, *Majma' al-Zawā'id* vi, 244; *Musnad* iii, 31, 33, 82; Ibn Ḥibbān, *Ṣaḥīḥ* ix, 46 no: 6898.

Prophet's Family, for it caused them to neglect their primary duty, the protection of religion and the service of Islam. When, on the other hand, they gave up worldly rule, they brilliantly and most successfully served Islam and the Qur'an.

Now see: of the poles of sainthood descended from Hasan, especially the Four Poles[28] and above all 'Abd al-Qadir Gilani, and the Imams of Husayn's line, especially Zayn al-'Abidin and Ja'far al-Sadiq, each became like a spiritual Mahdi, dispelled wrongdoing and spiritual darkness, and spread the light of the Qur'ān and the truths of belief. And in so doing each showed he was a true heir of his noble forefather.

It may then be asked: "What was the wisdom in the awesome and bloody dissension that was visited on blessed Islam and the luminous Age of Bliss, and what aspect of mercy was there in it, for they did not deserve such distress?

The Answer: Just as a heavy spring rainstorm stirs into action the potentialities of all the varieties of plants, seeds, and trees, and causes them to develop, so each blossoms in its particular way and performs the duties inherent in its nature, so too, the dissension visited on the Companions and their successors stirred their potentialities into action, which were all different and like seeds; it spurred them on. Exclaiming, "Islam is in danger! Fire! Fire!", it put fear into all the groups and made them hasten to protect Islam. According to its abilities, each of the groups shouldered one of the numerous different duties of the Islamic community and strove in utmost earnestness. Some working for the preservation of the prophetic Hadiths, some for the preservation of the Shari'a, some for the preservation of the truths of belief, some for the preservation of the Qur'an, and so on; each group undertook a particular duty. They strove in performing the duties of Islam. Numerous multicoloured flowers

28. The Four Poles of sainthood, namely, 'Abd al-Qādir Gīlānī, Aḥmad Rufā'ī, Aḥmad Badawī, and Ibrāhīm Dasūqī. (Tr.)

opened. And through the storm, seeds were cast to all the corners of the most extensive world of Islam; half the earth was transformed into a rose-garden. But sadly, together with the roses, the thorns of the deviant sects appeared in the garden.

It was as if the Hand of Power had shaken that era in wrath, rotated it with intense vigour, and electrified the men of zeal. Through the centrifugal force of that movement, a great many enlightened interpreters of the Law, luminous scholars of Hadith, holy memorizers of the Qur'an, gifted scholars, men of purity, and poles of sainthood were flung off and caused to emigrate to the remote corners of the world of Islam. It fired with enthusiasm all the people of Islam from East to West and awakened them to the treasures of the Qur'an. Now we return to our subject.

There are thousands of events that God's Noble Messenger (Upon whom be blessings and peace) predicted and that happened as he foretold. Here we shall mention a few of them. The majority of those we will cite are agreed upon by the six well-known and most authentic books of Hadith, particularly by Bukhari and Muslim. There is 'consensus in meaning' concerning the reports, while others, on account of being verified by meticulous researchers, may also be considered to have this certainty.

According to an authentic and certain narration, the Noble Messenger (Upon whom be blessings and peace) said to his Companions: "You will be victorious over all your enemies, will succeed in the conquest of Makkah,[29] Khaybar,[30] Damascus and Iraq,[31] Persia, and Jerusalem,[32] and will share among yourselves the treasures of the rulers of the greatest empires, the Byzantines and the Persians."[33] He did not say this as a matter

29. 'Alī al-Qārī, *Sharḥ al-Bukhārī* i, 678, 679. See, Concordance.
30. 'Alī al-Qārī, *Sharḥ al-Shifā'* i, 679. See, Concordance.
31. 'Alī al-Qārī, *Sharḥ al-Shifā'* i, 678. See, Concordance.
32. 'Alī al-Qārī, *Sharḥ al-Shifā'* i, 678, 679. See, Concordance.
33. *Bukhārī*, Jihād 15; Manāqib 25; Īmān 3; *Muslim*, Fitan 75, 76; *Tirmidhī*, Fitan 41.

of conjecture or personal opinion; he said it as if he had seen it, and what he said came true as predicted. This was despite the fact that at the time he foretold this he had to migrate to Madinah with a handful of followers, with the rest of the world, including the environs of Madinah, hostile to him!

He also repeatedly declared, according to authentic and certain narrations, that Abu Bakr and 'Umar would outlive him and be his Caliphs, that they would act for God's sake and within the bounds of the pleasure of God and that of the Prophet, that Abu Bakr's rule would be short, and that 'Umar would remain a long time to succeed in many conquests. Thus he said: "*Incumbent upon you is following the path of those who come after me, Abu Bakr and 'Umar.*"[34]

He also declared: "*The earth was laid out before me, and its eastern and western extremities were displayed to me; the realm of my community shall extend over whatever was laid out before me.*"[35] And his words proved to be true.

According to an authentic and certain narration, before the Battle of Badr, he pointed out one by one the places where the leaders of the Quraysh would be killed, saying: "*Abu Jahl will be killed here, 'Utba here, Umayya here, etc.,*"[36] and added, "*I shall kill 'Ubay b. Khalif with my own hands.*"[37] His predictions all proved to be true.

Again, according to an authentic and certain narration, he informed his Companions about what was happening in the celebrated Battle of Mu'ta, near Damascus —at a distance of one month's journey from where he was— as if he were seeing his Companions fighting in the battle, and said: "*Zayd has taken*

34. *Tirmidhī*, Manāqib 16, 37; *Ibn Māja*, Muqaddima 11; *Musnad* v, 382, 385, 399, 402.

35. *Muslim*, Fitan 19, 20; *Abū Dā'ūd*, Fitan 1; *Tirmidhī*, Fitan 14; *Ibn Māja*, Fitan 9; *Musnad* iv, 123, 278, 284.

36. *Muslim*, Jihād 83; Janna 76; *Abū Dā'ūd*, Jihād 115; *Nasā'ī*, Janā'iz 117; *Musnad* i, 26; iii, 219, 258.

37. al-Ḥākim, *al-Mustadrak* ii, 327.

the banner and been struck; now Ibn Rawaha has taken the banner and been struck; now Ja'far has taken the banner and been struck; now one of God's swords [i.e. Khalid] has taken it."[38] Two to three weeks later Ya'la b. Munabbih returned from the battlefront. In his presence, the Noble Prophet described the details of the battle, and Ya'la swore by God that what had taken place at the battle was exactly the same as the Prophet had described.[39]

According to an authentic and certain narration, the Noble Messenger (Upon whom be blessings and peace) said: "*After me, the Caliphate will last thirty years; then it will be rapacious monarchy.*"[40] "*The beginning of this affair is prophethood and mercy; then it will be mercy and Caliphate; then it will be rapacious monarchy; then it will be arrogance and tyranny.*"[41] He thus predicted the six-month-long caliphate of Hasan and the period of the Four Rightly-Guided Caliphs, and, following that, the transition of Caliphate to monarchy and monarchy's being beset by intrigues and tyranny. This is exactly what later occurred.

Again, according to an authentic narration, he declared: "*'Uthman will be killed while reading the Qur'an.*"[42] "*And it may be that God will cause him to be dressed in a shirt at that time. His deposal may also be sought.*"[43] These events, too, all took place exactly as predicted.

Also according to an authentic narration, while cupping the Prophet (PBUH), 'Abd Allah b. Zubayr tasted his blessed blood. And then the Prophet said: "*Woe unto the people for what shall befall them at your hands, and woe unto you for*

38. al-Ḥākim, *al-Mustadrak* iii, 298; *Bukhārī*, Maghāzī 44.
39. al-Khafājī, *Sharḥ al-Shifā'* iii, 210; Ibn al-Qayyim al-Jawzī, *Zād al-Ma'ād* (*Taḥqīq*: Arnavūd) iii, 385.
40. *Musnad* v, 220, 221.
41. Qāḍī Iyāḍ, *al-Shifā'* i, 340; *Musnad* iv, 273.
42. al-Ḥākim, *al-Mustadrak* iii, 103.
43. See, al-Ḥākim, *al-Mustadrak* iii, 100.

what shall befall you at their hands,"[44] predicting that 'Abd Allah would lead the Muslims with extraordinary bravery, would face terrible attacks, and that because of him fearsome events would befall people. What he foretold came about exactly: during the Umayyad rule, 'Abd Allah b. Zubayr declared his Caliphate in Makkah, heroically fought in many battles, until finally Hajjaj the Tyrant attacked him with a large force, and following a fierce battle the illustrious hero was martyred.

Again, according to an authentic narration, he foretold the characteristics of the Umayyad dynasty[45] and the tyrannical rule of many of its monarchs, including Yazid and Walid,[46] and Mu'awiya's taking the leadership of the Muslims. He advised justice and gentleness, and said: "*When ruling, act with forebearance.*"[47] He predicted that the 'Abbasid dynasty would emerge after the Umayyads to remain in power for a long time, and said: "*The 'Abbasids will come forth with black banners and rule for much longer than they [the Umayyads] rule.*"[48] All these predictions proved to be true.

According to an authentic narration, the Noble Messenger (Upon whom be blessings and peace) also said: "*Woe to the Arabs for the evil that has drawn near,*"[49] suggesting the dreadful disorders to be caused by Jenghiz and Hulagu, and their destruction of the 'Abbasid state. All this proved to be true.

According to an authentic narration, when Sa'd b. Abi Waq-

44. al-'Asqalānī, *al-Maṭālib al-'Alīya* iv, 21; al-Haythamī, *Majma' al-Zawā'id* no: 2708; al-Ḥākim, *al-Mustadrak* iii, 554.

45. Qāḍī Iyāḍ, *al-Shifā'* i, 338; 'Alī al-Qārī, i, 683; al-Khafājī, *Sharḥ al-Shifā'* i, 179.

46. al-Albānī, *Ṣaḥīḥ al-Jāmi' al-Ṣaghīr* no: 2579; al-Albānī, *Silsilat al-Aḥādīth al-Ṣaḥīḥa* no: 1749; al-'Asqalānī, *al-Maṭālib al-'Aliya* no: 4528.

47. al-Haythamī, *Majma' al-Zawā'id* v, 186; Ibn Ḥajar, *al-Maṭālib al-'Aliya* (*Taḥqīq*: 'Abd al-Raḥmān al-A'zamī) no: 4085.

48. Qāḍī Iyāḍ, *al-Shifā'* i, 338; *Musnad* iii, 216-218; al-Ḥākim, *al-Mustadrak* iii, 326.

49. *Bukhārī*, Fitan 4, 28; *Muslim*, Fitan 1; *Abū Dā'ūd*, Fitan 1; *Tirmidhī*, Fitan 23; *Ibn Māja*, Fitan 9; *Musnad* ii, 390, 399; al-Ḥākim, *al-Mustadrak* i, 108; iv, 439, 483.

qas was gravely ill, the Prophet said to him: "*It may be that you will be spared so that some may benefit by you, and others harmed by you,*"[50] thus predicting that he would be a great commander winning many victories, and many peoples would benefit from him entering the fold of Islam, while others would be destroyed by him. His words proved to be true; Sa'd led the Muslim armies, wiped out the Persian Empire, and caused many peoples to reach guidance, the path of Islam.

Also according to an authentic narration, when the Negus, the Abyssinian ruler, who had accepted faith earlier, died in the seventh year of the Hijra, God's Prophet (Upon whom be blessings and peace) informed his Companions about it; he even performed funeral prayers for him.[51] One week later came the news confirming the death of the Negus on the very same day as the Prophet had said.

According to an authentic narration, when the Noble Prophet was with his closest four Companions on the top of Mount Uhud (or Hira), the mountain began to tremble. He said, "*Steady! For on you are a prophet, a veracious one [siddiq], and a martyr,*"[52] and foretold the martyrdom of 'Umar, 'Uthman, and 'Ali. It too proved true.

Now, O unfortunate, wretched man without heart who says that Muhammad (PBUH) was only a clever person and then closes his eyes to that Sun of Truth! Of all his fifteen different kinds of miracle, you have thus far heard only the hundredth part of one kind, that relating to his predictions which have the certainty of 'consensus in meaning.' To discover future events through one's own sagacity and thus succeed even in one hundredth part of the Prophet's predictions, one would have to be

50. *Bukhārī*, Janā'iz 36; Manāqib al-Anṣār 49; Farā'iḍ 6; al-Khafājī, *Sharḥ al-Shifā'* iii, 209; 'Alī al-Qārī, *Sharḥ al-Shifā'* i, 699; Abū Na'īm, *Ḥilyat al-Awliyā'* i, 94.

51. *Bukhārī*, Janā'iz 57; Manāqib al-Anṣār 38; *Muslim*, Farā'iḍ 14; *Abū Dā'ūd*, Jihād 133; Buyū' 9; *Tirmidhī*, Janā'iz 69; *Nasā'ī*, Janā'iz 66, 67; *Ibn Māja*, Ṣadaqāt 9, 13.

52. *Bukharī*, Faḍā'il al-Ṣaḥāba 101; *Ibn Māja*, Janā'iz 64; *Musnad* iv, 240, 282, 283; Qāḍī Iyāḍ, *al-Shifā* i, 340.

of the highest genius. Even if we merely called him a genius as you call him, could such a man with the sagacity of a hundred geniuses have ever seen anything wrongly? Or could he have ever stooped to reporting it wrongly? Not to heed the word of such a hundredfold genius concerning happiness in both worlds is therefore the sign of a hundredfold madness!

■ SIXTH SIGN

According to an authentic narration, the Noble Messenger (Upon whom be blessings and peace) said to Fatima: "*You will be the first of my Family to join me [after my death].*"[53] Six months later, what he said took place.

He also told Abu Dharr: "*You will be expelled from here [Madinah], will live alone, and will die alone.*"[54] All this came true twenty years later.

Once, as he awakened in the house of Anas b. Malik's aunt, Umm Haram, he smilingly said: "*I saw my community waging war on the seas like kings sitting on thrones.*"[55] Umm Haram requested: "Pray that I too will be with them." He said: "*You shall be.*" Forty years later she accompanied her husband, 'Ubada b. Samit, on the conquest of Cyprus. She died there, and her grave has ever since been visited by the believers. Thus, what the Prophet foretold proved to be true.

Also according to an authentic narration, he declared: "*From the tribe of Thaqif, a liar will claim prophethood, and a blood-thirsty tyrant will appear.*"[56] With this, he gave tidings of the

---

53. *Bukhārī*, Manāqib 25; *Muslim*, Fadā'il al-Ṣaḥāba 101; *Ibn Māja*, Janā'iz 64; *Musnad* vi, 240, 282, 283; Qāḍī Iyāḍ, *al-Shifā'* i, 340.

54. al-Ḥākim, *al-Mustadrak* iii, 345; Qāḍī Iyāḍ, *al-Shifā'* i, 343; 'Alī al-Qārī, *Sharḥ al-Shifā'* i, 700; al-'Asqalānī, *al-Maṭālib al-'Alīya* iv, 116 no: 4109; Ibn Kathīr, *al-Bidāya wa'l-Nihāya* v, 8-9; al-'Asqalānī, *al-Iṣāba* iv, 64.

55. *Bukhārī*, Ta'bīr 12; Jihād 3, 8, 63, 75; Isti'dhān 41; *Muslim*, 'Imāra 160, 160; *Abū Dā'ūd*, Jihād 9; *Tirmidhī*, Faḍā'il al-Jihād 15; *Nasā'ī*, Jihād 40; *Ibn Māja*, Jihād 10; *Dārimī*, Jihād 28; *Muwaṭṭa'*, Jihād 39; *Musnad* iii, 240, 264; al-Albānī, *Ṣaḥīḥ al-Jāmi' al-Ṣaghīr* vi, 24 no: 6620; al-Ḥākim, *al-Mustadrak* iv, 556.

56. *Muslim*, Faḍā'il al-Ṣaḥāba 229; *Tirmidhī*, Fitan 44; Manāqib 73; al-Ḥākim, *al-Mustadrak* iii, 450; iv, 254.

infamous Mukhtar, who claimed prophethood, and of the barbarous Hajjaj, who killed a hundred thousand people.

According to an authentic narration, he said: "*Istanbul will be conquered, and blessed are the ruler and the toops that will conquer it.*"[57] He thus gave tidings that Istanbul would be conquered by Muslim hands, and that Mehmed the Conqueror would attain a high spiritual rank. His prediction again proved to be true.

He also said, according to an authentic narration: "*Were religion to be hung on the Pleiades, men from Persia would reach up and lay hold of it,*"[58] indicating that matchless scholars and saints like Abu Hanifa would emerge from Iran. In addition, he foretold Imam Shafi'i, saying: "*A scholar from Quraysh who will fill all regions of the earth with learning.*"[59]

According to an authentic narration, he said: "*My community will be divided into seventy-three sects, and only one among them will attain salvation.*" He was asked: "Who are they?" He replied: "*Those who follow me and my Companions,*"[60] meaning the *Ahl al-Sunna wa'l-Jama'a*.

He also declared: "*The Qadariyya are the Magians of this community,*"[61] foretelling the emergence of the Qadariyya sect, which would be divided into different branches and reject Divine Determining or Destiny. He also foretold the Rafida, who would produce various offshoots.

Again according to an authentic narration, he said to 'Ali:

57. al-Ḥākim, *al-Mustadrak* iv, 422; *Bukhārī*, Ta'rīkh al-Ṣaghīr, no: 139; *Musnad* iv, 335; al-Haythamī, *Majma' al-Zawā'id* vi, 218.

58. *Bukhārī*, al-Tafsīr 62; *Tirmidhī*, 47; Tafsīr Sūra 3.

59. al-Ajlūnī, *Kashf al-Khafā'* ii, 52, 54.

60. *Abū Dā'ūd*, Sunna 1; *Ibn Māja*, Fitan 17; *Tirmidhī*, Īmān 18; *Musnad* ii, 232; iii, 120, 148; 'Alī al-Qārī, *Sharḥ al-Shifā'* i, 679. See also, page 130.

61. al-Albānī, *Saḥīḥ Jāmi' al-Saghīr* iv, 150; al-Ḥākim, *al-Mustadrak* i, 185; *Abū Dā'ūd*, Sunna 5; Suyūṭī, *al-Fatḥ al-Kabīr* iii, 23; *Musnad* ii, 86, 125; v, 406.

62. al-Sā'atī, *al-Fatḥ al-Rabbānī* xxiii, 134; Aḥmad b. Ḥanbal, *Faḍā'il al-Ṣaḥāba* (*Tahqīq*: Vasiyyullāh) ii, 565; al-Ḥākim, *al-Mustadrak* iii, 123.

"As was true of Jesus, two groups of people will perish on your account: one because of excessive love, the other because of excessive enmity.[62] *Christians, on account of their deep love for Jesus, transgressed the limits and called him—God forbid!—'the son of God,' while the Jews, because of their hostility, went to another extreme by denying his message and virtue. Similarly, some will also incur loss through their exaggerated affection toward you. For them is the insulting name of Rafida.*[63] *And certain others will be excessively hostile to you. They are the Kharijites and the extremist partisans of the Umayyads, who will be called Nasiba."*

It may be asked here: Love for the Prophet's Family is a command of the Qur'an and was greatly encouraged by the Prophet. The affection of the Shi'a may therefore serve as an excuse for them, since deep affection may be likened to intoxication. Why, then, can the Shi'a, especially the Rafida not benefit from their love, and why is their love described by the Prophet (PBUH) as transgression?

The Answer: Love is of two kinds:

The First is to love something or someone for the meaning it or he signifies. This means to love 'Ali, Hasan, Husayn, and the Prophet's Family in the name of God and of His Messenger. This kind of love augments the love of the Prophet, and becomes a means to love God Almighty. Thus, it is permissible, and its excess is not harmful or aggressive, nor does it call for reproach and hostility towards others.

The Second Kind of love takes the means as the object, it is to love something or someone for itself or himself. In it, one does not think of the Prophet, (PBUH) but devotes one's love to 'Ali on account of his bravery, and to Hasan and Husayn on

62. al-Sā'atī, *al-Fatḥ al-Rabbānī* xxiii, 134; Aḥmad b. Ḥanbal, *Faḍā'il al-Ṣaḥāba* (*Taḥqīq*: Vasiyyullāh) ii, 565; al-Ḥākim, *al-Mustadrak* iii, 123.

63. al-Haythamī, *Majma' al-Zawā'id* x, 22; al-Sā'atī, *al-Fatḥ al-Rabbānī* xxiv, 20-1.

account of their greatness and lofty qualities, no matter if one knows the Prophet or recognizes God. This love is not a means of love for God and His Prophet; besides, when excessive, it results in censure and enmity for others. It is on account of this kind of love that such people held themselves at a distance from Abu Bakr and 'Umar, and fell into loss. Their negative love, indeed, is the source of misfortune.

According to an authentic narration, God's Most Noble Messnger declared: "*When Persian and Roman girls serve you, then calamity and misfortune will be with you, and your struggles will be between yourselves, with the wicked preying on the virtuous.*"[64] After thirty years, his predictions came true.

Again, according to an authentic narration, he declared: "*The fortress of Khaybar will be conquered at 'Ali's hand.*"[65] As a miracle of his prophethood and beyond all expectation, the following day 'Ali ripped off the gate of the fortress of Khaybar, used it as a shield, and seized the fortress. When he threw it aside after the conquest, eight strong men —or according to another version, forty— tried to lift it, but could not do so.[66]

The Noble Messenger (Upon whom be blessings and peace) also predicted the Battle of Siffin between 'Ali and Mu'awiya, saying: "*The hour shall not come until two parties with a single claim fight each other.*"[67]

He also declared that a group of rebels would kill 'Ammar.[68] When 'Ammar was killed at the Battle of Siffin, 'Ali cited this

64. *Tirmidhī* (*Taḥqīq*: Aḥmad Shākir) no: 2262; al-Albānī, *Silsilat al-Aḥādith al-Ṣaḥīḥa* 954; al-Haythamī, *Majma' al-Zawā'id* x, 232, 237.

65. *Bukhārī*, Jihād 102, 143; al-Maghāzī 38; *Muslim*, Faḍā'il al-Ṣaḥāba 34, 35; *Musnad* ii, 484; v, 333; Bayhaqī, *Dalā'il al-Nubūwwa* iv, 205.

66. Suyūṭī, *al-Durar al-Muntathira* (Muṣṭafā al-Bābī al-Ḥalabī 1960) 118; Ibn Kathīr, *al-Bidāya wa'l-Nihāya* iv, 189-190; al-Ajlūnī, *Kashf al-Khafā'* i, 365.

67. *Muslim*, Fitan 4; Ibn Ḥibbān, *Ṣaḥīḥ* viii, 259; 'Alī al-Qārī, *Sharḥ al-Shifā'* i, 704; al-Albānī, *Saḥīḥ Jāmi' al-Ṣaghīr* vi, 174 no: 7294.

68. *Bukhārī*, Ṣalāt 63; *Muslim*, Fitan 70, 72, 73; *Tirmidhī*, Manāqib 34; Kattānī, *Naẓm al-Mutanāthir* 126; Ibn Ḥibbān, *Ṣaḥīḥ* viii, 260; al-Ḥākim, *al-Mustadrak* ii, 155; iii, 191, 397; Qāḍī Iyāḍ, *al-Shifā'* i, 339; al-Sā'atī, *al-Fatḥ al-Rabbānī* xxiii, 142.

as a proof that Mu'awiya's followers were rebellious; but Mu'awiya interpreted it differently, and also 'Amr b. al-'As said: "The rebels are murderers, not all of us."

The Noble Prophet (PBUH) also said: "*As long as 'Umar is alive, no sedition will erupt among you.*"[69] And so it happened.

Before accepting faith, Sahl b. 'Amr was once captured in a battle. 'Umar said to the God's Messenger: "Allow me to pull out his teeth, for he, with his eloquent speech, incited the idolatrous Quraysh to wage war against us." God's Messenger replied: "*It may be that he will assume a stance pleasing to you, O 'Umar.*"[70] In fact, at the time of the Prophet's demise, which caused panic and agitation, Sahl, with his well-known eloquence, calmed and comforted the Companions in Makkah with an address; while in Madinah Abu Bakr, with his great firmness, was also giving a very important address to comfort the Companions. Surprisingly, the two addresses resemble each other in regard to their wording.

To Suraqa, the Prophet once said: "*You will wear the two bracelets of Khusraw.*"[71] Khusraw was wiped out during the Caliphate of 'Umar. When Khusraw's jewelry arrived, 'Umar put the bracelets on Suraqa, saying, "Praise be to God Who took these off Khusraw and put them on Suraqa."[72] This confirmed the report of the Prophet.

The Noble Messenger (Upon whom be blessings and peace) also declared: "*Once Khusraw the Persian has gone, there will be no other.*"[73] So it turned out.

---

69. *Bukhārī*, Mawāqit 4; Fitan 22; *Muslim*, Īmān 231; Fitan 27; *Ibn Māja*, Fitan 9; *Musnad* v, 401, 405.

70. 'Alī al-Qārī, *Sharḥ al-Shifā'* i, 704; al-Khafājī, *Sharḥ al-Shifā'* iii, 218; al-'Asqalānī, *al-Iṣāba* ii, 93-94; al-Ḥākim, *al-Mustadrak* iv, 282.

71. 'Alī al-Qārī, *Sharḥ al-Shifā'* i, 703; al-'Asqalānī, *al-Iṣāba* no: 3115.

72. See, fn. 71. Also, Qāḍī Iyāḍ, *al-Shifā'* i, 344.

73. *Bukhārī*, Īmān 31; *Muslim*, Fitan 76; *Tirmidhī*, Fitan 41; *Musnad* ii, 233, 240; v, 92, 99; Qāḍī Iyāḍ, *al-Shifā'* i, 337; al-Mubārakfūrī, *Tuḥfat al-Aḥwazī* (*Taḥqīq*: 'Abd al-Wahhāb) iv, 462, 663.

He once said to Khusraw's envoy: "*Khusraw has now been killed by his son Shirviya Parviz.*"[74] Upon investigating and finding out that he had indeed been murdered at that very time, the envoy accepted Islam. The name of the envoy occurs in some narrations as Firuz.

According to an authentic narration, the Noble Prophet (PBUH) once mentioned a secret letter that Khatib b. Balta'a had sent to the Quraysh. He sent 'Ali and Miqdad to fetch it, saying, "There is a person at such-and-such a location bearing such-and-such a letter. Take it and bring it here." They went and brought exactly the letter he had described from exactly the place. The Prophet summoned Khatib and asked him why he had done it. Khatib apologized, and the Prophet pardoned him.[75]

Again, according to an authentic narration concerning 'Utba b. Abi Lahab, God's Messenger prayed: "*May he be eaten by one of the dogs of God!*",[75] predicting the terrible fate of 'Utba. For while on his way to the Yemen, 'Utba was devoured by a lion. Both the malediction and the prediction of the Prophet were thus confirmed.

At the conquest of Makkah, as is also related in an authentic narration, Bilal al-Habashi went up onto the roof of the Ka'ba and made the call to prayer, while Abu Sufyan, 'Attab b. Asid, and Harith b. Hisham, from among the leaders of the Quraysh, were sitting together nearby. 'Attab said: "My father was fortunate enough not to witness this moment." Harith said contemptuously about Bilal: "Could Muhammad have not found someone other than this black crow to make the *mu'ezzin*?" Abu Sufyan said: "I am afraid to say anything, for he will come to know of

---

74. Qāḍī Iyāḍ, *al-Shifā'* i, 343; al-Khafājī, *Sharḥ al-Shifā'* iii, 211; 'Alī al-Qārī, *Sharḥ al-Shifā'* i, 700; al-Albānī, *Silsilat al-Aḥādīth al-Ṣaḥīḥa* 1427.

75. *Bukhārī*, Jihād 141; Tafsīr 60:1; Maghāzī 46; *Muslim*, Faḍā'il al-Ṣaḥāba, 161; *Abū Dā'ūd*, Jihād 98; *Tirmidhī*, lx, 1; *Musnad* i, 79; al-Ḥākim, *al-Mustadrak* iii, 301; Qāḍī Iyāḍ, *al-Shifā'* i, 342.

76. al-Khafājī, *Sharḥ al-Shifā'* iii, 139; 'Alī al-Qārī, *Sharḥ al-Shifā'* i, 664; Suyūṭī, *Kanz al-'Ummāl* no: 438, 439.

whatever I say. Even if nothing else informs him, the rocks of this Batha [Makkah] will do so." Indeed, a little later the Noble Messenger (Upon whom be blessings and peace) encountered them and repeated to them their conversation word for word.[77] That very moment 'Attab and Harith became Muslims.

See, wretched denier who does not recognize the Prophet! Two stubborn leaders of the Quraysh came to believe on hearing this single report of his from the Unseen. How corrupted your heart must be, for you hear about thousands of miracles having the certainty of 'consensus in meaning' like this one, and still you are not completely satisfied! However, to return to our subject.

According to an authentic narration, 'Abbas was captured by the Companions in the Battle of Badr. When he was asked for ransom, he said he did not have money. God's Messenger (Upon whom be blessings and peace) said to him: "*You and your wife Umm Fadl hid that much money* [he gave the exact amount] *in such-and-such a place.*"[78] 'Abbas confirmed this, saying: "This was a secret known by only the two of us," and became a Muslim.

Also according to an authentic narration, a dangerous Jewish sorcerer named Labid once concocted a strong and effective spell to harass the God's Messenger (PBUH). He wrapped hair and thread around a comb, bewitched it, and threw it into a well. The Noble Messenger told his Companions including 'Ali to go and bring the spell in the well, which they did, finding it exactly as described. As they unwrapped the hair, the Messenger's discomfort lessened.[79]

77. al-Khafājī, *Sharḥ al-Shifā'* i, 219, 220; al-'Asqalānī, *al-Maṭālib al-'Alīya* no: 4366; Ibn al-Qayyim al-Jawzī, *Zād al-Ma'ād* (*Taḥqīq*: al-Arnavūd) iii, 409-410; Ibn Ḥishām, *Sīrat al-Nabī* ii, 413.

78. Qāḍī Iyāḍ, *al-Shifā'* i, 343; 'Alī al-Qārī, *Sharḥ al-Shifā'* i, 699; al-Khafājī, *Sharḥ al-Shifā'* iii, 206, 207; al-Haythamī, *Majma' al-Zawā'id* iv, 85.

79. *Bukhārī*, Ṭibb 47, 49, 50; Adab 56; Da'wāt 57; Badu'l-Khalq 11; *Muslim*, Salām 43; *Ibn Māja*, Ṭibb 45; *Musnad* vi, 57, 63, 96; 'Alī al-Qārī, *Sharḥ al-Shifā'* i, 706; Tabrīzī, *Mishkāt al-Maṣābīh* (*Taḥqīq*: al-Albānī) iii, 174 no: 5893.

Again, according to an authentic narration, the Noble Messenger once gave the news of the awesome fate of an apostate to a group that included such important persons as Abu Hurayra and Hudhayfa, saying: "*One of you will enter the Fire with a tooth bigger than Mount Uhud.*"[80] Abu Hurayra related: "I was afraid, as later only two remained from that group, one of which was me. Finally, the other man was killed in the Battle of Yamama as one of the followers of Musaylima."[81] The truth of the Prophet's (PBUH) prediction was thus confirmed.

It is related through an authentic chain of reports that 'Umayr and Safwan, before they became Muslims, once decided to kill the Prophet for a handsome reward that had been offered them. When 'Umayr arrived in Madinah with this intention, the Noble Messenger summoned him, and, putting his hand on 'Umayr's chest, told him about what he had planned with Safwan. 'Umayr answered, "Yes," and became a Muslim.[82]

Like those mentioned above, many predictions which the Noble Messenger (Upon whom be blessings and peace) gave concerning the Unseen have been recorded in the six best-known, authentic books of Hadith, together with the chains of the narrators. As for the occurrences related in this work, they are definite to the degree of 'consensus in meaning,' being related in Bukhari and Muslim—which are accepted by the scholars as the most authentic sources after the Qur'an, and in the other collections like Tirmidhi, Nasa'i, Abu Da'ud, Musnad al-Hakim, Musnad al-Ahmad b. Hanbal, and Dala'il al-Bayhaqi.

Now, unthinking denier! Do not shrug these off, saying, "Muhammad the Arabian was clever!" Because the accurate predictions of Muhammad (PBUH) concerning the Unseen can-

80. Qāḍī Iyāḍ, *al-Shifā'* iv, 342; al-Khafājī, *Sharḥ al-Shifā'* iii, 203; al-Haythamī, *Majma' al-Zawā'id* viii, 289-290; Tabrīzī, *Mishkāt al-Maṣābīḥ* iii, 103.

81. Qāḍī Iyāḍ, *al-Shifā'* i, 342; 'Alī al-Qārī, *Sharḥ al-Shifā'* i, 298.

82. Qāḍī Iyāḍ, *al-Shifā'* i, 342, 343; original: al-Haythamī, *Majma' al-Zawā'id* viii, 286-7; viii, 284-6.

not be explained except in either of the following two ways: you will either suppose that this blessed person had such piercing vision and expansive genius that he saw and knew the past and the future and all the world; beheld the East, the West, and the whole universe; and discovered what happened in the past and what will happen in the future. Such a quality is not to be found in a human being, but if it was to be, it would certainly be a wonder, a gift, bestowed on him by the Creator of the world, which would itself be the greatest of miracles. Or you will believe this blessed person to be an official and a student of One under Whose disposal and observation everything stands, under Whose command are all ages and all the species and realms of beings in the cosmos, in Whose great ledger is recorded everything, so that He may show and communicate them to his student whenever He wishes. Thus, Muhammad the Arabian (Upon whom be blessings and peace) instructs others as he himself is instructed by the Lord of Pre-Eternity.

It is related in an authentic narration that when the Prophet appointed Khalid b. Walid to fight against Ukaydir, the head of the Dawmat al-Jandal, he informed Khalid that he would find Ukaydir on a wild ox hunt, and that he would be captured without resistance. Khalid captured Ukaydir in exactly this way.[83]

According to an authentic narration, when the Quraysh hung up on the wall of the Ka'ba a leaf on which were written words against the Bani Hashim, the Prophet said to them: "*Worms have eaten the leaf, except the parts bearing the Names of God.*"[84] They examined the leaf to find it in the same condition as had been described.

According to an authentic narration, the Noble Messenger

83. Qāḍī Iyāḍ, *al-Shifā'* iii, 218; 'Alī al-Qārī, *Sharḥ al-Shifā'* i, 704; Ibn al-Qayyim, *Zād al-Ma'ād* v, 538-9; al-Ḥākim, *al-Mustadrak* iv, 519; Ibn Kathīr, *al-Bidāya wa'l-Nihāya* iv, 30.

84. Qāḍī Iyāḍ, *al-Shifā'* i, 345; al-Khafājī, *Sharḥ al-Shifā'* iii, 720; 'Alī al-Qārī, *Sharḥ al-Shifā'* i, 706; Ibn Kathīr, *al-Bidāya wa'l-Nihāya* iii, 96-7; Ibn Ḥishām, *Sīrat al-Nabī* i, 371.

(Upon whom be blesssings and peace) said: *"There will be a big epidemic during the conquest of Jerusalem."*[85] When Jerusalem was conquered during the Caliphate of 'Umar, a widespread epidemic caused in three days the death of about seventy thousand people.

Again, according to an authentic narration, the Prophet (PBUH) predicted that Basra[86] and Baghdad[87] would come into existence, which at that time had not been founded, that the treasure of the world would enter Baghdad, and that the Turks and the people living on the shores of the Caspian Sea would do battle with the Arabs and that the majority of them would later enter the fold of Islam,[88] and that among the Arabs they would come to dominate them. He said: *"The Persians [non-Arabs] will almost predominate among you, consuming your booty and smiting you."*[89]

He also said: *"The ruin of my community will be at the hands of the wicked ones from Quraysh,"*[90] suggesting the disorder caused by the wicked leaders of the Umayyads, such as Walid and Yazid.

He furthermore predicted that apostasy would take place in such areas as Yamama.[91]

85. *Bukhārī*, Ṭibb 30; Khiyal 13; *Muslim*, Salām 98, 100; *Muwaṭṭa'*, Madīna 22, 24; *Musnad* iv, 195-6; Bayhaqī, *Dalā'il al-Nubūwwa* vi, 383; Suyūṭī, *al-Khaṣā'iṣ al-Kubrā* ii, 477-8.

86. al-Albānī, *Ṣaḥīḥ al-Jāmi' al-Ṣaghīr* vi, 268 no: 7736; Tabrīzī, *Mishkāt al-Maṣābīḥ* no: 5433.

87. Qāḍī Iyāḍ, *al-Shifā'* i, 344; 'Alī al-Qārī, *Sharḥ al-Shifā'* i, 703; Ibn Kathīr, *al-Bidāya wa'l-Nihāya* x, 102; Tabrīzī, *Mishkāt al-Maṣābīḥ* no: 5433.

88. Bukhārī, Muslim, Abū Dāwūd, Tirmidhī, and Ibn Māja narrated it. See, Tabrīzī, *Mishkāt al-Maṣābīḥ* vi, 173.

89. Qāḍī Iyāḍ, *al-Shifā'* i, 341; al-Khafājī, *Sharḥ al-Shifā'* iii, 194; 'Alī al-Qārī, *Sharḥ al-Shifā'* i, 692; al-Haythamī, *Majma' al-Zawā'id* vii, 310; al-Ḥākim, *al-Mustadrak* iv, 519; *Musnad* ii, 288, 296, 304, 324, 377, 520, 536; iv, 66; v, 38.

90. *Bukhārī*, Manāqib 25; al-Ḥākim, *al-Mustadrak* iv, 479, 527, 572; *Musnad* ii, 288, 296, 301, 304, 324, 377, 520, 536; iv, 66; v, 38; (different wording): Ibn Ḥibbān, *Ṣaḥīḥ* viii, 215, 252.

91. *Bukhārī*, Manāqib 25; Maghāzī 70; Ta'bīr 40; *Muslim*, Ru'yā 21, 22; *Tirmidhī*, Ru'yā 10; *Musnad* ii, 319, Bayhaqī, *Dalā'il al-Nubūwwa* v, 334-6; vi, 358, 360, 524.

During the famous Battle of Khandaq, he declared: "*From now on, I will make assaults on the Quraysh and their confederates, not they on me.*"[92] This was also verified.

According to an authentic narration, he said a few months prior to his death: "*One of God's bondsmen has been given a choice, and he chose that which is with God.*"[93]

About Zayd b. Suwahan, he said: "*One of his limbs will precede him to Paradise.*"[94] In the Battle of Nihawand, one of his hands was martyred and in effect reached heaven first.

The incidents we have so far mentioned concerning predictions relating to the Unseen comprise only one out of his ten different kinds of miracle. Yet of this kind alone, we have not even mentioned one tenth. In addition to what is mentioned here, four general kinds of miracle concerning predictions of the Unseen have been described briefly in the Twenty-Fifth Word, which is about the miraculousness of the Qur'an. Now consider the kinds mentioned here together with the four extensive sorts communicated from the Unseen by the tongue of the Qur'an, you will see what conclusive, indisputable, sound, brilliant, and firm proof of his messengership they form. Indeed, anyone whose heart and mind are not corrupted will of a surety believe that Muhammad is the Messenger of, and receives knowledge from, a Glorious One Who is the Creator of all things, the One All-Knowing of the Unseen.

■ SEVENTH SIGN

We will give in this Sign a few examples from among the Prophet's (PBUH) miracles that relate to his effecting increase

92. *Bukhārī*, Maghāzī 29; *Musnad* iv, 262; vi, 394; Ibn Ḥibbān, *Ṣaḥīḥ* vi, 272.

93. *Bukhārī*, Manāqib al-Anṣār 45; Ṣalāt 80; Faḍā'il al-Ṣaḥāba 2; *Tirmidhī*, Manāqib 15; *Abū Dā'ūd*, Muqaddima 14; *Musnad* iii, 18, 478; iv, 211; v, 139; Ibn Ḥibbān, *Ṣaḥīḥ* viii, 200; ix, 58.

94. Qāḍī Iyāḍ, *al-Shifā'* i, 343; 'Alī al-Qārī, *Sharḥ al-Shifā'* i, 702; al-Khafājī, *Sharḥ al-Shifā'* iii, 214; al-Haythamī, *Majma' al-Zawā'id* ix, 398; al-'Asqalānī, *al-Maṭālib al-'Alīya* iv, 91 no: 4047.

in food and that are definite to the degree of 'consensus in meaning.' But before going into the subject, some introductory comments will be appropriate.

Introduction

Each of the following examples of miracles is narrated, as authentic, through various—sometimes as many as sixteen—chains of transmission. Most of them occurred in the presence of large assemblies, and were narrated by many truthful persons of good repute from among those present. For example, from among seventy men who partook of four handfuls of food and were filled, one relates the incident, and the others do not contradict him. Their silence thus indicates their confirmation. For if in that era of truth and truthfulness the Companions, who were lovers of the truth and earnest and honest, had witnessed even the tiniest lie, they would have rejected and denied it. But the incidents we will be citing were narrated by many, and the others who witnessed them remained silent. Thus, each of these incidents has the certainty of 'consensus in meaning.'

Furthermore, books of both history and the Prophet's biography testify that, next to the preservation of the Qur'an and its verses, the Companions worked with all their strength to preserve the deeds and words of God's Most Noble Messenger (Upon whom be blessings and peace), and especially those relating to the injuctions of the Shari'a and to miracles, paying extreme attention to their accuracy. They never neglected even the tiniest aspect of his conduct, actions, and states. This and the fact that they recorded them is testified to by books of Hadith.

In addition, in the Era of Bliss, they wrote down and recorded very many of the Hadiths concerning the injunctions of the Law and his miracles. The 'Seven 'Abd Allah's' in particular recorded them in writing. And especially 'Abd Allah b. 'Abbas, known as 'the Interpreter of the Qur'an,' and 'Abd

Allah b. 'Amr b. al-'As some thirty to forty years later, and the thousands of exacting scholars of the generation that followed the Companions recorded the Hadiths and miracles in writing. And still later, chiefly the four great interpreters of the Law and thousands of exacting scholars of Hadith related them and preserved them in writing. Then two hundred years after the Hijra, foremost Bukhari and Muslim and the six accepted books of tradition, undertook the duty of their preservation. Many severe critics such as Ibn al-Jawzi emerged who identified false reports which had been produced by deniers, the unthinking, the ignorant, or those who had recalled them wrongly. Later, learned and exacting scholars like Jalal al-Din al-Suyuti, who seventy times was honoured in a waking state by the presence and conversation of the Noble Messenger, differentiated the diamonds of authentic traditions from other sayings and fabrications.

Thus, the incidents and miracles we shall speak of, have come down to us through numerous, perhaps uncountable, strong and trustworthy hands, and have reached us in sound condition.

All praise be to God, this is from the bounty of my Lord.

It is for this reason that one's mind should be freed from the notion that these incidents have been distorted or confused in any way in being passed down all the way from that time to the present.

The First Example of definite miracles concerning the Prophet's increase of food through his blessing. The six accurate books of tradition, Bukhari and Muslim included, unanimously relate that during the feast on the occasion of the Prophet's (PBUH) marriage to Zaynab, Anas's mother, Umm Sulaym, prepared a dish by frying two handfuls of dates in oil and sent it with Anas to the Prophet. The Noble Prophet told him: "*Go and invite so-and-so* [naming some person], *and also invite whomever you encounter on your way.*" Anas invited those named and those he met. About three hundred Companions came and filled the Prophet's room and anteroom. Then the Prophet said: "*Make circles of ten.*" He placed his blessed hand on that little amount of food, uttered supplications, and told them to help themselves. All of them ate and was fully satisfied. Afterwards the Prophet asked Anas to remove the food. Anas later related: "I could not tell if there was more of it when I set it down, or when I removed it."[95]

Second Example: Abu Ayyub al-Ansari, the Prophet's host, relates that when the Noble Prophet (Upon whom be blessings and peace) honoured his house, he had prepared a meal for two, which would suffice the Prophet and Abu Bakr. But the Prophet told him: "*Invite thirty men from among the distinguished Ansar!*"[96] Abu Ayyub said: "Thirty men came and ate. He then said: '*Invite sixty men,*' which I did, and they also came and ate. The Prophet said again: '*Invite seventy more.*' I invited them; they came, and when they finished eating, there was still food left in the bowls. All who came embraced Islam and took the oath of allegiance after witnessing this miracle. One hundred and eighty men ate the food of two men."[97]

Third Example: It is reported through many chains of transmission from 'Umar b. al-Khattab, Abu Hurayra, Salama b. Akwa', Abu 'Amrat al-Ansari and others that on one expedition, the army went hungry. They referred themselves to the Noble Prophet (Upon whom be blessings and peace), and he told them: "*Gather whatever food is left in your saddle-bags.*" Everyone brought a few pieces of dates and put them on a mat. The most they could put together was four handfuls. Salama

95. *Bukhārī*, Nikāḥ 64; *Muslim*, Nikāḥ 94, 95; *Tirmidhī*, xxxiii, 21; *Nasā'ī* Nikāḥ 84; *Abū Dā'ūd*, Adab 95; *Musnad* iii, 29; v, 462; Qāḍī Iyāḍ, *al-Shifā'* i, 294.

96. *Anṣār*—Helpers: those of the Madīnan Companions who had the migrants from Makka to stay in their houses. (Tr.)

97. Qāḍī Iyāḍ, *al-Shifā'* i, 292; al-Haythami, *al-Majma' al Zawā'id* vii, 303; al-Khafājī, *Sharḥ al-Shifā'* iii, 33; 'Alī al-Qārī, *Sharḥ al-Shifā'* i, 604.

related: "I estimated it amounted to the size of a sitting goat." Then the Noble Messenger (Upon whom be blessings and peace) announced: "*Everyone bring his dish!*" They pressed forward, and no one in the whole army remained with an empty dish, all the dishes were filled. There was even some left over. One of the Companions later said: "I realized from the way that increase was obtained that if the whole world had come, the food still would have been sufficient."[98]

Fourth Example: As recorded in all of the Six Books including Bukhari and Muslim, 'Abd al-Rahman b. Abu Bakr al-Siddiq relates: "We, one hundred and thirty Companions, were with the Noble Messenger (Upon whom be blessings and peace) on an expedition. Dough was prepared to the amount of about four handfuls, a goat was slaughtered and cooked, and its liver and kidneys were roasted. I swear by God that from that roasted meat [liver and kidneys] God's Messenger gave a small piece to each and put the cooked meat into two large bowls. After we had all eaten until we were filled there was still some left over, which I loaded onto a camel."[99]

Fifth Example: As is recorded in the Six Books, Jabir al-Ansari related under oath: "During the Ahzab expedition on the celebrated day of Khandaq, about a thousand people ate from four handfuls of rye bread and a young cooked goat; yet food was still left over. That day the food had been cooked in my house, and after the one thousand people had left, the pot was still boiling with meat in it, and bread was being made from the dough; for the Prophet had wetted the dough and the pot with his blessed mouth, beseeching God for plenty."[100]

Sixth Example: According to an authentic narration

98. *Bukhārī*, Sharīka 1; Jihād 123; *Muslim*, Īmān 44, 45; *Musnad* iii, 11, 418.

99. *Bukhārī*, Hiba 28; Aṭ'ima 6; *Muslim*, Ashriba 175; *Musnad* i, 197, 198; al-Sā'atī, *al-Fatḥ al-Rabbānī* xx, 55.

100. *Bukhārī*, Maghāzī 29; *Muslim*, Ashriba 141; al-Ḥākim, *al-Mustadrak* iii, 31; 'Alī al-Qārī, *Sharḥ al-Shifā'* i, 290; Suyūṭī, *Kanz al-'Ummāl* xii, 409, 424.

from Abu Talha, the uncle of Anas who served God's Messenger, the Messenger fed seventy to eighty men with a small amount of rye bread that Anas had brought under his arm. The Messenger ordered: "*Break the bread into small pieces!*", and prayed for increase. Because the house was small, they came ten at a time, and left having filled themselves.[101]

Seventh Example: It is related as authentic in accurate books such as *Shifa' al-Sharif* and Muslim that Jabir al-Ansari narrated: "Once a man asked the Noble Messenger (Upon whom be blessings and peace) for food for his household. The Messenger gave him a half load of barley. For a long time he ate of the barley together with his family and guests. They would look and see that it did not finish. So they measured it to see by how much it decreased. After that the blessing of abundance was gone and the barley began to dwindle rapidly. The man went to the Messenger and related what had happened. God's Messenger replied: "*If you had not put it to the test by measuring it, it would have lasted you a life-time.*"[102]

Eighth Example: According to accurate books such as Tirmidhi, Nasa'i, Bayhaqi, and *Shifa' al-Sharif*, Samura b. Jundub related that a bowl of meat was brought to the Prophet (PBUH). From morning to evening, many groups of men came and ate from it.[103]

In accordance with the explanation we gave in the introduction to this section, this is not the narration of Samura alone, since Samura narrated this incident on behalf of, and with the approval of, all those present.

Ninth Example: It is also narrated by reliable and trusted scholars such as the well-known author of *Shifa' al-*

101. *Bukhārī*, Aṭ'ima 6, 48; *Muslim*, Ashriba 142, 143; *Musnad* iii, 218; 'Alī al-Qārī, *Sharḥ al-Shifā'* i, 291, 297; al-Ḥākim, *al-Mustadrak* iii, 31.
102. *Muslim*, Faḍā'il 3 No: 2281; Bayhaqī, *Dalā'il al-Nubūwwa* vi, 114.
103. *Tirmidhī* (*Taḥqīq*: Aḥmad Shākir) no: 2629; *Abū Dā'ūd*, Muqaddima 9; *Musnad* v, 12, 18; al-Ḥākim, *al-Mustadrak* ii, 618.

Sharif, Ibn Abi Shayba, and Tabarani, that Abu Hurayra related: "The Noble Messenger commanded me, '*Invite the poor Makkan migrants who have made the Bench* [*suffa*][104] *of the Mosque their home and who number more than a hundred.*' So I went and searched for them and gathered them together. A tray of food was set before us, and we ate as much as we wanted, then we arose. The dish remained full as it was when set down, only, the traces of fingers on the food were visible.[105]

Thus, this incident is related by Abu Hurayra in the name of all the People of the Bench, supported by their confirmation. Hence, the incident is as definite as if all the People of the Bench had related it. Is it at all possible that if it had not been true those men of truth and perfection would have remained silent and not denied it?

Tenth Example: According to an authentic narration from 'Ali, the Noble Messenger (Upon whom be blessings and peace) once gathered the Bani 'Abd al-Muttalib. They were about forty, including some who would eat a young camel and drink a gallon of milk in one meal. Yet for them he had prepared only a handful of food. All ate and were satisfied, and the food remained just as it had been before. Later he brought milk in a wooden bowl that would have been sufficent for only three or four persons. They all drank their fill.[106]

Thus, a miracle of plenty as definite as 'Ali's courage and loyalty!

Eleventh Example: According to an authentic narration, on the occasion of 'Ali's marriage to Fatima al-Zahra,

---

104. The People of the Bench: those among the Makkan migrants (*Muhājirīn*) who lived in the outer part of the Mosque, who devoted their lives to the preservation and dissemination of the Qur'ān, Sunna, and Ḥadīth, and whose livelihood was provided by the Prophet (PBUH). (Tr.)

105. Qāḍī Iyāḍ, *al-Shifā'* i, 293; 'Alī al-Qārī, *Sharḥ al-Shifā'* i, 606; al-Haythamī, *Majma' al-Zawā'id* viii, 308; Bayhaqī, *Dalā'il al-Nubūwwa* vi, 101.

106. Qāḍī Iyāḍ, *al-Shifā'* i, 293; 'Alī al-Qārī, *Sharḥ al-Shifā'* i, 607; al-Khafājī, *Sharḥ al-Shifā'* iii, 36; al-Haythamī, *Majma' al-Zawā'id* viii, 302-3; Aḥmad b. Ḥanbal, *Faḍā'il al-Ṣaḥāba* (*Taḥqīq*: Vasiyyullāh) 1220; *Musnad* i, 159.

The Noble Messenger (Upon whom be blessings and peace) ordered Bilal al-Habashi: "Have bread made from a few handfuls of flour; also slaughter a young camel!" Bilal relates: "I brought the food and he put his hand on it to bless it. Later, the Companions arrived in groups, ate, and left. From the remaining food, he sent a full bowl to each of his wives, saying that they should eat and feed anyone who visited them."[107]

Such blessed plenty was indeed necessary for such a blessed marriage!

Twelfth Example: Imam Ja'far al-Sadiq related from his father Muhammad al-Baqir, and he from his father, Zayn al-'Abidin, and he from 'Ali, that Fatima al-Zahra had prepared enough food for herself and 'Ali. She then sent 'Ali to invite the Noble Messenger (Upon whom be blessings and peace) to come and eat with them. God's Messenger came and told them to send a dish of food to each of his wives. Fatima said that after a dish of food had been set aside for himself, 'Ali, Fatima, and their children, they lifted up the saucepan and it was full to overflowing. Through God's will, they ate of the food for a long time afterwards.[108]

Why do you not believe this miracle of plenty just as if you had witnessed it with your own eyes, since it comes from this luminous, elevated chain of transmission? Satan himself could find no excuse in this face of this one.

Thirteenth Example: Veracious authorities such as Abu Da'ud, Ahmad b. Hanbal, and Bayhaqi, narrate from Dukayn al-Ahmasi b. Sa'id al-Muzayn, and from Nu'man b. Muqarrin al-Ahmasi al-Muzayn, who with his six brothers was honoured with the Prophet's conversation and was a Companion, and by way of Jarir through numerous chains of transmis-

107. Qāḍī Iyāḍ, *al-Shifā'* i, 297; 'Alī al-Qārī, *Sharḥ al-Shifā'* i, 613; Bayhaqī, *Dalā'il al-Nubūwwa* iii, 160.

108. Qāḍī Iyāḍ, *al-Shifā'* i, 294; 'Alī al-Qārī, *Sharḥ al-Shifā'* i, 608; Ibn Ḥajar al-'Asqalānī, *al-Maṭālib al-'Alīya* iv, 73 no: 4001.

sion from 'Umar b. al-Khattab that God's Noble Messenger (Upon whom be blessings and peace) ordered 'Umar b. al-Khattab: "*Equip with provisions for a journey four hundred horesemen from the Ahmasi tribe!*" 'Umar replied: "O Messenger of God! What we have in hand is the equivalent of a seated young camel." The Messenger said: "*Go and give it to them!*" So he went, and out of that half load of dates, gave the four hundred horsemen sufficient provisions. And he stated that it remained as before, without diminishing.[109]

Thus, this miracle of plenty occurred in connection with four hundred men and 'Umar in particular. They are behind the narrations, supporting them, and their silence confirms them. Do not ignore these narrations because they are related by a few individuals only, for if the incident had only been reported by a single individual, it still would have the certainty of 'consensus in meaning.'

Fourteenth Example: All the accurate books of tradition, and foremost Bukhari and Muslim, narrate that when Jabir's father died, he was heavily in debt. His creditors were Jews. Jabir offered the creditors all his father's possessions but they did not accept them. The fruit produced by his orchard over many years would have been insufficient to defray the debt. The Noble Messenger (Upon whom be blessings and peace) said: "*Pick and gather in all the fruit in the orchard!*" They did so, then the Noble Messenger walked around the crop and prayed. Then Jabir gave from the amount corresponding to his father's debt. What was left was as much as the annual produce of the orchard. And according to another narration, it was equal to the amount he gave the creditors. The Jews were amazed and astounded at this.[110]

---

109. al-Sā'atī, *al-Fatḥ al-Rabbānī* xx, 85; *Musnad* v, 445; Qāḍī Iyāḍ, *al-Shifā'* i, 294; 'Alī al-Qārī, *Sharḥ al-Shifā'* i, 609; Bayhaqī, *Dalā'il al-Nubūwwa* v, 365.

110. *Bukhārī,* Vaṣāyā 36; Buyū' 51; Sulḥ 13; Istiqrāḍ 18; *Nasā'ī* Vaṣāya 3, 4; *Musnad* iii, 313, 365, 373, 391, 395, 398; Ibn Ḥibbān, *Ṣaḥīḥ* viii, 167; al-Sā'atī, *al-Fatḥ al-Rabbānī* xx, 60; Qāḍī Iyāḍ, *al-Shifā'* i, 295.

See, this clear miracle of plenty was not only reported by a few narrators like Jabir; many people connected with it described and narrated it, thus giving it the degree of 'consensus in meaning.'

Fifteenth Example: Exact scholars, and foremost Tirmidhi and Imam Bayhaqi, related through a sound chain of authorities from Abu Hurayra that Abu Hurayra said: "During one expedition —that of Tabuk according to another narration— the army went hungry. God's Noble Messenger (Upon whom be blessings and peace) asked: '*Is there nothing?*' I said: 'I have one or two dates in my saddle-bag.' —According to another narration, it was fifteen.— He said: '*Bring them here!*' I took them to him, and he plunged his hand into them and took a handful. He put them into a dish, and offered a supplication for their increase. Then he called the men in groups of ten and they all ate of them. Then he said: '*Take what you brought, hold it, and do not turn it upside down.*' I put my hand in the bag; there were in my hands as many dates as I had brought. Later, during the lifetime of the Prophet (PBUH), and those of Abu Bakr, 'Umar, and 'Uthman, I ate of those dates." —It is narrated through another chain of transmission: "I gave several loads of those dates to be used 'in God's way.' Later the bag containing the dates was plundered when 'Uthman was assassinated."[111]

Abu Hurayra was a constant and important student and disciple among the People of the Bench, the sacred school and *tekke* of the Teacher of the Universe, the Pride of the World (PBUH). In addition, the Prophet had prayed for his strength of memory. The miracle of plenty he reported which occurred in a large gathering like the expedition of Tabuk, should therefore be as sound and certain as the word of a whole army.

---

111. *Tirmidhī,* Manāqib 47 no: 3839; Bayhaqī, *Dalā'il al-Nubūwwa* vi, 110 (through various lines of transmission); Qāḍī Iyāḍ, *al-Shifā'* i, 295; al-Sā'atī, *al-Fatḥ al-Rabbānī* xx, 56; Tabrīzī, *Mishkāt al-Maṣābīḥ* iii, 191 no: 5933.

Sixteenth Example: Foremost Bukhari, and the accurate books relate, through an authentic narration, that once Abu Hurayra was hungry, so he followed the Noble Messenger (Upon whom be blessings and peace) into his house. There they saw that a cup of milk had been brought as a gift. God's Messenger said to him: "*Call all the People of the Bench!*" Abu Hurayra relates: "I said to myself, I could drink all the milk myself, as I was most in need of it. But since it was God's Messenger's order, I fetched the People of the Bench, who numbered more than a hundred. God's Messenger told me to offer milk to them. I gave the cup to each one by one, and each drank until satisfied. At the end, the Messenger told me,'*The rest is for me and you.*' As I drank, God's Messenger kept telling me to drink more, until I said, 'I swear by the Glorious One who sent you with the truth that I am too full to drink any more.' Then God's Messenger drank the rest, invoking the name of God and offering Him thanks."[112] May it be a blessing for him a hundred thousand times!

This indubitable, manifest miracle, as pure and sweet as milk itself, is related by all Six Books with their sound narrations, and foremost Bukhari, who committed to memory five hundred thousand Hadiths. Moreover, it is narrated by a celebrated, loyal, and brilliant student of the Prophet's blessed school of the Bench, Abu Hurayra, who also cited as witness —rather, represented— all the other students of the Bench. Therefore, not to regard such a report as having the certainty of 'consensus,' either one's heart should be corrupted, or one's brain, destroyed! Is it ever possible that such a truthful person as Abu Hurayra, who devoted all his life to the Prophet's Hadiths and to religion, and who heard and himself transmitted the Hadith, "*Whoever knowingly tells a lie concerning me should prepare*

112. *Bukhārī*, Riqāq 17; *Tirmidhī*, Ṣifāt al-Qiyāma 36 no: 2477; *Musnad* ii, 515; *Tirmidhī* (*Taḥqīq*: Aḥmad Shākir) no: 2479; al-Ḥākim, *al-Mustadrak* iii, 15; Qāḍī Iyāḍ, *al-Shifā'* i, 296.

for a seat in Hell-fire,"[113] should have related an unfounded incident or saying that would have made him the target of the contradiction of the People of the Bench, and that would have caused doubt concerning the value and soundness of all the other Hadiths he had memorized? God forbid!

O our Sustainer! For the sake of the blessings You bestowed on Your Most Noble Messenger, bestow the blessings of abundance on the favours with which You have provided us!

An Important Point: It is well-known that when assembled together, weak things become strong. Fine threads are twisted, and they become a strong rope; strong ropes are wound together, and no one can break them. In this Sign, we have shown from among fifteen different kinds of miracles only one, that related to the blessings of increase and plenty, and the sixteen examples we have given constitute barely a fifteenth of this one kind. However, each of the examples mentioned is a proof on its own, with enough strength to prove prophethood. Even if some of them —supposing the impossible— were to be regarded as weak, they could still not properly be called such, since whatever is united with the strong also becomes strong.

When considered together, the sixteen examples given above constitute a great and strong miracle through the strength of definite, indisputable 'consensus in meaning.' And, when this miracle is joined by fourteen other miracles of plenty that have not been mentioned, it manifests a supreme miracle which is as unbreakable as a collection of strong ropes. Now add this supreme miracle to the fourteen other kinds of miracle, and see what a definite, decisive and irrefutable proof they provide for the prophethood of Muhammad (PBUH)! Thus, the pillar of Muhammad's prophethood, formed by such a collection, has the strength of a mountain. Now you have understood how

113. *Bukhārī*, 'Ilm 39; Janā'iz 33; Anbiyā' 50; Adab 109; *Muslim*, Zuhd 72; *Abū Dā'ūd*, 'Ilm 4; *Tirmidhī*, Fitan 70; 'Ilm 8, 13; Tafsīr 1; Manāqib 19; *Ibn Māja*, Muqaddima 4; *Dārimī*, Muqaddima 25, 46; *Musnad* i, 70, 78.

unreasonable it is to regard as unstable and liable to fall that lofty, firm heaven, due to doubts arising from lack of understanding in particular matters and examples. Certainly those miracles concerning increase and plenty show that Muhammad the Arabian (Upon whom be blessings and peace) was the beloved official and honoured servant of One All-Compassionate and Munificent Who creates all sustenance and provides all beings with it, for contrary to His practice, He sent him banquets of different varieties of food out of nothing, from the pure Unseen.

It is well-known that the Arabian Peninsula is a place where water and agriculture are scarce. For this reason, its people, and particularly the Companions in the early days of Islam, suffered want and scarcity. They were also frequently afflicted with thirst. Due to this, the important of the manifest miracles of Muhammad (Upon whom be blessings and peace) concerned food and water. Rather than being miracles proving his claim to prophethood, these wonders were on account of need and like Divine gifts, dominical bounty, and banquets of the Most Merciful One for His Most Noble Messenger. For those who saw the miracles had already assented to his prophethood. However, as the miracles took place, their belief increased and became more luminous.

■ EIGHTH SIGN

This section relates miracles which were manifested in connection with water.

Introduction

It is known that when such events as take place among groups of people are related individually and not contradicted by others, this indicates the veracity of the reports. For by virtue of his very nature, man is inclined to call a lie a lie. In particular if the people in question were the Companions who were more intolerant of lies than anyone else, if the incidents concerned

God's Noble Messenger (Upon whom be blessings and peace), and if the narrator was a renowned Companion, then certainly the narrator gives his report on behalf of all who witnessed the incident. However, each of the miracles involving water that we will cite below was transmitted through many channels, entrusted by many Companions to thousands of precise scholars of the following generation, who in turn passed them down, authentically, to the great interpreters of the Law of the second century. They too received them with complete seriousness and reverence, accepted them, then handed them down to the exacting scholars of succeeding centuries. Thus the traditions have reached our times, passing through thousands of strong, reliable hands. Moreover, the texts of Hadiths written down in the Era of Bliss, the era of the Prophet, were handed down in accurate form till they reached the brilliant scholars of the science of Hadith like Bukhari and Muslim. And they, through punctilious examination and classification, collected together those of the Hadiths that were undoubtedly authentic, and presented and taught them to us. May God reward them abundantly!

Thus, the flowing of water from the fingers of God's Messenger (Upon whom be blessings and peace) and many men drinking from it has the certainty of consensus. It is impossible that the gathering who narrated it would have agreed on a lie. The miracle is most definite. Moreover, it was repeated three times in the presence of three vast assemblies. A great many accurate scholars, primarily, Bukhari, Muslim, Imam Malik, Imam Shu'ayb, and Imam Qatada, recorded from definitely authenticated narrations from a great many of the well-known Companions, primarily, the Prophet's servants, Anas, Jabir, and Ibn Mas'ud how abundant water had flowed from his fingers and the army drunk from it. From numerous narrations of this kind of miracle, we will cite here only nine examples.

First Example: Accurate books of tradition, in particular Bukhari and Muslim, report from an authentic narration from Anas: "About three hundred of us were together with God's Noble Messenger (Upon whom be blessings and peace) in the place named Zawra'. He ordered us to perform the ablution for the afternoon prayer, but we could find no water. He then told us to bring a little water, which we did, and he dipped his auspicious hands into it. I saw water flow from his fingers like a fountain. His three hundred men performed the ablution with the water and drank from it."[114]

Anas relates this incident in the name of three hundred men. Is it possible that those three hundred people did not in effect assent to it, or in the event of their not assenting to it, not deny it?

Second Example: As narrated in accurate books, and foremost Bukhari and Muslim, Jabir b. 'Abd Allah al-Ansari said: "We fifteen hundred people were thirsty during the Battle of Hudaybiyya. The Noble Messenger (Upon whom be blessings and peace) performed the ablutions from a leather water-bag called a *qirba*, then he dipped his hand into it. Then I saw that water was flowing from his fingers like a spring. Fifteen hundred men drank from it and filled their water-bags." Once, Salim b. Abi'l-Ja'd asked Jabir: "How many of you were there?" He replied: "The water would have been enough even if there had been a hundred thousand people, but we were fifteen hundred."[115]

Thus, the narrators of this clear miracle in effect number fifteen hundred, for it is man's nature to reject lies. As for the Companions of the Prophet, who sacrificed their tribes and peoples, their fathers and mothers, their lives and all they possessed for the sake of truth and veracity, they could not have remained silent in the face of a lie, especially in the light of the warning given by the tradition, "*Whoever knowingly tells a lie concern-*

114. *Bukhārī,* Wuḍū' 32, 46; Manāqib 25; *Muslim,* Faḍā'il 45, 46; Ṭahāra 60; *Abū Dā'ūd,* Muqaddima 5; *Tirmidhī,* Manāqib 6; *Muwaṭṭa',* Ṭahāra 32; *Musnad* iii, 132, 147, 170, 215, 289; Ibn Ḥibbān, *Ṣaḥīḥ* viii, 171; *Tirmidhī* (Aḥmad Shākir) no: 3635.

115. *Bukhārī,* Manāqib 25; Maghāzī 35; Tafsīr Sūra al-Fatḥ 5; Ashriba 31; *Muslim,* 'Imāra 72, 73; *Musnad* iii, 329; Ibn Ḥibbān, *Ṣaḥīḥ* viii, 159.

ing me should prepare for a seat in Hell-fire." Since they remained silent concerning this report, they accepted it, in effect joined Jabir, and confirmed him.

Third Example: Again as related in the accurate books of Hadith and foremost Bukhari and Muslim, Jabir reported: "During the Buwat expedition, the Noble Prophet (Upon whom be blessings and peace) commanded: '*Call for the ablutions!*' They said there was no water. He said, '*Find a small amount!*' We brought a very small amount. He held his hand over the water while reciting something I could not hear, and then commanded: '*Bring the caravan's big trough!*' They brought it to me and I placed it before God's Messenger. He put his hands in the trough and spread his fingers. I poured that very small amount of water onto his blessed hands, and I saw that abundant water was flowing from his blessed fingers and filling the trough. Then I summoned those who needed water. When they had all performed the ablutions with the water and drunk from it, I told the Noble Messenger that there was no one else. He lifted his hands, leaving the trough full to the brim."[116]

Thus, this clear miracle of Muhammad (PBUH) has the certainty of 'consensus in meaning,' for since Jabir was most prominent in the matter, he had the right to recount it and proclaim it in everybody else's name. Ibn Mas'ud relates exactly the same thing in his narration: "I saw water flowing from the fingers of God's Messenger as from a spring."[117] If a truthful, well-known group of Companions composed of Anas, Jabir, and Ibn Mas'ud said: "We have seen it," is it possible that they should not have seen it? Now combine these three examples and see how powerful and manifest a miracle it was, and how, if the three chains of transmission are combined, it proves the flowing of water from his fingers like 'true consensus.' Indeed,

116. *Muslim*, Zuhd 74 no: 3013; Ibn Ḥibbān, *Ṣaḥīḥ* viii, 159.
117. *Bukhārī*, Manāqib 25; *Tirmidhī*, Manāqib 6; *Tirmidhī* (*Taḥqīq*: Aḥmad Shākir) no: 3637; *Dārimī*, Muqaddima 5.

even Moses' making water flow from twelve different places in a rock cannot be equated with the water flowing from Muhammad's ten fingers, for water may gush out of rock —examples are to be found among ordinary events— but there is no equivalent of, no parallel for, water flowing in abundance, like from the Spring of Kawthar, from flesh and bone.

Fourth Example: Foremost Imam Malik in his esteemed book, *Muwatta'*, relates from the renowned Companion Mu'adh b. Jabal: "During the Tabuk expedition we came across a spring flowing as meagrely as a piece of fine string. The Noble Messenger (Upon whom be blessings and peace) ordered: '*Collect a little of the water!*' They collected some in the palms of their hands. God's Messenger washed his hands and face in it, and we returned it to the spring. Suddenly the outlet of the spring opened up and water gushed forth; it was sufficient for the whole army."[118]

Another narrator, even, Imam Ibn Ishaq, stated: "The water gushed forth from the spring under the earth making a roar like thunder. God's Noble Messenger told Mu'adh: '*If you live long enough, you will see that this miraculous water will transform this place into gardens.*' And so it did."

Fifth Example: Foremost Bukhari relates from al-Bara', and Muslim from Salama b. Akwa' and other authentic books of Hadith, unanimously relate: "During the Hudaybiyya expedition we came across a well. We numbered four hundred while the water in the well was barely sufficient for fifty. We drew the water and left nothing. Then God's Messenger (Upon whom be blessings and peace) came and sat at the head of the well. He asked for a bucket of water and we fetched one. He put some of his blessed spittle into the bucket and prayed, then poured the water into the well. Suddenly the well filled and

118. *Muwaṭṭa'*, Safar 2; *Musnad* ii, 308, 323; v, 228, 237; Ibn Ḥibbān, *Ṣaḥīḥ* viii, 167; Bayhaqī, *Dalā'il al-Nubūwwa* ii, 64; v, 236.

frothed with water, filling to the top. The whole army drank their fill and watered their animals. They also replenished their water bags.[119]

Sixth Example: Again, foremost brilliant authorities of the science of Hadith like Muslim and Ibn Jarir al-Tabari, and the authentic books of Hadith, relate from a sound narration from the famous Abu Qatada: "We were going for help on the leaders being martyred in the celebrated Battle of Mu'ta. I had a water-bag with me. The Noble Prophet commanded: '*Keep your water bag carefully; there will be great need for it.*' Soon after, we began to suffer from thirst. We were seventy-two people. [According to Tabari, three hundred.] The Prophet said: '*Bring me your water-bag!*' I did so, he took the bag and placed his lips on its mouth. I do not know whether or not he blew into it. Then seventy-two men came and drank from the bag and filled their bags. When I took it back, it was just as I had given it.[120]

See this decisive miracle of Muhammad (PBUH) and say: "O God! Grant him blessings and peace to the number of drops of water, and to his Family!"

Seventh Example: The authentic books and foremost Bukhari and Muslim narrate from 'Imran b. Husayn: "On one journey we and God's Messenger (Upon whom be blessings and peace) were without water. He said to me and 'Ali: '*There is a woman in such-and-such a place together with her beast which is laden with two full water-bags. Go and fetch her!*' 'Ali and I went and found the woman and the water in exactly the place described, and brought her to God's Messenger. He ordered: '*Pour a little of the water into a vessel.*' We did so and he prayed for the blessing of increase. He then commanded everyone to come to fill his water-bag. All the people

119. *Bukhārī*, Manāqib 25; Maghāzī 35; *Musnad* iv, 290, 301; Bayhaqī, *Dalā'il al-Nubūwwa* iv, 110.
120. *Muslim*, Masājid 311.

came, drank, and filled their water-bags. Afterwards he gave an order to collect something for the woman, and they filled her skirt." 'Imran said: "I imagined the two water-bags were constantly filling. The Noble Messenger told the woman: '*You can go now. We did not take water from you; rather God gave us water from His treasury.*'"[121]

Eighth Example: Scholars of Hadith, primarily Ibn Khuzayma in his *Sahih*, narrate from 'Umar: "We ran out of water during the Tabuk expedition. Some people even slaughtered their camels, wrung out the innards and drank the liquid. Abu Bakr the Veracious requested the Noble Messenger (Upon whom be blessings and peace) to pray. The Messenger raised his hands, and before he had lowered them clouds gathered, and such rain fell that we filled our containers. Then the rain stopped, and it had not fallen beyond the limits of the army."[122] That is to say, no chance was involved in the incident; it was purely a miracle of Muhammad (Upon whom be blessings and peace).

Ninth Example: Relating from 'Amr b. Shu'ayb, the grandson of 'Abd Allah b. 'Amr b. al-'As, on whom they relied for explanations of Hadiths, the Four Imams narrated—from a sound narration: "Before his prophetic mission, the Noble Messenger (Upon whom be blessings and peace) once came by camel to the place called Dhu'l-Mijaz near 'Arafat with his uncle Abu Talib. Abu Talib said he was thirsty. The Prophet dismounted from the camel and struck the ground with his foot. Water gushed out and Abu Talib drank from it."[123]

One of the researchers, however, stated that this incident

---

121. *Bukhārī*, Tayammum 6; Manāqib 25; *Muslim*, Masājid 312; *Musnad* iv, 434-5; Bayhaqī, *Dalā'il al-Nubūwwa* iv, 216; vi, 130.

122. al-Haythamī, *Majma' al-Zawā'id* vi, 194; al-Hindī, *Kanz al-'Ummāl* xii, 353; Qāḍī Iyāḍ, *al-Shifā'* i, 190; 'Alī al-Qārī, *Sharḥ al-Shifā'* i, 600; Bayhaqī, *Dalā'il al-Nubūwwa* ii, 63; Suyūṭī, *al-Khaṣā'iṣ al-Kubrā* ii, 105.

123. Qāḍī Iyāḍ, *al-Shifā'* i, 290; al-Khafājī, *Sharḥ al-Shifā'* iii, 29; Bayhaqī, *Dalā'il al-Nubūwwa* ii, 15-20.

should be considered to be of the category of *irhasat*,[124] because it occurred before his prophethood; however, since that time the spring of 'Arafat has flowed from the spot, and may therefore be considered a wonder of Muhammad (PBUH).

Similar to these nine examples, ninety different narrations—if not ninety instances—have reported miracles concerning water. The first seven examples are as sound and definite as 'consensus in meaning.' For sure the last two are not supported by the narrations of numerous narrators or a strong chain of transmitters, but supporting and confirming the incident mentioned in the eighth example as narrated by 'Umar, is another miracle reported by the authentic books of Hadith, including Bayhaqi and al-Hakim; it is as follows:

"'Umar requested of God's Noble Messenger (Upon whom be blessings and peace) that he should pray for rain, because the army was in need of water. The Messenger raised his hands, and at once clouds gathered and rain fell, enough for the army's needs, then they dispersed."[125] It was quite simply as though they were officials charged with watering the army; they came, poured down sufficient for its needs, then went.

Just as this narration corroborates and proves decisively the eighth example, so too the famous learned scholar, Ibn al-Jawzi, who was extremely fastidious in verifying Hadiths even rejecting as spurious many authentic ones, said that this event took place, but at the famous Battle of Badr. He stated that the verse,

> *And He caused rain to descend on you from heaven to clean you therewith*[126]

refers to the incident. Since that is the case, certainly no room for doubt can remain. Furthermore, rain falling on the Prophet praying for it, suddenly, swiftly, before he lowered his hands,

124. For *irhāṣāt*, see definition on page 124ff.
125. al-Khafājī, *Sharḥ al-Shifā'* iii, 128; 'Alī al-Qārī, *Sharḥ al-Shifā'* i, 601; Suyūṭī, *al-Durar al-Manthūr* iii, 170.
126. Qur'ān, 8:11.

occurred on many occasions, and was on its own a miracle, concerning the reports for which there is consensus. It is also narrated with 'consensus,' that several times he raised his hands while in the pulpit and that rain fell before he lowered them.

■ NINTH SIGN

One of the various kinds of miracles of God's Most Noble Messenger (Upon whom be blessings and peace) is that like human beings, trees obeyed his orders, and moving from their places, came to him. There is also 'consensus in meaning' in the reports of these miracles, like those of water flowing from his fingers. They have been narrated in numerous forms and through numerous channels. Indeed, the consensus concerning trees leaving their places and coming to him may be considered as 'explicit,'[127] because the best-known of the Companions such as 'Ali, Ibn 'Abbas, Ibn Mas'ud, Ibn 'Umar, Ya'la b. Murra, Jabir, Anas b. Malik, Burayda, Usama b. Zayd, and Ghaylan b. Salama, each reported the same miracle with certainty. Hundreds of scholars of the succeeding generation narrated the miracle from one of the above-mentioned Companions through a different line of transmission, as though transmitting it to us in the form of multiple 'consensus.' Thus, this miracle of the trees has decisively and indisputably the certainty of 'consensus in meaning.' We will now cite only a few examples of this great miracle, although it was repeated many times.

First Example: Foremost, Imam Maja, and al-Darimi narrate from Anas b. Malik and 'Ali, and Imam Bayhaqi from 'Umar, that the Noble Messenger (Upon whom be blessings and peace) was saddened at the denial of the unbelievers. He prayed: "*O my Sustainer! Give me a sign that I shall no longer see anyone who contradicts me!*"[128] According to Anas,

127. Kattānī, *Naẓm al-Mutanāthir* 137.

128. *Ibn Māja*, Fitan 23 no: 4028; *Dārimī*, Muqaddima 3; *Musnad* i, 223; iii, 113; iv, 177; Qāḍī Iyāḍ, *al-Shifā'* i, 302; 'Alī al-Qārī, *Sharḥ al-Shifā'* i, 620; al-Haythamī, *Majma' al-Zawā'id* ix, 10; al-Hindī, *Kanz al-'Ummāl* ii, 354.

Gabriel was also present, upon whose instruction God's Messenger called to a tree at the side of the valley. It came near him. He then told the tree to go back; it returned and settled itself in its place.

Second Example: In *Shifa' al-Sharif*, Qadi Iyad, the leading scholar of the Maghrib, relates from 'Abd Allah b. 'Umar through an exalted and sound chain of narrators: "On one expedition, a beduin approached the Noble Messenger (Upon whom be blessings and peace). God's Messenger asked him: '*Where are you going?*' He replied: 'To my family.' God's Messenger asked him: '*Don't you want something better than that?*' The beduin asked: 'What is that?' The Messenger said: '*That you bear witness that there is no god but God, He is One, He has no partner, and that Muhammad is His servant and Messenger.*' The beduin asked: 'What is witness to this testimony?' God's Messenger said: '*The tree beside the valley shall bear witness.*'" Ibn 'Umar said: "Shaking, the tree cleft the earth and came to God's Messenger. He asked the tree three times to testify; each time it testified to his truthfulness. When he ordered, it went back and settled in its place."[129]

According to the authentic narration of Ibn Sahib al-Aslami, Burayda reports: "When we were with the Noble Messenger (Upon whom be blessings and peace) on an expedition, a beduin came and asked for a sign, that is, a miracle. The Messenger said: '*Tell that tree that God's Messenger summons it!*' Then he pointed to a tree; it swayed to right and left, brought itself out of the ground with its roots, and came to the presence of the Messenger, saying: 'Peace be upon you, O Messenger of God!' The beduin said: 'Now let it go to its place again!' He commanded, and it went. Then the beduin said: 'Allow me to prostrate before

129. Qāḍī Iyāḍ, *al-Shifā'* i, 298; 'Alī al-Qārī, *Sharḥ al-Shifā'* i, 615; Bayhaqī, *Dalā'il al-Nubūwwa* vi, 14; al-Haythamī, *Majma' al-Zawā'id* viii, 292; Ibn Kathīr, *al-Bidāya wa'l-Nihāya* vi, 125; al-'Asqalānī, *al-Maṭālib al-'Alīya* iv, 16 no: 3836; al-Ḥākim, *al-Mustadrak* ii, 620; Ibn Ḥibbān, *Ṣaḥīḥ* viii, 150.

you.' The Messenger replied: '*No one is permitted to do that.*' The beduin said: 'Then I will kiss your hands and feet,' and he permitted him."[130]

Third Example: Foremost the *Sahih* of Muslim, and the authentic books of Hadith relate that Jabir said: "We were together with God's Noble Messenger (Upon whom be blessings and peace) on an expedition when he searched for a place to answer the call of nature. There was no secluded place. So he went towards two trees, caught hold of the branches of one of them, and pulled. Obeying him, the tree went together with him to the second tree. It was like an obedient camel being led by its reins. Having in this way brought the two trees together, he said: '*Join together over me, with God's permission!*' The two trees joined together and formed a screen. After relieving himself behind them, he ordered them to go back, and they returned to their places."[131]

According to another narration, Jabir said: "God's Messenger commanded me: '*Tell those trees to join together for the relief of God's Messenger!*' I told them to do so, and they joined together. Then, while I was waiting, God's Messenger (Upon whom be blessings and peace) emerged, and indicated to left and right with his head. The two trees returned to their places."[132]

Fourth Example: Usama b. Zayd, one the brave commanders and servants of the Noble Messenger (Upon whom be blessings and peace), reports in an authentic narration: "We were together with God's Messenger on an expedition. There was no secluded, private place in which to answer the call of nature. He asked: '*Can you see any trees or rocks?*' I replied: 'Yes, I can.' He ordered: '*Speak to them and tell them to join*

---

130. Qāḍī Iyāḍ, *al-Shifā'* i, 299; al-Khafājī, *Sharḥ al-Shifā'* iii, 49.

131. *Muslim*, Zuhd no: 3012.

132. *Dārimī*, Muqaddima 4; Qāḍī Iyāḍ, *al-Shifā'* i, 299; 'Alī al-Qārī, *Sharḥ al-Shifā'* i, 616; al-Khafājī, *Sharḥ al-Shifā'* iii, 51.

together for the relief of God's Messenger; also tell the rocks to gather together as a wall.' I went and said as he commanded. I swear that the trees joined together and the rocks formed a wall. God's Messenger after relieving himself, again commanded: '*Tell them to separate!*' I swear by the Glorious One in the grasp of Whose power I am that the trees and rocks separated, and returned to their places."[133]

These two incidents which were reported by Jabir b. Usama were also rreported by Ya'la b. Murra, Ghaylan b. Salama al-Thaqafi, and Ibn Mas'ud, referring to the Battle of Hunayn.[134]

Fifth Example: Reported by Imam b. Fawrak, known as 'the foremost scholar of his time' and 'Shafi'i the Second' for his excellence in interpretation: "While travelling on horseback one night during the Ta'if expedition, sleep overcame God's Noble Messenger (Upon whom be blessings and peace). While in that state a lote-tree loomed up before him. To make way for him and not to hurt his horse, the tree split in two, and the Noble Messenger, on the horse, passed between the two parts of the tree." The tree has remained as two trunks, in that honoured position, up to our time.[135]

Sixth Example: Ya'la b. Murra relates in an authentic narration: "During an expedition, a tree —called either *talha* or *samura*— came, passed around God's Noble Messenger (Upon whom be blessings and peace) as if circumambulating, and went back to its place. God's Messenger said: '*The tree requested of God that it should salute me.*'"[136]

Seventh Example: Scholars of Hadith relate from

133. Qāḍī Iyāḍ, *al-Shifā'* i, 300; 'Alī al-Qārī, *Sharḥ al-Shifā'* i, 617-9; al-Khafājī, *Sharḥ al-Shifā'* iii, 51; al-'Asqalānī, *al-Maṭālib al-'Alīya* iv, 8-10 no: 3830.

134. Qāḍī Iyāḍ, *al-Shifā'* i, 301; al-Hindī, *Kanz al-'Ummāl* xii, 403.

135. Qāḍī Iyāḍ, *al-Shifā'* i, 301; 'Alī al-Qārī, *Sharḥ al-Shifā'* i, 619; al-Khafājī, *Sharḥ al-Shifā'* iii, 57.

136. Qāḍī Iyāḍ, *al-Shifā'* i, 301; 'Alī al-Qārī, *Sharḥ al-Shifā'* i, 619; al-Khafājī, *Sharḥ al-Shifā'* iii, 53; al-Haythamī, *Majma' al Zawā'id* ix, 6-7; *Musnad* iv, 170, 172; al-Ḥākim, *al-Mustadrak* ii, 617.

Ibn Mas'ud with an authentic narration: "When the jinn of Nusaybin came to the Noble Messenger (Upon whom be blessings and peace) in the place called Batn al-Nakhl in order to find guidance, a tree informed him of their coming." Also, Imam Mujahid relates from Ibn Mas'ud in the Hadith: "The jinn asked for a proof of his prophethood, so the Noble Prophet commanded the tree, and it left its place, came to him, then returned to its place."[137] That single miracle was sufficient for the race of jinns. So if a human being does not come to believe having heard of a thousand miracles like this one, is he not more of a devil than those described by the jinn as, "*Some foolish ones among us*"?[138]

Eighth Example: Tirmidhi reports in his Sahih from Ibn 'Abbas through a sound narration: "God's Noble Messenger (Upon whom be blessings and peace) asked a beduin: '*Will you testify that I am the Messenger of God if a branch of that tree comes to me when I call to it?*' He replied: 'Yes.' The Messenger called to the branch. It broke off and jumped over near him, then jumped back when he told it to do so."[139]

Like these eight examples, there are many others related through many chains of transmission. Seven or eight strands of rope form a strong cable when they come together. Similarly, these miracles concerning trees, which were reported on the authority of the best-known and most veracious Companions in thus numerous chains of transmission, certainly have the strength of 'consensus in meaning,' indeed, 'true consensus.' In fact, they take on the form of 'consensus' when passed down by the Companions to the following generation. In particular, the accurate books of Hadith such as Bukhari, Muslim, Ibn Hibban,

137. *Bukhārī*, Manāqib al-Anṣār 32 (Bāb: Dhikr al-Jinn); *Muslim*, Ṣalāt 150; 'Alī al-Qārī, *Sharḥ al-Shifā'* i, 619.

138. Qur'ān, 72:4.

139. *Tirmidhī*, Manāqib 6; al-Mubārakfūrī, *Tuḥfat al-Aḥwazī* no: 3707; al-Haythamī, *Majma' al-Zawā'id* ix, 10.

and Tirmidhi, made the chains leading back to the time of the Companions so sound, and they kept them thus, that reading a Hadith, say in Bukhari, is like hearing it directly from the Companions.

If, as seen in the above examples, trees recognize God's Messenger (Upon whom be blessings and peace) testify to his prophethood, visit and salute him, and obey his orders, and those lifeless, unreasoning creatures who call themselves human beings do not recognize him or believe in him, will they not be more worthless than a dead tree, and like a piece of wood, fit for the fire?

■ TENTH SIGN

Corroborating the miracles concerning trees and reported in the form of 'consensus,' is the miracle of the moaning of the pole. Yes, the pole's moaning in the Prophet's mosque before a vast crowd because of its temporary separation from the Prophet (PBUH) both confirms and strengthens the instances of miracles related to trees. For the pole also was of wood; their substance was the same. However, the reports of this miracle itself form a consensus, whereas the others are thus as a group in one class, most of them individually or separately not attaining the degree of 'explicit consensus.'

When delivering the sermon in the mosque, God's Noble Messenger (Upon whom be blessings and peace) used to lean against a pole consisting of a date-palm. But when the pulpit was made, he began to give the sermon from there. Whereupon the pole moaned and wailed like a camel; the whole congregation heard it. Only when the Prophet came down from the pulpit to it, and placed his hand on it, speaking to it and consoling it, did the pole stop moaning. This miracle of Muhammad (PBUH) was narrated through numerous chains of transmission, at the degree of 'consensus.'

Indeed, the miracle of the moaning of the pole is very widely known and there is 'true consensus' concerning it.[140] Hundreds of authorities on Hadith of the subsequent generation narrated the miracle through fifteen chains of transmission from an illustrious group of Companions, and passed it down to succeeding centuries.[141] From that group, eminent scholars among the Companions and leading experts on Hadith such as Anas b. Malik[142] and Jabir b. 'Abd Allah al-Ansari[143]—both servants of the Prophet, 'Abd Allah b. 'Umar,[144] 'Abd Allah b. 'Abbas,[145] Sahl b. Sa'd,[146] Abu Sa'id al-Khudri,[147] Ubayy b. Ka'b,[148] Burayda,[149] and Umm Salama, the Mother of Believers,[150] each at the head of a chain of transmission, reported this same miracle to the Prophet's community. Foremost Bukhari, Muslim, and the authentic books of Hadith gave accounts of this great miracle, concerning which there is consensus of reports, together with its lines of transmission for succeeding generations.

Jabir, in his chain of transmission, says: "God's Messenger (Upon whom be blessings and peace) used to lean against a wooden pole called 'the palm trunk' while delivering the sermon in the mosque. The pole could not endure it when the pul-

---

140. See, al-Kattānī, *Naẓm al-Mutanāthir* 134-5.

141. Ibn Kathīr, *al-Bidāya wa'l-Nihāya* 125-132.

142. *Bukhārī*, Manāqib 25; *Tirmidhī*, Manāqib 6; Jum'a 10; *Ibn Māja*, Iqāmat al-Ṣalāt 199; *Dārimī*, Muqaddima 6; Ṣalāt 202; *Musnad* i, 249, 267, 363; iii, 226; Ibn al-Asīr al-Jawzī, *al-Jāmi' al-Uṣūl* no: 8899.

143. *Bukhārī*, Manāqib 25l; *Tirmidhī*, Manāqib 6; Jum'a 10; *Nasā'ī*, Jum'a 17; *Ibn Māja*, Iqāmat al-Ṣalāt 199; *Dārimī*, Muqaddima 6 (3 different lines from Jābir); Ṣalāt 202; *Musnad* iii, 293, 295, 306, 324.

144. *Bukhārī*, Manāqib 25; *Tirmidhī*, Jum'a 10; *Tirmidhī* (*Taḥqīq*: Aḥmad Shākir) no: 505; Manāqib 6; *Dārimī*, Muqaddima 6.

145. *Tirmidhī*, Manāqib 6; Jum'a 10; *Dārimī*, Muqaddima 6; Ṣalāt 202; *Musnad* i, 249; *Musnad* i, 363.

146. *Tirmidhī*, Manāqib 6; Jum'a 10; *Dārimī*, Muqaddima 6; Ṣalāt 202; al-Khafājī, *Sharḥ al-Shifā'* iii, 62.

147. *Dārimī*, Muqaddima 6.

148. *Tirmidhī*, Jum'a 10; *Ibn Māja*, Iqāmat al-Ṣalāt 199; *Dārimī*, Muqaddima 6; *Musnad* 139; al-Khafājī, *Sharḥ al-Shifā* iii, 62; al-Mubārakfūrī, *Tuḥfat al-Aḥwazī* iii, 22.

149. *Dārimī*, Muqaddima 6.

150. *Tirmidhī*, Manāqib 6; Jum'a 10.

pit was made and the Messenger used that for the sermon, and began to moan and wail like a pregnant camel."[151] In his narration, Anas says: "It moaned like a water-buffalo causing the mosque to tremble."[152] In his narration, Sahl b. Sa'd says: "And weeping increased among the people, on the pole's moaning." In his narration, Ubayy b. Ka'b says: "It wept so much it split." While in another narration, the Noble Messenger said: "*It is weeping at being separated from the recitation of God's Names and the mentioning of God during the sermon.*" Still another narration reports that God's Messenger said: "*If I had not embraced and consoled it, it would have wept at being separated from God's Messenger until Doomsday.*" In his narration, Burayda reports: "When the pole began to moan, God's Messenger put his hand on it and said, '*If you wish, I will return you to the grove you came from; your roots will grow and you will flourish; you will produce new fruits. Of if you wish, I will plant you in Paradise, and God's friends, the saints, will eat of your fruit.*' He then listened to the pole. The people behind God's Messenger could hear it as it spoke, saying: 'Plant me in Paradise, where there is no decay, so that Almighty God's beloved servants will eat of my fruit.' The Messenger said: '*I will,*' and added: '*It has preferred the eternal realm to that of transitoriness.*'" Abu Ishaq Isfara'ini, one of the great authorities on theology, narrated: "God's Messenger (Upon whom be blessings and peace) did not go to the pole, but it came to him, at his command. Then, at his command, it returned to its place."[153] Ubayy b. Ka'b says: "After this extraordinary event, God's Messenger ordered that the pole be put under the pulpit. It was put there and remained there until the mosque was pulled down before being rebuilt. Then Ubayy b. Ka'b took it and kept it until it decayed.[154]

151. See, *Bukhārī*, Manāqib 25.
152. See, *Dārimī*, Muqaddima 6.
153. Qāḍī Iyāḍ, *al-Shifā'* i, 304.
154. Qāḍī Iyāḍ, *al-Shifā'* i, 304; *Ibn Māja*, Iqāmat al-Ṣalāt 199; *Dārimī*, Muqaddima 6.

The famous scholar Hasan al-Basri would weep while teaching this miraculous event to his students, and say to them: "A piece of wood demonstrated love and longing for God's Noble Messenger (Upon whom be blessings and peace), so you should feel more love than that."[155] As for us, we say, Yes, and love and longing for him is shown through following his illustrious Practices and sacred Shari'a.

An Important Point

If it is asked : Why were the other miracles which were demonstrated in relation to food —to satisfy fully a thousand men with four handfuls of food in the Battle of Khandaq, and another thousand men with water flowing from the Messenger's blessed fingers— not narrated through numerous chains of transmission as the miracle of the moaning of the pole, although the former two miracles occurred in the presence of larger crowds?

The Answer: The miracles that were manifested were of two kinds: one were manifested at the hands of God's Messenger (Upon whom be blessings and peace), in order to make people assent to his prophethood. The moaning of the pole was of that kind. It occurred solely as a proof, an affirmation, of prophethood, to increase the believers' faith, to urge the dissemblers to sincerity and belief, and to bring to belief the unbelievers. That is why everyone, the low and the high, saw it, and great attention was paid to broadcasting it. However, the miracles concerning food and water were wonders rather than miracles, or Divine favours rather than wonders, or, more than favour, they were banquets bestowed by the All-Merciful One because of need. For sure, they were proofs of his claim to prophethood and miracles, but their basic aim was this: the army was hungry so Almighty God provided a feast for a thousand men out of a handful of food from His treasury in the Unseen, just as He creates a thousand pounds of dates from a single seed. And for a

155. Qāḍī Iyāḍ, *al-Shifā'* i, 305.

thirsty army fighting in His way, He caused water to flow like the water of Kawthar from the fingers of the Commander-in-Chief, and gave them to drink.

It is for this reason that all the examples of the miracles concerning food and water do not attain the degree of the miracle of the moaning of the pole. However, in their entirety, the various kinds of these two miracles are as numerous and unanimously reported as the moaning of the pole. Moreover, not everyone could see the increase of food and water flowing from his fingers; they could only see the results. Whereas everyone heard the pole moaning, so it was more widely broadcast.

If it is asked: All the actions and conduct of God's Messenger (Upon whom be blessings and peace) were recorded and transmitted by his Companions with extreme care. Why then are such great miracles only narrated through ten or twenty chains of transmission, when they should have been narrated through a hundred? Also, why are many narrated from Anas, Jabir, and Abu Hurayra, and few related from Abu Bakr and 'Umar?

The Answer: The answer to the first part of the question has been given in the Third Principle in the Fourth Sign. Regarding the second part: just as someone in need of medicine goes to a doctor, mathematicians are consulted on mathematical problems, and questions to do with the Shari'a are asked of the Mufti, and so on; so too, some of the scholars among the Companions were charged with the duty of instructing succeeding centuries in the Hadiths of the Prophet, working with all their strength for this end. Yes, Abu Hurayra devoted his entire life to memorizing Hadiths, while 'Umar was occupied with the world of politics and the Caliphate. 'Umar therefore narrated very few traditions, relying on persons like Abu Hurayra, Anas, and Jabir, to teach the Hadiths to the Muslim community. Furthermore, on a well-known, truthful, sincere, honest, and trusted Companion reporting an incident through one chain, it was regarded as sufficient, and no need remained for another to narrate it. This is why some significant events were narrated through only two or three chains of transmission.

ELEVENTH SIGN

As the Tenth Sign explained miracles of the Prophet related to trees, the Eleventh Sign will describe how rocks and mountains among lifeless creatures also demonstrated prophetic miracles. Here we cite a few out of numerous instances.

First Example: The great scholar of the Maghrib, Qadi Iyad, in his *Shifa' al-Sharif*, with a celebrated chain of authorities, and great imams like Bukhari, report through an authentic narration, from Ibn Mas'ud, the Prophet's servant: "While eating together with God's Noble Messenger (Upon whom be blessings and peace), we used to hear the food glorifying God."[156]

Second Example: Accurate books of Hadith report from Anas and Abu Dharr through an authentic narration: "Anas, the Prophet's servant, said: 'We were together with God's Messenger (Upon whom be blessings and peace) when he took up a handful of small stones and they began to praise God in his blessed palm. Then he put them in Abu Bakr the Veracious's hand and again they glorified God.'"[157] In his line of transmission, Abu Dharr al-Ghifari says: "Then he put them into 'Umar's hand, and again they glorified God. Then he took them and put them on the ground, and they were silent. Then he again took them, and put them in 'Uthman's hand, where again they began to glorify God." Abu Dharr and Anas relate: "He put them in our hands and they were silent."[158]

---

156. *Bukhārī*, Manaqib 25; *Tirmidhī*, Manāqib 6 (*Taḥqīq*: Ibrāhīm A'wād) no: 3633; *Musnad* i, 460; Qāḍī Iyāḍ, *al-Shifā'* i, 306; 'Alī al-Qārī, *Sharḥ al-Shifā'* i, 627; Ibn Kathīr, *al-Bidāya wa'l-Nihāya* vi, 97-8, 133.

157. Qāḍī Iyāḍ, *al-Shifā'* i, 306; al-Khafājī, *Sharḥ al-Shifā'* iii, 70; 'Alī al-Qārī, *Sharḥ al-Shifā'* i, 627.

158. Qāḍī Iyāḍ, *al-Shifā'* i, 306; al-Haythamī, *Majma' al-Zawā'id* v, 179; vii, 298-9; Ibn Kathīr, *al-Bidāya wa'l-Nihāya* vi, 132-3

Third Example: It is established through a sound narration from 'Ali, Jabir, and 'A'isha al-Siddiqa: "Rocks and mountains would say to God's Messenger (Upon whom be blessings and peace), 'Peace be upon you, O Messenger of God!'" In 'Ali's chain of narration, it says: "Whenever we went around in the environs of Makkah in the early of days of his prophethood, the trees and rocks we encountered would declare: 'Peace be upon you, O Messenger of God!'"[159] While in his chain of transmission, Jabir says: "Whenever the Noble Messenger came across rocks and trees, they would prostrate before him, that is, demonstrating obedience to him, they would declare: 'Peace be upon you, O Messenger of God!'"[160] In one of Jabir's narrations, the Messenger said: "*I know a rock that salutes me.*"[161] Some said that he intended the Black Stone of the Ka'ba. In her line of transmission, 'A'isha said: "God's Messenger said: '*When Gabriel brought me the message, I would never pass by a rock or a tree without it saying, 'Peace be upon you, O Messenger of God!*'"[162]

Fourth Example: Reported through an authentic narration from 'Abbas: "God's Messenger (Upon whom be blessings and peace) covered 'Abbas and his four sons ('Abd Allah, 'Ubayd Allah, Fadl, and Qusam) with a piece of cloth called *mula'at*, praying: '*O my Sustainer! This is my uncle; protect through me these his sons and veil them from the Fire, as I veil them with this cloth!*' The roof, door, and the walls of the house joined in the prayer at once, saying, Amen! Amen!"[163]

Fifth Example: Accurate books, notably Bukhari, Ibn Hibban, Da'ud, and Tirmidhi, unanimously report from Anas[164]

160. Qāḍī Iyāḍ, *al-Shifā'* i, 307; al-Khafājī, *Sharḥ al-Shifā'* iii, 71.

161. *Muslim*, Faḍā'il 2; *Tirmidhī*, Manāqib 5; *Musnad* v, 89, 95, 105; Ibn Ḥibbān, *Ṣaḥīḥ* viii, 139.

162. Qāḍī Iyāḍ, *al-Shifā'* i, 307; al-Khafājī, *Sharḥ al-Shifā'* iii, 71; al-Haythamī, *Majma' al-Zawā'id* viii, 259.

163. Qāḍī Iyāḍ, *al-Shifa'* i, 608; 'Alī al-Qārī, *Sharḥ al-Shifā'* i, 628; al-Ḥākim, *al-Mustadrak* ii, 309; al-Haythamī, *Majma' al-Zawā'id* ix, 269-70.

164. *Bukhārī*, Faḍā'il al-Aṣḥāb 5, 6, 7; *Tirmidhī*, Manāqib 19, no: 3697; *Abū Dā'ūd*, Sunna 9 (Bāb: Fi'l-Khulafā').

Abu Hurayra[165] 'Uthman Dhi'n-Nurayn,[166] and Sa'd b. Zayd,[167] from among the ten promised Paradise: "God's Noble Messenger (Upon whom be blessings and peace) climbed Mount Uhud together with Abu Bakr al-Siddiq, 'Umar al-Faruq, and 'Uthman Dhi'n-Nurayn. Either due to their awesomeness, or out of its own joy and happiness, the mountain began to tremble and stir. God's Messenger said: *'Steady! For upon you are a prophet, a veracious one (siddiq), and two martyrs!'*

This tradition is giving news from the Unseen that 'Umar and 'Uthman were going to be martyred. As a supplement to this tradition, it is narrated that when God's Noble Messenger (Upon whom be blessings and peace) migrated from Makkah pursued by the unbelievers, they climbed the mountain called Thubir. The mountain said: "Leave me, O Messenger of God! I am afraid that God will punish me if they strike you on me." Then Mount Hira called to him: "Come to me, O Messenger of God!" For this reason, men of intuition feel fear on Mount Thubir and a sense of safety on Mount Hira.

As can be understood from this example, these vast mountains are each an individual servant of God; each glorifies and praises Him; each is charged with duties. They recognized and loved God's Messenger; they are not without purpose or owner.

Sixth Example: Reported through an authentic narration from 'Abd Allah b. 'Umar:[168] "While delivering the sermon from the pulpit, God's Messenger (Upon whom be blessings and peace) recited the verse:

> *No just estimate have they made of God, such as is due to Him: on the Day of Judgement the whole earth will be but His handful, and the heavens will be rolled up in His right hand,*[169]

165. *Muslim*, Faḍā'il al-Ṣaḥāba 6 no: 2417; *Tirmidhī*, Manāqib 19.
166. *Tirmidhī*, Manāqib 19.
167. *Tirmidhī*, Manāqib 19; al-Ḥākim, *al-Mustadrak* iii, 450.
168. Qāḍī Iyāḍ, *al-Shifa'* i, 308; al-Khafājī, *Sharḥ al-Shifā'* iii, 75.
169. Qur'ān, 39:67.

and said: '*God the Compeller is exalting Himself and saying: I am the Compeller! I am the Compeller! I am the Mighty! I am the Most High!*' As he said this, the pulpit so trembled and shook that we were frightened it would cause God's Messenger to fall."[170]

Seventh Example: It is reported through an authentic narration from Ibn 'Abbas,[171] known as 'the Scholar of the Muslim Community' and 'Interpreter of the Qur'an,' and Ibn Mas'ud, the servant of the Prophet and one of the great scholars of the Companions,[172] that they said: "On the conquest of Makkah, there were three hundred and sixty idols around the Ka'ba, fixed with lead to the stone. That day, the Noble Prophet (Upon whom be blessings and peace) pointed to each of the idols in turn with a stick he was holding curved like a bow, saying,

> *The Truth has arrived and falsehood has perished; indeed, falsehood is ever bound to perish.*[173]

Whichever one he pointed to, it fell down.[174] If he pointed to the face of the idol, it fell backwards; otherwise it fell on its face. Thus they all toppled over and fell to the ground.[175]

Eighth Example: This is the famous story of the well-known monk Bahira. Before the beginning of his prophethood, God's Noble Messenger (Upon whom be blessings and peace) was travelling towards Damascus to trade together with his uncle Abu Talib and some of the Quraysh. They rested when they came near the church of Bahira the monk. Bahira,

---

170. *Muslim*, Ṣifāt al-Qiyāma 19-26; *Musnad* ii, 88; al-Ḥākim, *al-Mustadrak* ii, 252; Qāḍī Iyāḍ, *al-Shifa'* i, 308; al-Khafājī, *Sharḥ al-Shifā'* iii, 75; 'Alī al-Qārī, *Sharḥ al-Shifā'* i, 630; Ibn Ḥibbān, *Ṣaḥīḥ* ix, 214.

171. *Muslim*, Jihād 87 no: 1781.

172. *Bukhārī*, Maghāzī 48; Maẓālim 32; Tafsīr al-Qur'ān 12; *Tirmidhī*, Tafsīr al-Qur'ān 18 (Bāb: Sūra Bani Isrā'īl); Ibn Ḥibbān, *Ṣaḥīḥ* no: 1702.

173. Qur'ān, 17:81.

174. In Bukhārī, Muslim, Tirmidhī, and other books, this much is recorded. Only in the following is the Ḥadīth complete.

175. al-Haythamī, *Majma' al-Zawā'id wa'l-Manbā' al-Fawā'id* vi, 176 (from Ibn Mas'ūd).

who was a hermit and did not mix with people, suddenly came out. He saw Muhammad the Trustworthy (PBUH) among the caravan, and said: "He is the Lord of the World; he will be a prophet." The Quraysh asked: "How do you know?" The holy monk replied: "I saw a small cloud over the caravan as you were coming. When you sat down, the cloud moved toward him and cast its shadow over him. I also saw trees and rocks prostrate themselves before him, which they do only before prophets."[176]

There are at least eighty examples of the same kind as these eight instances. When they come together, these eight instances form a chain so strong that no doubt can break it or shake it. Taken as a whole, this sort of miracle, that is, the speaking of inanimate beings in order to testify to his prophethood, expresses the same certainty as 'consensus in meaning.' Each example receives strength greater than its own from the strength of the whole. Yes, a slender pole becomes strong on coming together with stout poles. On becoming a soldier and joining the army, a weak, powerless man becomes so strong he may challenge a thousand men.

■ TWELFTH SIGN

This consists of three examples related to the Eleventh Sign, but which are examples of the greatest importance.

First Example:

And when you threw, it was not you who threw; it was rather God that threw.[177]

As established by the researches of all Qur'anic commentators, and by the reports of the scholars of Hadith, this verse refers to the following incident during the Battle of Badr:

---

176. Qāḍī Iyāḍ, *al-Shifa'* i, 308; 'Alī al-Qārī, *Sharḥ al-Shifā'* i, 631; *Tirmidhī*, Manāqib 3 (Bāb: Mājā' fī Badī' al-Nubūwwa); al-Mubārakfūrī, *Tuḥfat al-Aḥwazī* no: 3699; al-Ḥākim, *al-Mustadrak* ii, 615; Ibn Ḥishām, *Sīrat al-Nabī* 115.

177. Qur'ān, 8:17.

God's Noble Messenger (Upon whom be blessings and peace) took up a handful of earth and small stones and threw them at the army of the unbelievers, saying: "*May your faces be deformed!*" Just as these words entered the ears of all of them despite being a single phrase, so too the handful of earth entered the eyes of each one of the unbelievers. Each became preoccupied with his eyes, and although on the attack, the army suddenly turned tail and fled.[178]

Also during the Battle of Hunayn, the authorities on Hadith and foremost Imam Muslim report that like at the Battle of Badr, he again threw a handful of earth while the unbelievers were staging a fierce attack. Saying: "*May your faces be deformed!*", the handful of earth struck the faces of each of them, with God's leave, the same as words of the phrase entered the ears of each. Busy with their eyes, they retreated and fled.[179] Since this extraordinary event at Badr and Hunayn is not within man's power and ordinary causes, the Qur'an of Miraculous Exposition states,

> *When you threw, it was not you who threw; it was rather God that threw.*

That is, "The event was outside human power. It occurred, not through human ability, but in an extraordinary manner, through Divine power."

Second Example: The accurate books and foremost Bukhari and Muslim narrate that during the Khaybar expedition, a Jewess roasted a goat, filling it with a very strong poison. She then sent it to God's Messenger (Upon whom be blessings and peace). The Companions had begun to eat it, when the Prophet suddenly said: "*Withdraw you hands! It tells me it is poisoned!*" Everyone pulled back his hand. But Bishr b. al-Bara' had eaten a single morsel and died from the effects of the severe poison. The Noble Messenger sent for the Jewess called

179. *Muslim*, Jihād 76, 81 (Bāb: Shāhat al-Vujūh); *Musnad* v, 286.

Zaynab and asked her why she had done it. The inauspicious woman said: "I considered that if you were a prophet, it would not harm you; and if you were a king, I would save the people from you."[180] According to some narrations, the Prophet did not have her put to death, but left her to Bishr's family to be killed.[181] Now listen to a few points demonstrating aspects of the miraculousness in this extraordinary incident:

The First: According to one narration, some of the Companions also heard the goat speaking.[182]

The Second: According to another narration, God's Messenger (Upon whom be blessings and peace) said: "*Say, Bismillah, then eat; the poison will not affect you.*"[183] Ibn Hajar al-'Asqalani does not accept this narration, but others do.

The Third: The treacherous Jews wanted to a deal a sudden blow at God's Messenger (Upon whom be blessings and peace) and his close Companions, but being informed about this from the Unseen, the Prophet's warning proved true, and their plot was uncovered and brought to naught. And when Muhammad (PBUH), from whom the Companions never heard an untrue statement, said: "This goat tells me that...., " everyone believed him with conviction as sure as if they themselves had heard the goat.

Third Example: This consists of three instances of another miracle which resembles 'the Shining Hand' and 'Staff' of Moses:

---

180. From Abū Hurayra: *Bukhārī*, Ṭibb 55; Jizya 7; Maghāzī 41; *Abū Dā'ūd*, Diyāt 6 nos: 4509, 4511, 1512; *Dārimī*, Muqaddima 11; *Musnad* ii, 451.

From Anas: *Muslim*, no: 2992; *Bukhārī*, al-Hiba 28; *Abū Dā'ūd*, Diyāt 6 no: 4508.

From Jābir b. 'Abd Allāh: *Dārimī*, Muqaddima 11; *Abū Dā'ūd*, Diyāt 6 no: 4510.

For the lines of transmission and narrations about this Ḥadīth, see, *Abū Dā'ūd*, Diyāt 6.

181. al-Ḥākim, *al-Mustadrak* iii, 219; iv, 109; Bayhaqī, *Dalā'il al-Nubūwwa* vi, 256, 264; Ibn al-Qayyim, *Zād al-Ma'ād* iii, 336.

182. al-Tabrīzī, *Mishkāt al-Maṣābīḥ* no: 5931; *Abū Dā'ūd*, Diyāt 6; *Dārimī*, Muqaddima 11; al-Jizrī, *Jāmi' al-Uṣūl* No: 8888; al-Haythamī, *Majma' al-Zawā'id* viii, 295-6.

183. Qāḍī Iyāḍ, *al-Shifā'* i, 317-9; 'Alī al-Qārī, *Sharḥ al-Shifā'* i, 645.

The First: Imam Ahmad b. Hanbal, explaining and authenticating a narration from Abu Sa'id al-Khudri, reports: "One dark and stormy night, the Noble Messenger (Upon whom be blessings and peace) gave Qatada b. al-Nu'man a staff, saying: *'This staff will light up ten yards all around you. You will see a dark shadow when you arrive at your house; it is Satan. Throw him out of the house and drive him away!'* Qatada took the staff and set off. It cast a light like Moses' shining hand. He came to his house, where he saw the shadowy figure, and he drove it away."[184]

The Second: While fighting the idolators during the great Battle of Badr, itself a source of wonders, 'Ukkasha b. Muhassin al-Asadi had his sword broken. God's Noble Messenger (Upon whom be blessings and peace) gave him a stout staff in place of it, saying: "Fight with this!" Suddenly, with God's leave, the staff became became a long white sword, and he fought with it. He carried the sword on his person for the rest of his life until he fell as a martyr during the Battle of al-Yamama.[185] This incident is certain, because throughout his life he carried the sword with pride and it became famous with the name of 'Succour.' Thus, two proofs of this incident are 'Ukkasha's pride, and the sword's name, 'Succour' and its widespread fame.

The Third: It is narrated by authorities on Hadith like Ibn 'Abd al-Barr,[186] a celebrated scholar known as 'the Scholar of the Age,' that at the Battle of Uhud a cousin of the God's Messenger (Upon whom be blessings and peace), 'Abd Allah b. Jahsh's sword was broken. God's Prophet gave him a staff

---

184. *Musnad* iii, 65; al-Sā'atī, *al-Fatḥ al-Rabbānī* xx, 66-7; al-Haythamī, *Majma' al-Zawā'id* ii, 166-7; al-Hindī, *Kanz al-'Ummāl* xii, 376; Qāḍī Iyāḍ, *al-Shifā'* i, 3323; 'Alī al-Qārī, *Sharḥ al-Shifā'* i, 671; al-'Asqalānī, *al-Iṣāba* no: 7076.

185. Qāḍī Iyāḍ, *al-Shifā'* i, 333; 'Alī al-Qārī, *Sharḥ al-Shifā'* i, 671; al-Khafājī, *Sharḥ al-Shifā'* iii, 156; Ibn Ḥishām, *Sīrat al-Nabī* i, 637; Ibn al-Qayyim, *Zād al-Ma'ād* (*Taḥqīq*: Arnavūdī) iii, 186.

186. Qāḍī Iyāḍ, *al-Shifā'* i, 333; al-Khafājī, *Sharḥ al-Shifā'* iii, 157; Ibn Sayyid al-Nās, *'Uyūn al-Athār* ii, 20; al-'Asqalānī, *al-Iṣāba* no: 4583.

which became a sword in his hand. He fought with it, and after the battle that product of a miracle remained a sword.

In his *Siyar*, the well-known Ibn Sayyid al-Nas reports that some time later 'Abd Allah sold the sword to a man called Bugha' al-Turki for two hundred liras. Thus these two swords were each miracles like the Staff of Moses. But while no aspect of miraculousness remained in his staff after Moses' death, these swords remained unchanged.

■ THIRTEENTH SIGN

Another of the miracles of Muhammad (Upon whom be blessings and peace) of which there are numerous instances, which are reported unanimously, is the sick and the wounded being healed through his blessed breath. The reports of this kind of miracle are, as a whole, 'unanimous in meaning.' Some of the instances of these miracles also are considered to be 'unanimous in meaning.' And if the others are single reports, since they have been rendered and confirmed as authentic by the exacting authorities of the science of Hadith, they afford the certainty of science. We shall mention a few instances of the miracles out of many.

First Example: The learned scholar of the Maghrib, Qadi Iyad, in his *Shifa' al-Sharif,*[187] narrates through an elevated chain of authorities and numerous lines of transmission, that Sa'd b. Abi Waqqas, the Prophet's servant and commander, and commander-in-chief of the army of Islam in the time of 'Umar, the conqueror of Iran, and one of the ten promised Paradise, said: "I was at the Noble Prophet's side during the Battle of Uhud. He shot arrows at the unbelievers until his bow broke. Then he gave arrows to me, telling me to shoot them. The arrows he gave me were without flights, that is, without the

187. Qāḍī Iyāḍ, *al-Shifā'* i, 322; 'Alī al-Qārī, *Sharḥ al-Shifā'* i, 651; al-Haythamī, *Majma' al-Zawā'id* vi, 113; *Muslim*, Faḍā'il al-Ṣaḥāba 42 no: 2412; Ibn Ḥibbān, *Ṣaḥīḥ* ix, 65.

feathers which help them fly. He was ordering me to shoot them, which I did, and they flew like flighted arrows, hitting the unbelievers' bodies and piercing them. At that point, Qatada b. Nu'man was hit in the eye by an arrow; it was struck out of his head, so that it was sitting on the side of his face. God's Messenger (Upon whom be blessings and peace) took the eye in his blessed, healing hand and placed it in its socket; it was healed as though nothing had happened to it and became the better of his two eyes. This event became very widely known. A grandson of Qatada, even, once described himself to 'Umar b. 'Abd al-'Aziz as, "I am the grandson of one who, when God's Most Noble Messenger placed his eye back in its socket after it had been struck out, it was suddenly healed and became his best eye."[188] He said this in verse, introducing himself to 'Umar in that way.

It is also related through an authentic narration that during the battle known as the *Yawm al-Dhi Qarad*, Abu Qatada was hit in the face by an arrow. God's Prophet touched his face with his blessed hand. Abu Qatada said: "I felt no pain at all, nor did the wound fester."[189]

Second Example: The authentic books of Hadith, and foremost Bukhari and Muslim, report that the Noble Prophet (Upon whom be blessings and peace) had appointed 'Ali al-Haydari as standard-bearer during the Battle of Khaybar, but his eyes were aching severly due to illness. The moment the Noble Messenger applied his healing spittle to his eyes, they were cured, with no trace of the discomfort remaining.[190] The following morning, 'Ali conquered the citadel of Khaybar by removing

188. Qāḍī Iyāḍ, *al-Shifā'* i, 322; al-Haythamī, *Majma' al-Zawā'id* vi, 113; al-Hindī, *Kanz al-'Ummāl* xii, 377; Ibn al-Qayyim, *Zād al-Ma'ād* (*Taḥqīq*: Arnavūdī) iii, 186-7; al-Ḥākim, *al-Mustadrak* iii, 295.

189. Qāḍī Iyāḍ, *al-Shifā'* i, 322; al-Khafājī, *Sharḥ al-Shifā'* iii, 113; 'Alī al-Qārī, *Sharḥ al-Shifā'* i, 653.

190. *Bukhārī*, Jihād 102, 144; Maghāzī 38; Faḍā'il al-Ṣaḥāba 32, 34; al-Ḥākim, *al-Mustadrak* iii, 38.

its extremely heavy gate and using it in his hand as a shield. During the same battle, Salama b. al-Akwa's leg was struck and split open by a sword; God's Messenger breathed onto it, and the leg was at once healed.[191]

Third Example: Authorities on the Prophet's life, and foremost Nasa'i, report from 'Uthman b. Hunayf, who said: "A blind man came to God's Noble Messenger (Upon whom be blessings and peace) and said: 'Pray so that my eyes may be healed and I may see!' The Prophet said: '*Go and take the ablutions, then pray two rak'ats, and say: O God! I beseech you and I turn to you, for the sake of the Prophet Muhammad, the Prophet of Mercy. O Muhammad! I turn to your Sustainer, for your sake and through you, asking that He uncover my sight. O God, make him my intercessor!*' He went and did this, and when he returned, we saw that his eyes had opened and he could see very well."[192]

Fourth Example: A great authority, Ibn Wahab, reports: "The hero Mu'awwidh b. 'Afra', one of the fourteen martyrs of the Battle of Badr, had his hand cut off by Abu Jahl the Accursed while fighting with him. He took the hand with his other hand and went to the Noble Messenger (Upon whom be blessings and peace). God's Messenger stuck the hand in its place and spread his spittle over it. It was at once healed. Mu'awwidh went again to fight and continued to do so until he was martyred."[193]

Imam Jalil b. Wahab also reports: "During that same battle, Hubayb b. Yasaf was struck on the shoulder by a sword so that he received a grievous wound with part of it almost severed. The Noble Messenger (Upon whom be blessings and peace)

191. *Bukhārī*, Maghāzī 38 (from Yazīd b. 'Ubayd); *Abū Dā'ūd*, Ṭibb 19; al-Sā'atī, *al-Fatḥ al-Rabbānī Sharḥ al-Musnad* xxii, 259.

192. *Tirmidhī*, Da'wāt 119 no: 3578; al-Ḥākim, *al-Mustadrak* i, 526; Bayhaqī, *Dalā'il al-Nubūwwa* vi, 166; Qāḍī Iyāḍ, *al-Shifā'* i, 322.

193. Qāḍī Iyāḍ, *al-Shifā'* i, 324; 'Alī al-Qārī, *Sharḥ al-Shifā'* i, 656; Ibn Sayyid al-Nās, *'Uyūn al-Athār* i, 261.

joined the arm and shoulder back together again and breathed on it, and it was healed.[194]

Thus, for sure these two incidents are separate, single reports, but if an authority like Ibn Wahab considered them to be sound, and if they occurred during a battle like that of Badr, which was a spring of miracles, and if there are many other examples which resemble these two incidents, for sure it may be said that they definitely occurred. Indeed, there are perhaps a thousand examples established in authentic traditions for which the blessed hand of God's Messenger (Upon whom be blessings and peace) was healing.

A Question: You describe many things as being reported unanimously through many channels, but we are hearing most of them for the first time. Surely something the various reports of which are numerous and unanimous cannot remain thus secret?

The Answer: There are numerous things concerning which there is consensus in their various reports and which are self-evident to the learned scholars of the Shari'a, but are unknown to those who are not one of them. For the scholars of Hadith there are many such things, which for poets have not even the status of isolated reports, and so on. The specialists of all the sciences explain the theories and axioms of their science, and the ordinary people rely on them, and either submit to them, or become one of them and see for themselves. Now, the events the reports of which we describe as forming 'true consensus,' 'consensus in meaning,' or which express certainty like 'consensus,' have been shown to be thus by both the scholars of Hadith, and the scholars of the Shari'a, and the scholars of the principles of religion, and by most of the other levels of the 'Ulama. If ordinary people in their heedlessness or the ignorant who close their eyes to the truth do not know this, the fault is theirs.

194. Qāḍī Iyāḍ, *al-Shifā'* i, 324; 'Alī al-Qārī, *Sharḥ al-Shifā'* i, 656; Ibn Kathīr, *al-Bidāya wa'l-Nihāya* vi, 164; Bayhaqī, *Dalā'il al-Nubūwwa* vi, 134.

A Passage Worthy of Being Written in Gold and Diamonds

Yes, it was mentioned above: small stones glorifying and praising God in his hand; and in accordance with the verse, **"When you threw, it was not you who threw,"** *earth and small stones in the same hand becoming missiles and projectiles against the enemy, routing them; and according to the verse,* **"And the moon split,"** *the moon splitting at a sign of the fingers of the same hand; and water flowing like a spring from the ten fingers of the same hand, and their providing a whole army with water; and the same hand being healing to the sick and wounded —all this shows what a wondrous miracle of Divine Power that blessed hand was. It was as if for friends its palm was a small place for the remembrance of God, for as soon as small stones entered it, they glorified God and recited His Names; while in the face of enemies, it was a small dominical ammunitions store which when pebbles and earth entered it, they were transformed into missiles and projectiles. And for the sick and the wounded it was a small pharmacy of the Most Merciful One which was a cure for whatever ills it touched. When it rose with Glory, it split the moon, giving it the shape of two bows, while when it was lowered with Beauty, it became like a spring of mercy with ten spigots pouring forth the water of Kawthar. If the single hand of such a one is the means of those wondrous miracles, is it not then to be understood clearly how acceptable he is before the Creator of the Universe, and how loyal he is to his cause, and how fortunate are those who declare their allegiance to him?*

Fifth Example: Having explained and authenticated it, Imam Baghawi relates: "At the Battle of Khandaq, 'Ali b. al-Hakam's leg was broken by the blow of an unbeliever. The Noble Messenger (Upon whom be blessings and peace) rubbed it. At the moment he did so, it was healed so that 'Ali b. al-Hakam did not even dismount from his horse."[195]

Sixth Example: The scholars of Hadith, and foremost Imam Bayhaqi, relate: "'Ali was very ill. In his distress, he was moaning and praying for himself. The Noble Messenger (Upon whom be blessings and peace) came and said: '*O God! Grant him healing,*' and touched 'Ali with his foot. He told him to stand, and 'Ali was at once cured. He stated: 'I never again suffered from that illness.'"[196]

Seventh Example: This is the well-known story of Shurahbil al-Ju'fi. He had a morbid growth in the palm of his hand so that he could hold neither his sword nor the reins of his horse. God's Messenger (Upon whom be blessings and peace) rubbed the growth with his blessed hand and massaged it; not a trace of it remained.[197]

Eighth Example: Six children each the object of a different miracle of Muhammad (PBUH).

The First: Ibn Abi Shayba, a meticulous researcher and well-known scholar of Hadith, relates that a woman brought her child to God's Messenger (Upon whom be blessings and peace). The child had an affliction; he could not speak and was an idiot. God's Messenger rinsed his mouth with water and washed his hands, then gave the water to the woman, telling her to give it to the child to drink. After the child had drunk it, noth-

195. Qāḍī Iyāḍ, *al-Shifā'* i, 324; 'Alī al-Qārī, *Sharḥ al-Shifā'* i, 656; al-Khafājī, *Sharḥ al-Shifā'* iii, 118; al-Haythamī, *Majma' al-Zawā'id* iv, 134.

196. *Tirmidhī*, Da'wāt 1121; *Musnad* i, 83, 107, 128; Qāḍī Iyāḍ, *al-Shifā'* i, 323; 'Alī al-Qārī, *Sharḥ al-Shifā'* i, 656; Ibn Ḥibbān, *Ṣaḥīḥ* ix, 47; al-Mubārakfūrī, *Tuḥfat al-Aḥwazī* 3635.

197. al-Haythamī, *Majma' al-Zawā'id* viii, 298; Qāḍī Iyāḍ, *al-Shifā'* i, 324; 'Alī al-Qārī, *Sharḥ al-Shifā'* i, 657.

ing remained of his illness and affliction, and he became so intelligent, he surpassed even the brightest of the rest.[198]

The Second: According to an authentic narration, Ibn 'Abbas said: "An insane child was brought to the Noble Messenger (Upon whom be blessings and peace). He placed his blessed hand on the child's chest and the child suddenly vomited a small black object like a cucumber. The child was healed and went home."[199]

The Third: Imam Bayhaqi and Nasa'i relate through an authentic chain of transmission that a child called Muhammad b. al-Hatib had been scalded by a pan of boiling water and his whole arm burnt. God's Noble Messenger (Upon whom be blessings and peace) touched the arm, spreading his spittle over it; the same instant it was healed.[200]

The Fourth: A child who was not young but was mute came to the Noble Messenger (Upon whom be blessings and peace). He asked the child: "*Who am I*?" The child, who had been mute from birth, replied: "You are the Messenger of God," and started to speak.[201]

The Fifth: Jalal al-Din Suyuti, who was honoured with conversing with God's Messenger (Upon whom be blessings and peace) on many occasions while awake and was the leading scholar of his age, explaining and authenticating a narration, reports: Soon after being born, a famous person called Mubarak al-Yamama was taken to the Prophet. On his turning to the baby, it started to speak, saying: "I testify that you are the Mes-

198. *Ibn Māja*, Ṭibb 40 no: 3532; Qāḍī Iyāḍ, *al-Shifā'* i, 324; 'Alī al-Qārī, *Sharḥ al-Shifā'* i, 657.

199. *Dārimī*, Muqaddima 4; *Musnad* iv, 172; Qāḍī Iyāḍ, *al-Shifā'* i, 324; 'Alī al-Qārī, *Sharḥ al-Shifā'* i, 657; al-Haythamī, *Majma' al-Zawā'id* ix, 2; Tabrīzī, *Mishkāt al-Maṣābīḥ* iii, 188.

200. Qāḍī Iyāḍ, *al-Shifā'* i, 324; 'Alī al-Qārī, *Sharḥ al-Shifā'* i, 657; al-Khafājī, *Sharḥ al-Shifā'* iii, 121; al-Haythamī, *Majma' al-Zawā'id* ix, 415; Ibn Kathīr, *al-Bidāya wa'l-Nihāya* i, 295; al-Ḥākim, *al-Mustadrak* iv, 62-3.

201. Qāḍī Iyāḍ, *al-Shifā'* i, 319; al-Khafājī, *Sharḥ al-Shifā'* iii, 105; Ibn Kathīr, *al-Bidāya wa'l-Nihāya* iv, 158-9.

senger of God." The Prophet exclaimed: "May God bless you!" The child never spoke again in his infancy, and later became famous as Mubarak al-Yamama (the blessed one, Yamama), since he had been the object of this miracle of the Prophet and his prayer.[202]

The Sixth: One time, an ill-mannered youth interrupted the prayer of the Noble Messenger (Upon whom be blessings and peace), by passing in front of him while he was performing it. God's Messenger said: "*O God, cut short his paces!*" After this the child was unable to walk as a punishment for his bad behaviour.[203]

The Seventh: A shameless woman, who was like a child, asked for a piece of the food God's Messenger (Upon whom be blessings and peace) was eating. He gave her some, but she said: "No, I want a piece from your mouth." So he gave her a piece, and, after eating the morsel, she became the most modest and bashful woman in Madinah.[204]

There are not eighty but perhaps eight hundred further examples of this miracle similar to the eight mentioned above, most of which are related in the Hadith books and books of the Prophet's biography. For sure, since the blessed hand of God's Messenger (Upon whom be blessings and peace) was like a pharmacy of Luqman the Wise, and his spittle was like a spring of Khidr's water of life, and his breath soothing and healing like that of Jesus (Upon whom be peace), certainly many people would have recourse to him; and the sick, children, and the insane did flock to him in great numbers, and they were all healed. Abu 'Abd al-Rahman al-Yamani, known as *'Tavus'*, even, who made the Hajj forty times and for forty years per-

---

202. Qāḍī Iyāḍ, *al-Shifā'* i, 319; al-Khafājī, *Sharḥ al-Shifā'* iii, 105; Suyūṭī, *Kanz al-'Ummāl* iv, 379; Ibn Kathīr, *al-Bidāya wa'l-Nihāya* iv, 159.

203. Qāḍī Iyāḍ, *al-Shifā'* i, 328; al-Khafājī, *Sharḥ al-Shifā'* iii, 137; 'Alī al-Qārī, *Sharḥ al-Shifā'* i, 663.

204. Qāḍī Iyāḍ, *al-Shifā'* i, 325; 'Alī al-Qārī, *Sharḥ al-Shifā'* i, 657; al-Haythamī, *Majma' al-Zawā'id* viii, 312.

formed the morning prayer with the ablution of the preceeding night prayers, and who met with many of the Companions and was one of the greatest scholars of the generation following them, stated and made the certain report that however many lunatics came to God's Messenger (Upon whom be blessings and peace), placing his hand on their chests, they were all healed; not one was not cured.[205]

Thus, since a great scholar such as that who had direct connections with the era of the Prophet, made such definite and general statements, for sure, none of the sick who came to God's Prophet were not healed; they were all healed. Since this was the case, certainly thousands would have had recourse to him.

FOURTEENTH SIGN

Another numerous sort of the various kinds of miracle of God's Most Noble Messenger (Upon whom be blessings and peace) were the wonders manifested as a result of his prayers. This kind is definite and there is 'true consensus' in their many reports. The instances and examples of it are so numerous as to be incalculable, and many of these have reached the degree of 'consensus,' or have become famous as such. Others have been related by such authorities that they bear the same certainty as well-known 'consensus.' As examples, we shall quote only some of the numerous instances of this kind of miracle that are very well-known and nearest in degree to 'consensus,' giving some particulars of each instance.

First Example: The fact that prayers of the Noble Messenger (Upon whom be blessings and peace) for rain were always accepted has been transmitted by authorities of Hadith, primarily Bukhari and Muslim. There were times when in the pulpit he raised his hands to pray for rain, and before he had

205. Qāḍī Iyāḍ, *al-Shifā'* i, 335; 'Alī al-Qārī, *Sharḥ al-Shifā'* i, 676.

lowered them even, rain began to fall. As mentioned above, once or twice when the army had run out of water, the clouds came and poured forth rain. Before his prophetic mission, even, during his childhood, the Prophet's grandfather 'Abd al-Muttalib would go to pray for rain with him, and the rain came out of respect for Muhammad (PBUH). The fact became celebrated through a poem of 'Abd al-Muttalib. And after the Prophet's death, 'Umar prayed making 'Abbas the means, saying: "O our Sustainer! This is the uncle of your Beloved. Send us rain for his sake!" And it rained.[206]

Bukhari and Muslim also relate that God's Messenger was asked to pray for rain. He did so and such rain fell that they were compelled to ask him to pray for it to stop. He did so, and it stopped at once.[207]

Second Example: It is almost as well-known as those incidents about which there are many unanimous reports that when the number of Companions and believers had still not reached forty, God's Noble Messenger (Upon whom be blessings and peace) prayed secretly while performing his worship: "*O God! Strengthen Islam by means of either 'Umar b. al-Khattab or 'Umar b. Hisham.*" A few days later, 'Umar b. al-Khattab came to believe and was the means to proclaiming and upholding Islam, so that he acquired the title of *Faruq* [Discerner between truth and falsehood].[208]

Third Example: God's Messenger prayed for various distinguished Companions for different purposes. His prayers were all accepted in so brilliant a fashion that the wonders of these prayers reached the degree of a miracle. For instance,

206. *Bukhārī*, Istisqā' 3; Faḍā'il Aṣḥāb al-Nabī 11.

207. *Bukhārī*, Istisqā' 19; *Ibn Māja*, Iqāma 154; *Muslim*, Salāt al-Istisqā' 8 no: 897; Ibn Kathīr, *al-Bidāya wa'l-Nihāya* vi, 91-2; Qāḍī Iyāḍ, *al-Shifā'* i, 327.

208. *Tirmidhī*, Manāqib 18 no: 1683; al-Albānī, *Mishkāt al-Maṣābīḥ* no: 6036; al-Mubārakfūrī, *Tuḥfat al-Aḥwazī* no: 3766; Ibn Asīr al-Jizrī, *Jāmi' al-Uṣūl* no: 7428; Ibn Ḥibbān, *Ṣaḥīḥ* ix, 17; al-Ḥākim, *al-Mustadrak* ii, 465; iii, 83, 502; Qāḍī Iyāḍ, *al-Shifā'* i, 327; Bayhaqī, *Dalā'il al-Nubūwwa* ii, 215.

foremost Bukhari and Muslim relate that he prayed for Ibn 'Abbas as follows: *"O God! Give him knowledge of religion and teach him interpretation."*[209] This supplication was accepted in such a way that Ibn 'Abbas gained the glorious title of 'Interpreter of the Qur'an' and reached the elevated degree of 'learned scholar of the Muslim community.' When still very young even, 'Umar used to include him in the gatherings of the religious scholars and leading Companions.[210]

Also, foremost Bukhari and the writers of books of authentic Hadith relate that the mother of Anas entreatied God's Noble Messenger (Upon whom be blessings and peace): "Pray that your servant Anas will be blessed with abundant wealth and offspring." The Prophet prayed, saying: *"O God! Grant increase to his wealth and offspring and bless what you bestow on him."* Towards the end of his life, Anas said swearing by God: "I have buried a hundred of my progeny with my own hand. No one has been as fortunate as myself in regard to wealth and possessions. You can see that my wealth is truly abundant. All these are the result of Prophet's prayer for the blessing of plenty."[211]

Also, foremost Imam Bayhaqi, and the scholars of Hadith relate that God's Messenger (Upon whom be blessings and peace) prayed that one of the ten promised Paradise, 'Abd al-Rahman b. 'Awf, be blessed with abundance of wealth. Through the blessing of that prayer, he acquired such wealth that on one occasion he donated seven hundred camels together with their

---

209. *Bukhārī*, Vuḍū' 10; 'Ilm 17; Faḍā'il al-Aṣḥāb 24; *Muslim*, Fadā'il al-Ṣaḥāba 138; Ibn Ḥibbān, *Ṣaḥīḥ* ix, 98; Qāḍī Iyāḍ, *al-Shifā'* i, 327; 'Alī al-Qārī, *Sharḥ al-Shifā'* i, 661; al-Khafājī, *Sharḥ al-Shifā'* iii, 130; Ibn al-Asīr, *Jāmi' al-Uṣūl* ix, 63; *Musnad* i, 264, 314, 328, 330; al-Ḥākim, *al-Mustadrak* iv, 534.

210. *Musnad* i, 338; Aḥmad b. Ḥanbal, *Faḍā'il al-Ṣaḥāba* no: 1871; al-Ḥākim, *al-Mustadrak* iii, 535; 'Alī al-Qārī, *Sharḥ al-Shifā'* i, 661.

211. *Bukhārī*, Da'wāt 19, 26, 47; *Muslim*, Fadā'il al-Ṣaḥāba 141, 142 nos: 2480-1; *Musnad* iii, 190; vi, 430; Ibn Ḥibbān, *Ṣaḥīḥ* ix, 155; al-Mubārakfūrī, *Tuḥfat al-Aḥwazī* x, 330.

loads to God's cause.[212] See the blessings of plenty resulting from the Prophet's prayer, and say: "How great are God's blessings!"

Also, narrators of Hadiths, and foremost Bukhari, relate: "God's Messenger (Upon whom be blessings and peace) prayed that 'Urwa b. Abi al-Ja'da might do profitably at trade. 'Urwa said: 'Sometimes I would go to the marketplace in Kufa and come home in the evening having made a forty thousandfold profit.'" Imam Bukhari says: "If he took earth in his hand, he still would make a profit from it!"[213]

Also, he prayed that 'Abd Allah b. Ja'far would acquire an abundance of wealth, and he became so rich he was famous for it. He also became as famous for his generosity as he was for the wealth he obtained through the Prophet's prayer for the blessing of plenty.[214]

There are numerous instances of this sort of miracle, but we consider the four described above to be sufficient as examples.

Also, foremost Imam Tirmidhi relates: "The Noble Messenger (Upon whom be blessings and peace) prayed for Sa'd b. Abi Waqqas: '*O God, answer his prayer!*'[215] After that everyone feared his malediction, and the answering of his prayers also became famous.

On another occasion, God's Messenger prayed for the famous Abu Qatada that he might remain young: "*May God*

---

212. Qāḍī Iyāḍ, *al-Shifā'* i, 326; 'Alī al-Qārī, *Sharḥ al-Shifā'* i, 659; al-Khafājī, *Sharḥ al-Shifā'* iii, 125.

213. *Bukhārī*, Manāqib 28; *Ibn Māja*, Ṣadaqāt 7; *Musnad* iv, 375; Qāḍī Iyāḍ, *al-Shifā'* i, 327; al-Sā'atī, *al-Fatḥ al-Rabbānī* xxii, 326.

214. Qāḍī Iyāḍ, *al-Shifā'* i, 327; 'Alī al-Qārī, *Sharḥ al-Shifā'* i, 661; al-Haythamī, *Majma' al-Zawā'id* v, 286; Ibn Ḥajar al-'Asqalānī, *al-Maṭālib al-'Alīya* no: 4077-8.

215. *Tirmidhī*, Manāqib 27 no: 3751; Ibn Ḥibbān, *Ṣaḥīḥ* no: 12215; al-Ḥākim, *al-Mustadrak* iii, 499; Abū Na'īm, *Ḥilyat al-Awliyā'* i, 93; Abū Na'īm, *Dalā'il al-Nubūwwa* iii, 206; al-Albānī, *Mishkāt al-Maṣābīḥ* iii, 251 no: 6116; al-Mubārakfūrī, *Tuḥfat al-Aḥwazī* x, 253-4 no: 3835; Aḥmad b. Ḥanbal, *Faḍā'il al-Ṣaḥāba* ii, 750 no: 1038; Ibn al-Asīr, *Jami' al-Uṣūl* x, 16 no: 6535.

prosper your face! O God, bless his hair and his skin!" When he died at the age of seventy, he was like a youth of fifteen.[216] This is related through a sound narration.

Also, the famous story of the poet Nabigha. He recited one of his poems before God's Messenger (Upon whom be blessings and peace), which ran: "Our glory and praise have reached to the skies; we want to ascend even higher." God's Messenger asked jokingly: "*Where, beyond the skies?*" Nabigha replied: "To Paradise." He then recited another of his meaningful poems, and the Prophet prayed: "*May God not spoil your mouth!*" It was through the blessing of this prayer of the Prophet that he did not have a single tooth missing when he was one hundred and twenty years old. Whenever he lost a tooth, another would appear in its place.[217]

Also, it is related through an authentic narration that he prayed for Imam 'Ali: "*O God, protect him from heat and cold!*" Through the blessing of this prayer, Imam 'Ali used to wear summer clothes in winter, and winter clothes in summer. He used to say: "I never suffer from heat or cold, thanks to that prayer."[218]

Also, he prayed for Fatima: "*O God, do not give her the pains of hunger!*" And Fatima used to say: "I never suffered from hunger after that prayer."[219]

Also, Tufayl b. 'Amr asked God's Messenger (Upon whom be blessings and peace) for a miracle to show to his tribe. The

---

216. Qāḍī Iyāḍ, *al-Shifā'* i, 327; 'Alī al-Qārī, *Sharḥ al-Shifā'* i, 660; al-Khafājī, *Sharḥ al-Shifā'* iii, 128.

217. 'Alī al-Qārī, *Sharḥ al-Shifā'* i, 661; Ibn Ḥajar, *al-Iṣāba fī Tamyīz al-Ṣaḥāba* no: 8639; al-'Asqalānī, *al-Maṭālib al-'Alīya* no: 4060; Ibn Kathīr, *al-Bidāya wa'l Nihāya* vi, 168.

218. al-Haythamī, *Majma' al-Zawā'id* ix, 122; Aḥmad b. Ḥanbal, *Faḍā'il al-Ṣaḥāba* no: 950; *Ibn Māja*, Muqaddima ii, 117; *Musnad* i, 99, 133; *Musnad* (*Taḥqīq*: Aḥmad Shākir) ii, 120 no: 1114; al-Khafājī, *Sharḥ al-Shifā'* iii, 133.

219. Qāḍī Iyāḍ, *al-Shifā'* i, 328; al-Khafājī, *Sharḥ al-Shifā'* iii, 134; al-Haythamī, *Majma' al-Zawā'id* ix, 203.

Prophet prayed: "*O God, illuminate him!*", and a light appeared between his eyes. Later it was transferred to the end of his staff, and he became famous as *Dhi'l-Nur,* the Possessor of Light.[220] This incidents are all from well-known Hadiths that are certain.

Also, Abu Hurayra once complained to the Noble Messenger (Upon whom be blessings and peace) that he sometimes suffered from forgetfulness. God's Messenger told him to spread out a piece of cloth. He then made some movements with his blessed hand as though taking some invisible objects and putting them on the cloth. He repeated this two or three times, then told him to gather up the cloth. Abu Hurayra later swore that through the mystery of this prayer of the Prophet's, he never again forgot anything.[221] This event is also among well-known Hadiths.

Fourth Example: We shall describe here a few events regarding maledictions of God's Messenger (Upon whom be blessings and peace).

The First: The Persian Shah Parviz tore up the letter sent to him by the Prophet. When God's Prophet received news of this, he prayed: "*O God, rend him as he rent my letter!*"[222] It was as a result of this malediction that Khusraw Parviz's son Shirviya cut him to pieces with a dagger. And Sa'd b. Waqqas broke his kingdom apart, so that in no part of the Sasanid empire did his sovereignty remain. However, the Emperor of Byzantium and other kings did not perish since they respected the Prophet's letters.

The Second: An event almost as well-known as those

220. Qāḍī Iyāḍ, *al-Shifā'* i, 328; al-Khafājī, *Sharḥ al-Shifā'* iii, 134; 'Alī al-Qārī, *Sharḥ al-Shifā'* i, 662.

221. *Bukhārī*, 'Ilm 42; Manāqib 28; Buyū' 1; Ḥarth 21; *Muslim*, Fadā'il al-Ṣaḥāba 159 no: 2492; *Tirmidhī*, Manāqib 46, 47; *Musnad* ii, 240, 274, 428; al-Mubārakfūrī, *Tuḥfat al-Aḥwazī* x, 334 no: 3923; Ibn al-Asīr, *Jāmi' al-Uṣūl* (*Taḥqīq*: Arnavūd) ix, 95; Ibn Kathīr, *al-Bidāya wa'l-Nihāya* vi, 162; al-Sā'atī, *al-Fatḥ al-Rabbānī* xxii, 405, 409-10; Abū Na'īm, *Ḥilyat al-Awliyā'* i, 381; al-'Asqalānī, *al-Iṣāba* no: 1190.

222. *Bukhārī*, 'Ilm 7; Jihād 101; Maghāzī 82; Qāḍī Iyāḍ, *al-Shifā'* i, 328; al-Sā'atī, *al-Fath al-Rabbānī* xxii, 159.

reported unanimously, which some verses of the Qur'an allude to, is this: in the early days of Islam, the Noble Messenger (Upon whom be blessings and peace) was performing the prayers in the Masjid al-Haram, when the chiefs of the Quraysh gathered and maltreated him. At the time, God's Prophet called down curses on them. Ibn Mas'ud stated: "I swear that at the Battle of Badr I saw the corpses of all those who had ill-treated him and received his curse."[223]

The Third: On their denying him, God's Noble Messenger (Upon whom be blessings and peace) prayed that a large Arab tribe called the Mudariyya would be afflicted with drought and famine. All rain ceased and drought and famine occurred. Then the Quraysh, a branch of the Mudariyya, pleaded with the Prophet, and he prayed. Whereupon the rains came and put an end to the drought.[224] Having been reported unanimously, this incident is also well-known.

Fifth Example: The fact that the Prophet's (PBUH) maledictions against particular persons were accepted and realized in a dreadful way is illustrated by numerous instances. We shall recount three of these by way of example.

The First: He uttered the following curse against 'Utba b. Abi Lahab: "*O God, beset a dog on him from among your dogs!*" Some time later 'Utba went on a journey during which a lion sought him out from among the caravan, and tore him to pieces.[225] This incident was famous and is narrated as authentic by the authorities on Hadith.

The Second: This is Muhallim b. Jaththama: he unjustly killed 'Amir b. Adbat, but God's Messenger had sent him as the commander of a force to fight in God's way. When the news of

223. *Bukhārī*, Ṣalāt 109; Manāqib al-Anṣār 45; *Muslim*, Jihād 107 no: 1794; *Musnad* i, 417.

224. *Bukhārī*, Tafsīr 30; 28:3; 44:3-4; Da'wāt 58; Istisqā' 13; Qāḍī Iyāḍ, *al-Shifā'* i, 328; 'Alī al-Qārī, *Sharḥ al-Shifā'* i, 663; Bayhaqī, *Dalā'il al-Nubūwwa* ii, 324.

225. See, page 140, fn. 76. Qāḍī Iyāḍ, *al-Shifā'* i, 329; 'Alī al-Qārī, *Sharḥ al-Shifā'* i, 664.

this reached the Messenger, he was angry and cursed him, saying: "*O God, do not grant forgiveness to Muhallim!*" Muhallim died a week later. They put him in his grave, but the grave cast him out. They buried him in several different places, but each time the grave rejected him. Finally they built a strong wall between two rocks, and in this way the corpse was housed.[226]

The Third: Once God's Noble Messenger (Upon whom be blessings and peace) saw a man eating with his left hand. He ordered him to eat with his right hand. The man replied: "I can't." The Messenger said as a malediction: "*Henceforth you will be unable to raise it.*" And after than he was unable to use it.[227]

Sixth Example: Here we shall mention several events which are certain, from among the numerous wonders resulting from prayers of the Noble Messenger (Upon whom be blessings and peace), and from his touch.

The First: God's Messenger gave Khalid b. al-Walid, known as God's Sword, several of his hairs and prayed for his victory in battle. Khalid put them in his cap. As the result of the hairs and the blessings of the prayer, there was never a battle in which he then fought, but he was victorious.[228]

The Second: Salman al-Farsi had formerly been a slave of the Jews. His masters had asked for a very high ransom, saying: "In order to gain your freedom, you must plant three hundred date-palms, and after they bear fruit, give us forty *okkas*[229] of gold in addition to the fruit." He went to the Noble Messenger (Upon whom be blessings and peace) and explained his situa-

---

226. *Ibn Māja*, Fitan 1 no: 3930; Qāḍī Iyāḍ, *al-Shifā'* i, 329; 'Alī al-Qārī, *Sharḥ al-Shifā'* i, 665; al-Khafājī, *Sharḥ al-Shifā'* iii, 142; Ibn Ḥishām, *Sīrat al-Nabī* iv, 247; Ibn Kathīr, *al-Bidāya wa'l-Nihāya* iv, 224-6.

227. *Muslim*, Ashriba 107 no: 2021; Ibn Ḥibbān, *Ṣaḥīḥ* viii, 152; Qāḍī Iyāḍ, *al-Shifā'* i, 328-9; 'Alī al-Qārī, *Sharḥ al-Shifā'* i, 666.

228. Qāḍī Iyāḍ, *al-Shifā'* i, 331; al-Haythamī, *Majma' al-Zawā'id* ix, 349; al-'Asqalānī, *al-Maṭālib al-'Alīya* iv, 90 no: 4044; al-Ḥākim, *al-Mustradrak* iii, 289.

229. 1 *okka* was the equivalent of 1,282 gr. or 2.8 lbs. (Tr.)

tion. God's Messenger then planted the three hundred palms in the region of Madinah; only one of them was planted by someone else. That year, all three hundred trees bore fruit, with the exception of the one planted by the other person. The Messenger uprooted it and planted another, and it too bore fruit. He then rubbed some of his spittle on a piece of gold the size of a hen's egg, and offered a prayer. He gave it to Salman, telling him to go and give it to the Jews. Salman al-Farsi went and gave them forty *okkas* of gold out of that piece, while it remained in its original state.[230] This miraculous incident, which was narrated by the most trustworthy and respected authorities, was the most significant event in Salman's entire life.

The Third: A woman Companion called Umm Malik used to give the Noble Messenger (Upon whom be blessings and peace) butter from a leathern bag called an *ukka*, as a gift. On one occasion God's Messenger uttered a prayer over it while returning it to her, and told her not to empty it and squeeze it. Umm Malik took the *ukka*, and thereafter as a result of the blessing of the Prophet's prayer, butter was found in it whenever her children asked for it. This continued for a long time, until they squeezed it, and the blessing disappeared.[231]

Seventh Example: There are also many examples of water becoming sweet and emitting a pleasant smell as the result of the Prophet's prayer and his touching it; we shall mention several by way of example:

The First: Scholars of Hadith, and foremost Imam Bayhaqi, report that the well known as Bi'r al-Quba would sometimes dry up. On God's Messenger (Upon whom be blessings and

230. *Musnad* v, 441-2; Ibn Sa'd, *Ṭabaqāt al-Kubrā* iv, 53-7; al-Haythamī, *Majma' al-Zawā'id* ix, 332-6; Qāḍī Iyāḍ, *al-Shifā'* 332; al-Ḥākim, *al-Mustadrak* ii, 16.

231. *Muslim*, Faḍā'il 8 no: 2280; *Musnad* iii, 340, 347; Qāḍī Iyāḍ, *al-Shifā'* i, 332.

232. Bayhaqī, *Dalā'il al-Nubūwwa* vi, 136; Qāḍī Iyāḍ, *al-Shifā'* i, 331; al-Khafājī, *Sharḥ al-Shifā'* iii, 149.

peace) pouring the water with which he had taken ablutions into the well and offering a prayer, its water became abundant and it never again dried up.[232]

The Second: Scholars of Hadith, including Abu Na'im in his *Dala'il al-Nubuwwa* (Evidences of Prophethood), report that when God's Messenger spat into the well in Anas' house and prayed, it became the sweetest water in Madinah.[233]

The Third: Ibn Maja reports that a bucketful of water from the spring of Zamzam was brought to the Messenger. He took a little of it into his mouth then emptied it into the bucket. The bucket then emitted a sweet scent like musk.[234]

The Fourth: Imam Ahmad b. Hanbal reports that a bucketful of water was drawn from a well. After God's Messenger (PBUH) had put some of his spittle in the bucket and poured it into the well, it began to emit a sweet scent like musk.[235]

The Fifth: Hammad b. Salama, who was a man of God and was trusted and accepted by Imam Muslim and the scholars of the Maghrib, reports that the Noble Messenger (Upon whom be blessings and peace) filled a leather bag with water, and breathed into it while praying. He then tied it up and gave it to some of the Companions, saying: "*Do not open it except when you perform the ablutions!*" When they opened the bag to take ablutions, they saw pure milk with cream at its opening.[236]

Thus, these five instances have been narrated by well-known and important authorities. Together with those that are not mentioned here, they prove the occurrence of this kind of miracle as definitely as those about the various reports of which there is 'consensus in meaning.'

Eighth Example: There were numerous instances of

233. Qāḍī Iyāḍ, *al-Shifā'* i, 331; 'Alī al-Qārī, *Sharḥ al-Shifā'* i, 668.

234. *Ibn Māja*, Ṭahāra 136 no: 659; Qāḍī Iyāḍ, *al-Shifā'* i, 332; 'Alī al-Qārī, *Sharḥ al-Shifā'* i, 669.

235. al-Sā'atī, *al-Fatḥ al-Rabbānī* xxii, 667.

236. Qāḍī Iyāḍ, *al-Shifā'* i, 334; al-Khafājī, *Sharḥ al-Shifā'* iii, 160.

barren and dry goats producing milk, and abundantly at that, through the touch and prayers of God's Noble Messenger (Upon whom be blessings and peace). We shall mention only two or three which are well-known and certain, as examples:

The First: All the reliable books of the Prophet's biography relate that when God's Prophet and Abu Bakr the Veracious were migrating to Madinah, they came to the house of Umm Ma'bad, called Atika Bint Khalid al-Khuza'i. There was an extremely thin, barren, and dry goat there. God's Messenger asked Umm Ma'bad: "*Has this no milk?*" She replied: "It has no blood in its body, how should it produce milk?" The Prophet stroked its loins and teets, and prayed. The he said: "*Bring a vessel, and milk it.*" They milked it, and after the Messenger and Abu Bakr had drunk, all the people of the house drank to repletion. The goat grew strong, and remained thus blessed.[237]

The Second: This is the famous story of Shat b. Mas'ud: before becoming a Muslim, Ibn Mas'ud used to act as a shepherd for certain people. God's Messenger (Upon whom be blessings and peace) went together with Abu Bakr the Veracious to the place where Ibn Mas'ud and his goats were. God's Messenger asked Ibn Mas'ud for some milk. On replying that they were not his but the property of someone else, God's Messenger told him to bring him a barren, dry goat. So he brought a nanny-goat who had not been mated for two years. God's Messenger stroked its teets with his hand and prayed. Then they milked it, and obtained sweet milk which they drank. Ibn Mas'ud came to believe after witnessing this miracle.[238]

The Third: This is the well-known story of Halima Sa'diya, the foster mother, that is, wet-nurse, of the Noble Messenger

---

237. Tabrīzī, *Mishkāt al-Maṣābīḥ* (*Taḥqīq*: al-Albānī) no: 5943: al-Haythamī, *Majma' al-Zawā'id* vi, 58; viii, 313; al-Ḥākim, *al-Mustadrak* ii, 109; Ibn Kathīr, *al-Bidāya wa'l-Nihāya* iii, 190-1; Ibn al-Qayyim, *Zād al-Ma'ād* iii, 55, 57; Ibn Sa'd, *Ṭabaqāt al-Kubrā* i, 230-1.

238. *Musnad* (*Taḥqīq*: Aḥmad Shākir) v, 210 no: 3598; Ibn Ḥibbān, *Ṣaḥīḥ* viii, 149; Ibn Kathīr, *al-Bidāya wa'l-Nihāya* vi, 102.

(Upon whom be blessings and peace). There was drought where the tribe was found, and all the animals were thin and without milk. They could not find sufficient to eat. But when the Messenger was sent to his foster mother there, through the blessing he brought, Halima Sa'diya's goats would return in the evening with both their stomachs and their teets full, contrary to everyone else's.[239]

There are further instances in the books of biography similar to these, but these examples are sufficient for our purpose.

Ninth Example: We shall recount here a few out of many instances of wonders which were manifest after God's Messenger (Upon whom be blessings and peace) had touched the faces and heads of certain people, and prayed.

The First: He passed his hand over the head of 'Umar b. Sa'd, and prayed. When the man died at the age of eighty, through the blessing of that prayer, there was not a single grey hair on his head.[240]

The Second: He placed his hand on Qays b. Zayd's head, and prayed. Through the blessing of the prayer and effect of his touch, when Qays reached a hundred years of age, his head was white except for where God's Messenger had placed his hand; that had remained totally black.[241]

The Third: 'Abd al-Rahman b. Zayd b. al-Khattab was both small and ugly. God's Messenger (Upon whom be blessings and peace) touched his head with his hand and prayed. Through the blessing of his prayer, 'Abd al-Rahman acquired the loftiest stature and most beautiful form.[242]

---

239. al-Sā'atī, *al-Fatḥ al-Rabbānī* xx, 192-3; al-Haythamī, *Majma' al-Zawā'id* viii, 220-1; Abū Na'īm, *Dalā'il al-Nubūwwa* i, 111-3; Ibn Kathīr, *al-Bidāya wa'l-Nihāya* ii, 273; Qāḍī Iyāḍ, *al-Shifā'* i, 366; 'Alī al-Qārī, *Sharḥ al-Shifā'* i, 750; al-Khafājī, *Sharḥ al-Shifā'* iii, 313.

240. Qāḍī Iyāḍ, *al-Shifā'* i, 334; 'Alī al-Qārī, *Sharḥ al-Shifā'* i, 673.

241. Qāḍī Iyāḍ, *al-Shifā'* i, 334; 'Alī al-Qārī, *Sharḥ al-Shifā'* i, 674.

242. Qāḍī Iyāḍ, *al-Shifā'* i, 335; 'Alī al-Qārī, *Sharḥ al-Shifā'* i, 676-7.

The Fourth: 'A'idh b. 'Amr received a wound on the face during the Battle of Hunayn. God's Messenger (Upon whom be blessings and peace) wiped away the blood on his face with his hand. The part of his face that the Messenger had touched acquired a shining brilliance, which the scholars of Hadith described as resembling a white blaze on a chestnut horse.[243]

The Fifth: He passed his hand over Qatada b. Malhan's face and prayed, and Qatada's face began to shine like a mirror.[244]

The Sixth: When Zaynab, the daughter of the Mother of Believers Umm Salama and the stepdaughter of God's Messenger was a child, the Noble Messenger (Upon whom be blessings and peace) sprinkled some of his ablution water on her face. With the touch of the water, her face acquired an extraordinary beauty.[245]

There are numerous further examples similar to these, most of which have been narrated by the leading scholars of Hadith. Even if we suppose each of these instances to be a single report and weak, as a whole they still demonstrate an absolute miracle of Muhammad (PBUH) which has the certainty of 'consensus in meaning.' For if an event is narrated in numerous different forms, the occurrence of the basic event becomes definite. Even if each form is itself weak, it still proves the basic event.

For example, a noise was heard; some people said that a house had collapsed. Others said it was a different house, and so on. Each narration may be a single report, and weak, and untrue, but the basic event was that a house had collapsed; that was certain and they were unanimous concerning it. However, the six instances we enumerated above were both authentic, and some of them became famous. Suppose we consider each of

243. Qāḍī Iyāḍ, *al-Shifā'* i, 334; al-Haythamī, *Majma' al-Zawā'id* ix, 412; al-Ḥākim, *al-Mustadrak* iii, 487.

244. Qāḍī Iyāḍ, *al-Shifā'* i, 334; al-'Asqalānī, *al-Iṣāba* iii, 225; al-Haythamī, *Majma' al-Zawā'id* v, 319.

245. Qāḍī Iyāḍ, *al-Shifā'* i, 334; al-Khafājī, *Sharḥ al-Shifā'* iii, 163; al-Haythamī, *Majma' al-Zawā'id* ix, 259.

these to be weak, all together they still demonstrate the certain existence of an absolute miracle of Muhammad (PBUH), like the absolute collapse of the house in the comparison.

Thus, God's Noble Messenger (Upon whom be blessings and peace) performed definite and clear miracles from every category. The instances of them are the forms or examples of those universal and absolute miracles. Just as the Messenger's hand, fingers, spittle, breath, and speech, that is, his prayer, were the means of numerous miracles, so too, his other subtle faculties and emotions and senses were the means of many wonders. The books of biography and history have described them and demonstrated that in his conduct, physical being, and senses were many evidences of his prophethood.

■ FIFTEENTH SIGN

Just as rocks, trees, the moon and the sun recognized him and affirmed his prophethood by each demonstrating a miracle, so too, animals, the dead, the jinn, and the angels recognized that blessed being and affirmed his prophethood. For by each of those species of beings displaying a number of miracles, they demonstrated that they recognized him and proclaimed their affirmation of his prophethood. This Fifteenth Sign contains three Branches.

First Branch

The animal realm recognized God's Noble Messenger (Upon whom be blessings and peace) and displayed his miracles. There are numerous examples of this Branch. Here as examples, we shall mention only those which are well-known and definite to the degree of 'consensus in meaning,' or have been accepted by authoritative scholars, or have been deemed acceptable by the Muslim community.

The First Incident: This is well-known to the degree of

'consensus in meaning,' and concerns the two pigeons coming and waiting at the entrance to the cave of Hira, where God's Messenger (Upon whom be blessings and peace) and Abu Bakr the Veracious hid from the pursuing unbelievers, and the spider veiling the entrance with a thick web, like a curtain holder. Ubayy b. Khalaf, one of the leaders of the Quraysh whom God's Messenger killed with his own hand at the Battle of Badr, looked at the cave. When his companions suggested that they enter, he replied: "Why should we? I see a large spider's web which appears to have been there since before Muhammad was born. And look, those two pigeons are there. Would they remain there if there was someone in the cave?"[246]

In an instance similar to this, a blessed pigeon cast a shadow over the head of God's Messenger (Upon whom be blessings and peace) during the conquest of Makkah, which was related by Imam Jalil b. Wahab.[247]

Also according to a sound narration, 'A'isha al-Siddiqa relates: "We had a bird in our house called a *dajin*, similar to a pigeon. When God's Messenger was present it would stay quiet, but as soon as he left the house, the bird would start hopping to and fro without stopping."[248] Thus, the bird was obedient to the Messenger, remaining quiet in his presence.

The Second Incident: This is the extraordinary story of the wolf, which has been narrated through a number of chains of transmission from some well-known Companions, and is like 'consensus in meaning.' In short, Abu Sa'id al-Khudri, Salama b. al-Akwa', Ibn Abi Wahab, and Abu Hurayra, and Uhban, a

---

246. Qāḍī Iyāḍ, *al-Shifā'* i, 313; 'Alī al-Qārī, *Sharḥ al-Shifā'* i, 368; *Musnad* i, 248; Ṣan'ānī, *al-Muṣannaf* v, 389; Ibn Kathīr, *al-Bidāya wa'l-Nihāya* iii, 179-81; al-Haythamī, *Majma' al-Zawā'id* vii, 27; Ibn al-Qayyim, *Zād al-Ma'ād* (*Taḥqīq*: Arnavūdī) iii, 52; al-Tabrīzī, *Mishkāt al-Maṣābīḥ* no: 5934; Marūzī, *Musnad Abū Bakr al-Ṣiddīq* no: 73; Zayla'ī, *Naṣb al-Ra'ya* i, 123; al-Haythamī, *Majma' al-Zawā'id* vi, 52-3.

247. Qāḍī Iyāḍ, *al-Shifā'* i, 313; 'Alī al-Qārī, *Sharḥ al-Shifā'* i, 637.

248. Qāḍī Iyāḍ, *al-Shifā'* i, 309; 'Alī al-Qārī, *Sharḥ al-Shifā'* i, 632; al-Khafājī, *Sharḥ al-Shifā'* iii, 79; al-Haythamī, *Majma' al-Zawā'id* ix, 403.

shepherd who was involved in another event, relate through numerous chains of transmission: "A wolf seized a goat and the shepherd saved it from the wolf. The wolf exclaimed: 'Don't you fear God? You have deprived me of my sustenance!' The shepherd muttered to himself: 'How strange! Can wolves speak?' The wolf said to him: 'You're the strange one, for beyond the hill is someone calling you to Paradise. He is a Messenger of God, yet you do not recognize him!'" Although all the lines of transmission agree on the wolf's speech, in his report, which has a strong line, Abu Hurayra says: "The shepherd said to the wolf: 'I am going to see him, but who will look after my goats?' The wolf replied: 'I'll look after them.' So the shepherd handed over the herd to the wolf and went to see the Noble Messenger (Upon whom be blessings and peace), believed in him, and returned to his herd. The shepherd found the wolf; not a goat had been lost. So he slaughtered one for the wolf, for it had become his teacher."[249]

According to one chain of transmission, one of the chiefs of Quraysh, Abu Sufyan, and Safwan saw a wolf pursuing a gazelle into the enclosure of the Ka'ba. As it returned, the wolf spoke, telling of the prophethood of Muhammad (PBUH). They were astonished. Abu Sufyan said to Safwan: 'Don't let's tell anyone of this; I'm frightened everyone will join him and Makkah will be emptied.'[250]

In Short: The story of the wolf gives one complete conviction, and is as certain as those unanimous reports about which there is 'consensus in meaning.'

The Third Incident: This is the narrative of the camel, which was unanimously related through some five or six chains

249. *Musnad* iii, 83, 88; *Musnad* (*Taḥqīq*: Aḥmad Shākir) xv, 202-3, nos: 8049, 11864, 11867; Qāḍī Iyāḍ, *al-Shifā'* i, 310; al-Ḥākim, *al-Mustadrak* iv, 467; Ibn Ḥibbān, *Ṣaḥīḥ* viii, 144; al-Haythamī, *Majma' al-Zawā'id* viii, 291-2; al-Sā'atī, *al-Fatḥ al-Rabbānī* xx, 240; Ibn Kathīr, *al-Bidāya wa'l-Nihāya* vi, 141.

250. Qāḍī Iyāḍ, *al-Shifā'* i, 311; al-Khafājī, *Sharḥ al-Shifā'* iii, 84.

of transmission by famous Companions such as Abu Hurayra, Tha'laba b. Malik, Jabir b. 'Abd Allah, 'Abd Allah b. Ja'far, and 'Abd Allah b. Abi Awfa, who are at the start of the chains. A camel approached God's Messenger (Upon whom be blessings and peace), prostrated itself before him as if saluting him, and spoke. According to a number of lines of transmission, the camel had been angered in a garden, and become wild, attacking anyone who approached it. When God's Messenger appeared, it came to him, prostrated as a sign of respect, and knelt down. The Messenger put a bridle on it, and the camel said to him: "They made me do the heaviest work and now they want to slaughter me. That's why I went wild." The Messenger asked its owner if this was true. "Yes," he replied.[251]

Also, God's Noble Messenger (Upon whom be blessings and peace) had a camel called 'Adba'. After he died, out of its grief, the camel neither ate nor drank, till it died.[252] A number of important authorities including Abu Ishaq Isfara'ini related that it spoke with the Prophet about a certain story.[253] In another instance, in an authentic narration, Jabir b. 'Abd Allah's camel became exhausted on a journey and could no longer continue. God's Messenger gave it a slight prod. Such joy and nimbleness did the camel receive from that prod of the Prophet that due to its speed it could not be caught up with, nor could its reins be seized.[254]

The Fourth Incident: The authorities on Hadith and foremost Bukhari report that it was rumoured one night that the enemy was attacking outside Madinah. Brave horsemen went out to investigate. On the way they saw someone coming. They

251. *Dārimī*, Muqaddima 4; *Musnad* iv, 173; al-Haythamī, *Majma' al-Zawā'id* ix, 4; al-Sā'atī, *al-Fatḥ al-Rabbānī* xxii, 50-1; al-Khafājī, *Sharḥ al-Shifā'* iii, 87; Ibn Kathīr, *al-Bidāya wa'l-Nihāya* vi, 135; al-Albānī, *Silsilat al-Aḥādith al-Ṣaḥīḥa* 485; al-Ḥākim, *al-Mustadrak* ii, 99, 100, 618.

252. Qāḍī Iyāḍ, *al-Shifā'* i, 313.

253. 'Alī al-Qārī, *Sharḥ al-Shifā'* i, 63.

254. *Muslim*, Mīthāqāt 109 no: 715; al-Khafājī, *Sharḥ al-Shifā'* iii, 145. .

looked and saw that it was the Noble Messenger (Upon whom be blessings and peace). He told them there was nothing. He had mounted Abu Talha's famous horse, as his sacred courage impelled him to, and had gone before everyone else to investigate, then returned. He told Abu Talha: "*Your horse is extremely swift and unfaltering.*" Whereas previously it had been extremely slow. After that night, there was no horse to compete with it.[255] On another occasion, as related in an authentic narration, while on a journey at the time for prayer, the Noble Messenger (Upon whom be blessings and peace) told his horse to stop. It stopped, and until he had finished praying the horse did not make the slightest movement.[256]

The Fifth Incident: Safina, the servant of the Noble Prophet (Upon whom be blessings and peace), was commanded by him to go to the Governor of Yemen, Mu'adh b. Jabal. He set off and on the way encountered a lion. Safina said to it: "I am the servant of God's Messenger!" Upon which the lion made a sound as if saying something, and left without molesting him.[257] According to another narration, Safina lost his way when returning, and met with a lion. Not only did the lion not molest him, it showed him the way.

Also, it is narrated from 'Umar that he said: "A beduin came to the Noble Messenger (Upon whom be blessings and peace). He was holding a lizard. He said: 'If this reptile testifies to you, I shall believe in you; otherwise I will not.' God's Messenger asked the lizard, and it testified to his messengership most eloquently."[258]

---

255. *Bukhārī*, Jihād 46, 82; Adab 39; *Muslim*, Faḍā'il 48 no: 2307; *Ibn Māja*, Jihād 9; *Abū Dā'ūd*, Adab 87 no: 4988; *Tirmidhī*, Faḍā'il al-Jihād nos: 1685-7.

256. Qāḍī Iyāḍ, *al-Shifā'* i, 315; al-Khafājī, *Sharḥ al-Shifā'* iii, 95.

257. Tabrīzī, *Mishkāt al-Maṣābīḥ* iii, 199 no: 5949; al-Ḥākim, *al-Mustadrak* iii, 606; al-'Asqalānī, *al-Maṭālib al-'Alīya* iv, 125 no: 4127; al-Haythamī, *Majma' al-Zawā'id* ix, 366-7; Abū Na'īm, *Ḥilyat al-Awliyā'* i, 368-9; Ibn Kathīr, *al-Bidāya wa'l-Nihāya* vi, 147.

258. al-Haythamī, *Majma' al-Zawā'id* viii, 293-4; al-Hindī, *Kanz al-'Ummāl* xii, 358; Ibn Kathīr, *al-Bidāya wa'l-Nihāya* vi, 149-60; 'Alī al-Qārī, *Sharḥ al-Shifā'* i, 632; al-Khafājī, *Sharḥ al-Shifā'* iii, 79.

Also, the Mother of Believers, Umm Salama relates: "A gazelle spoke with the Noble Messenger (Upon whom be blessings and peace), and testified to his messengership."[259]

Thus, there are numerous examples similar to these. We described a few that are famous and certain. And to those who do not recognize and obey the Noble Messenger (Upon whom be blessings and peace), we say this: O man! Take a lesson from these! The lion and the wolf recognized and obeyed him; you, then, should try not to fall lower than an animal!

Second Branch

This concerns corpses, jinns, and angels recognizing God's Noble Messenger (Upon whom be blessings and peace). There were very many instances of this. We shall describe a few examples which are famous and have been related by reliable scholars, firstly about corpses. As for jinns and angels, the many reports concerning them are unanimous, and examples of them number not one but a thousand. And so, examples of the dead speaking:

The First is this: Hasan al-Basri, an important and loyal student of Imam 'Ali and the greatest authority among the scholars of the external and esoteric sciences in the time of the generation subsequent to the Companions, related: "A man came weeping to God's Messenger. He said: 'I had a little girl; she drowned in such-and-such stream nearby. I left her there.' God's Messenger pitied the man and said they would go there together. They went, and the Messenger called to the dead girl, saying her name. At once the dead girl replied: 'I am present and answer your call gladly.' God's Messenger asked her: '*Do you want to return to your father and mother?*' She replied: 'No, I have found something better here!'"[260]

259. Qāḍī Iyāḍ, *al-Shifā'* i, 314; al-Khafājī, *Sharḥ al-Shifā'* iii, 91; al-Haythamī, *Majma' al-Zawā'id* viii, 295.

260. Qāḍī Iyāḍ, *al-Shifā'* i, 320; al-Khafājī, *Sharḥ al-Shifā'* iii, 106.

The Second: Important authorities like Imam Bayhaqi and Imam b. 'Adiyy relate from Anas b. Malik: Anas said: "An elderly woman had a single son who suddenly died. The righteous woman was very grieved and prayed: 'O God, I left my home and migrated here only to obtain Your pleasure and to pay allegiance to God's Noble Messenger (Upon whom be blessings and peace) and to serve him. For the sake of Your Messenger, return my son to me, who was the only person to look after me.'" Anas said: "The dead man rose up and came and ate with us."[261]

In the following lines from the celebrated poem *Qasida al-Burda*, Imam Busiri refers to this extraordinary event: *Were his wonders to correspond to his virtue in greatness / Mere mention of his name would have animated decayed bones.*

The Third: Scholars like Imam Bayhaqi relate from 'Abd Allah b. 'Ubayd Allah al-Ansari: 'Abd Allah said: "I was present when Thabit b. Qays b. Shammas fell as a martyr in the Battle of Yamama and was buried. As he was being put in his grave, a voice suddenly came from him, saying: 'Muhammad is the Messenger of God, Abu Bakr is the Veracious [*Siddiq*], 'Umar, the martyr, and 'Uthman pious and merciful.' We uncoveered him and looked: he was dead and lifeless, yet he was foretelling 'Umar's martyrdom even before he had succeeded to the Caliphate.[262]

The Fourth: Imam Tabarani, and Abu Na'im in his *Dala'il al-Nubuwwa,* relate from Nu'man b. Bashir: "Zayd b. Kharija suddenly dropped down dead in the marketplace. We took his body to his house. That evening between sunset and the night prayer, while the women were weeping all around him, he exclaimed: 'Silence! Silence!' Then, saying: 'Muhammad is God's Messenger! Peace be upon you, O Messenger of God!',

261. Qāḍī Iyāḍ, *al-Shifā'* i, 320; Ibn Kathīr, *al-Bidāya wa'l-Nihāya* vi, 292.
262. Qāḍī Iyāḍ, *al-Shifā'* i, 320; 'Alī al-Qārī, *Sharḥ al-Shifā'* i, 649; Ibn Kathīr, *al-Bidāya wa'l-Nihāya* vi, 157-8.

he spoke most eloquently for a while. We looked: he was dead, without life."[263]

Thus, if lifeless corpses affirm his prophethood and the living do not, for sure they are more dead than the dead and more lifeless than corpses!

As regards angels appearing and serving God's Messenger (Upon whom be blessings and peace), and jinns believing in him and obeying him, these facts have been reported numerously and unanimously. They have been stated explicitly in many verses of the Qur'an. At the Battle of Badr, according to the Qur'an, five thousand angels served him as soldiers in the front line, like the Companions. Indeed, those angels acquired distinction among the angels, like the men who fought in that battle.[264] There are two aspects to be considered in this matter:

The First is the fact that the existence of the different sorts of jinn and angels is as definite as that of the varieties and species of animals and human beings, and that they have relations with us. We have proved this decisively in the Twenty-Ninth Word as certainly as two plus two equals four, and we refer their proof to that Word.

The Second Aspect is members of the community of God's Messenger (Upon whom be blessings and peace) seeing them and speaking with them, as a miracle of his.

Thus, the leading scholars of Hadith, and foremost Bukhari and Muslim, unanimously relate: "One time, an angel, that is, Gabriel, appeared in the form of a man dressed in white. He approached God's Messenger (Upon whom be blessings and peace), who was sitting among his Companions, and asked: 'What is Islam, what is belief, and what is goodness? Explain them.' The Messenger explained them, and the Companions

---

263. Ibn Kathīr, *al-Bidāya wa'l-Nihāya* viii, 291(through various lines); al-Haythamī, *Majma' al-Zawā'id* v, 179-80 (through two lines of transmission).
264. *Bukhārī*, Maghāzī 11.

gathered there both received valuable instruction, and saw the person clearly. Although he seemed like a traveller, he displayed no sign of a journey. He suddenly rose and disappeared. God's Messenger then said: *'Gabriel did that in order to teach you!'*"[265]

Also, the authorities on Hadith relate through certain and authentic narrations of the degree of 'consensus in meaning': "The Companions saw Gabriel with God's Messenger (Upon whom be blessings and peace) many times in the form of Dihya, who was very handsome." For instance, 'Umar, Ibn 'Abbas, Usama b. Zayd, Harith, 'A'isha al-Siddiqa, and Umm Salama established and related certainly: "We frequently saw Gabriel with the God's Messenger in the form of Dihya."[266] Is it at all possible that such people would say that they had seen him if they had not?

Also, the conqueror of Persia, Sa'd b. Abi Waqqas, who was one of the ten promised Paradise, relates in an authentic narration: "At the Battle of Uhud we saw two white-dressed persons either side of God's Messenger (Upon whom be blessings and peace), guarding him like sentries. We understood that they were the angels, Gabriel and Michael."[267] Is it possible that if such a hero of Islam says he saw them, he had not seen them?

Also, Abu Sufyan b. Harith b. 'Abd al-Muttalib, the Prophet's cousin, relates in an authentic narration: "At the Battle of Badr, we saw horsemen dressed in white between the sky and the earth."[268]

Also, Hamza pleaded with the Noble Prophet (Upon whom

265. *Bukhārī*, Īmān 37; *Muslim*, Īmān 1-7.

266. *Bukhārī*, Faḍā'il al-Aṣḥāb 30; al-Haythamī, *Majma' al-Zawā'id* ix, 276-7; Aḥmad b. Ḥanbal, *Faḍā'il al-Ṣaḥāba* (*Taḥqīq*: Vasiyyullāh) no: 1817, 1853, 1918; *Musnad* i, 212; al-'Asqalānī, *al-Iṣāba* i, 598.

267. *Bukhārī*, Maghāzī 18; Libās 24; *Muslim*, Faḍā'il 46-7 no: 2306; Qāḍī Iyāḍ, *al-Shifā'* i, 361.

268. *Musnad* i, 147, 353; Qāḍī Iyāḍ, *al-Shifā'* i, 362; al-Khafājī, *Sharḥ al-Shifā'* iii, 281; 'Alī al-Qārī, *Sharḥ al-Shifā'* i, 735.

be blessings and peace) to see Gabriel. So he showed him to Hamza in the Ka'ba, but he could not endure it and fell to the ground unconscious.[269]

There were numerous occurrences like these of angels being seen. They all demonstrated one sort of the Miracles of Muhammad (PBUH), and show that the angels too were like moths drawn to the lamp of his prophethood.

When it comes to jinns, it was not only the Companions, it frequently occurs that ordinary members of the Muslim community meet with them and see them. But the most certain and authentic reports are given us by the leading scholars of Hadith, who say: Ibn Mas'ud related: "I saw the jinn on the night they accepted Islam at Batn al-Nakhl. I likened them to the Zut, a tall-statured Sudanese tribe; they resembled them."[270]

There is also the incident concerning Khalid b. Walid, which is famous and has been authenticated and accepted by the leading scholars of Hadith: when the idol called 'Uzza was destroyed, a jinn came out of it in the form of a black woman. Khalid cut it into two with his sword. The Noble Messenger (Upon whom be blessings and peace) said in connection with this: "They used to worship it inside the idol 'Uzza; it can no longer be worshipped."[271]

Also, is a narration from 'Umar: he said: "While we were with God's Messenger, a jinn called Hama came in the form of an old man carrying a staff; he accepted Islam. The Noble Messenger (Upon whom be blessings and peace) instructed him in some of the short Suras of the Qur'an, which he listened to and

269. Qāḍī Iyāḍ, *al-Shifā'* i, 362; al-Khafājī, *Sharḥ al-Shifā'* iii, 282; 'Alī al-Qārī, *Sharḥ al-Shifā'* i, 736.

270. *Musnad* (*Taḥqīq*: Aḥmad Shākir) vi, 165 no: 4353; Suyūṭī, *al-Khaṣā'iṣ al-Kubrā* i, 343; ii, 361.

271. Qāḍī Iyāḍ, *al-Shifā'* i, 362; al-Khafājī, *Sharḥ al-Shifā'* iii, 287; 'Alī al-Qārī, *Sharḥ al-Shifā'* i, 738; Ibn Kathīr, *al-Bidāya wa'l-Nihāya* iv, 316; al-Haythamī, *Majma' al-Zawā'id* vi, 176.

then departed."[272] Some scholars of Hadith have questioned this last incident, but the most important of them declared it to be authentic. In any event, it is unnecessary to describe this sort at length, for the examples of it are many. We would only add this:

Through the light of God's Most Noble Messenger (Upon whom be blessings and peace), through his training, and through following him, thousands of spiritual poles and purified scholars like Shaykh 'Abd al-Qadir Gilani have met and spoken with angels and jinn. This fact has reached the degree of 'consensus' a hundred times over through innumerable instances.[273] Yes, members of the community of Muhammad (PBUH) being in contact with angels and jinn, and speaking with them, occurs through the miraculous guidance and instruction of the Noble Messenger (Upon whom be blessings and peace).

Third Branch

The protection and preservation of God's Messenger (Upon whom be blessings and peace) was a clear miracle, and many instances of it are indicated by the clear truth of the verse, *And God will defend you from men.*[274] For sure, when God's Messenger appeared, he was not only challenging one group, or one people, or a few rulers, or one religion; he was rather challenging single-handed all kings and the people of all religions. And yet until he died in perfect ease and happiness and rose to the heavenly court, for twenty-three years he was without guard or protector and was exposed to numerous plots, with his own uncle his greatest enemy and his own tribe and people hostile to him. This shows what a powerful truth the above-mentioned verse expresses and what a firm point of support it was. We shall mention only a few events classed as definite as examples.

---

272. Qāḍī Iyāḍ, *al-Shifā'* i, 363; al-Khafājī, *Sharḥ al-Shifā'* iii, 287; Bayhaqi, *Dalā'il al-Nubūwwa* v, 416-8.

273. Ibn Taymiyya, *al-Tawassul wa'l-Wasila* 24; Ibn Taymiyya, *Majmū' al-Fatāwā* xi, 307.

274. Qur'ān, 5:70.

First Event: Scholars of Hadith and the Prophet's biography report unanimously that the Quraysh had made a certain agreement to kill God's Messenger (Upon whom be blessings and peace). Upon the suggestion of a demon in human form, so as to prevent discord within the Quraysh, at least one member of every branch of the tribe formed a group of nearly two hundred men under the leadership of Abu Jahl and Abu Lahab, and they staged a surprise attack on the Prophet's house. 'Ali was together with God's Messenger. He had told him to sleep that night in his bed. The Messenger waited till the Quraysh came and completely surrounded the house, then he went out and threw a handful of earth at their heads, and not one of them saw him. He passed through them and disappeared.[275] When he reached the cave of Hira, two pigeons and a spider became his guards, and protected him against all the Quraysh.[276]

The Second Event: It certainly occurred that when they emerged from the cave and set off towards Madinah, they were followed by a very brave man called Suraqa, who, for a large reward, had been sent by the leaders of the Quraysh to kill them. God's Messenger (Upon whom be blessings and peace) and Abu Bakr the Veracious had seen Suraqa coming when they came out of the cave. Abu Bakr had been anxious, but God's Messenger said: "*Do not be anxious, God is with us!*",[277] as he had in the cave. Abu Bakr looked at Suraqa: his horse's hooves were stuck in the sand. He was freed and started following them again. Then again the horse became transfixed, and something like smoke was rising from where its hooves were stuck. At that point he understood that it was beyond his power and anyone else's power, to harm God's Messenger. He cried for mercy. The Messenger freed him, but said: "Go back, but

275. Qāḍī Iyāḍ, *al-Shifā'* i, 349; *Musnad* (*Taḥqīq*: Aḥmad Shākir) iv, 269 no: 2009; al-Haythamī, *Majma' al-Zawā'id* ii, 228.

276. Qāḍī Iyāḍ, *al-Shifā'* i, 349; al-Khafājī, *Sharḥ al-Shifā'* iii, 236; see page, fn. 246, 247.

277. Qur'ān, 9:40.

make sure no one else comes after us."[278]

In connection with this incident, we should also mention that a shepherd spotted them and immediately set off for Makkah to inform the Quraysh. But on arriving at the city, he forgot why he had come. No matter how much he tried, he could not remember. He was obliged to return. Then later he understood that he had been made to forget it.[279]

The Third Event: The leading scholars of Hadith relate through many chains of transmission that at the Battle of Ghatfan and Anmar, a bold tribal chief called Ghurath got close to the Noble Prophet (Upon whom be blessings and peace) without anyone seeing him, his sword ready in his hand. He said to God's Messenger: "Who will save you from me?" God's Messenger replied: "*God!*" Then he prayed: "*O God, save me from him, if You thus will!*" Suddenly, Ghurath received a blow from the Unseen between the shoulders and his sword fell to the ground. The Noble Messenger picked up the sword and said: "*Now who will save you from me?*" Then he forgave him. The man returned to his tribe. Everyone was astonished at the bold, valiant fighter, and asked him what had happened to him and why he had done nothing. He replied to them: "That's the way it happened. I have come now from the best of men."[280]

In an incident similar to this at the Battle of Badr, a dissembler approached the Noble Messenger (Upon whom be blessings and peace) from behind when no one was aware of it. Just as he was raising his sword to strike, God's Messenger turned and looked at him; the man trembled and his sword slipped to the ground.[281]

---

278. *Bukhārī*, Anbiyā' (Bāb: 'Alāmat al-Nubūwwa fi'l-Islām, Faḍā'il Aṣḥāb al-Nabī, Manāqib al-Muhājirīn wa Faḍlihim, Hijrat al-Nabī wa Aṣḥābihi); *Muslim*, no: 2009; Ibn Ḥibbān, *Ṣaḥīḥ* 65; ix, 11. See, Concordance.

279. Qāḍī Iyāḍ, *al-Shifā'* i, 351; 'Alī al-Qārī, *Sharḥ al-Shifā'* i, 715.

280. *Bukhārī*, Jihād 84, 87; Maghāzī 31-2; *Muslim*, Ṣalāt al-Musāfirīn, 311 no: 843; Qāḍī Iyāḍ, *al-Shifā'* i, 347-8; al-Haythamī, *Majma' al-Zawā'id* ix, 7-8; al-Ḥākim, *al-Mustadrak* iii, 29-30.

281. Qāḍī Iyāḍ, *al-Shifā'* i, 347; 'Alī al-Qārī, *Sharḥ al-Shifā'* i, 710.

The Fourth Event: This is well-known almost to the degree of 'consensus in meaning,' and is given by most Qur'anic commentators as the immediate reason for the revelation of the verse,

Indeed We have put yokes round their necks right up their chins, so that they heads are forced up [and they cannot see]. And We have put a bar in front of them and a bar behind them, and further, We have covered them up, so that they cannot see.[282]

It is also related by the most learned commentators and scholars of Hadith. They relate that Abu Jahl took an oath, saying: "I shall strike Muhammad with a stone if I see him prostrating." He took a large stone and went to find God's Messenger. He lifted his hands to cast the stone, when he saw him prostrating, and they remained raised. God's Messenger (Upon whom be blessings and peace) stood up on completing the prayers, and Abu Jahl's hand was released. He could move it either because the Prophet permitted, or because there was no longer any need for it to remain thus.[283]

In another similar incident, a man from the same tribe as Abu Jahl, al-Walid b. Mughira according to one narration, went to the Ka'ba with a large stone in his hand, to strike the Noble Messenger (Upon whom be blessings and peace) while he was prostrating, but the man's eyes were sealed and he could not see the Messenger entering, nor was he able to see the people who had sent him; he could only hear their voices. When God's Messenger finished praying, his eyes were opened, for no need remained for them to be sealed.[284]

Also, it is related through an authentic narration from Abu

282. Qur'ān, 36:8-9.

283. Qāḍī Iyāḍ, *al-Shifā'* i, 351; al-Khafājī, *Sharḥ al-Shifā'* iii, 241; al-Haythamī, *Majma' al-Zawā'id* viii, 227; *Muslim*, No: 2797; Ibn Kathīr, *al-Bidāya wa'l-Nihāya* iii, 42-3.

284. Qāḍī Iyāḍ, *al-Shifā'* i, 351; al-Khafājī, *Sharḥ al-Shifā'* iii, 242.

Bakr the Veracious that after the Sura about Abu Lahab had been revealed, his wife, *Hammalat al-Hatab* (the wood carrier) Umm Jamil, came to the Ka'ba with a stone in her hand. She saw Abu Bakr, who was sitting beside the Noble Messenger (Upon whom be blessings and peace), and asked him, "Where's your friend? I hear that he mocked me. If I see him, I will hit him in the mouth with this rock." She could not see God's Messenger, although he was sitting beside him.[285] Of course, a wood-carrier of Hell like that could not enter the presence of the 'Sultan of Lawlak',[286] who was under Divine protection, and see him. How could she?

The Fifth Event: It is related through a sound narration that 'Amir b. Tufayl and Arbad b. Qays conspired to assassinate God's Noble Messenger (Upon whom be blessings and peace). 'Amir said: "I'll keep him busy, and you strike him." They went, but Arbad did not do anything. Amir asked him later why he did not strike him. Arbad answered: "How could I? Every time I intended to hit him, I saw you between us. How could I have struck you?"[287]

The Sixth Event: It is related through an authentic narration that at the battle either of Uhud or Hunayn, Shayba b. 'Uthman al-Hajabayya whose uncle and father Hamza had killed, crept up stealthily on the Noble Messenger (Upon whom be blessings and peace), in order to avenge them. On his raising his drawn sword, it suddenly slipped from his hand. God's Messenger turned and looked at him, putting his hand on his chest. Shayba later said: "At that moment there was no one in the world I loved more." He believed in him. The Messenger told him to go and fight. Shayba said: "I went and fought in front of God's

285. Qāḍī Iyāḍ, *al-Shifā'* i, 349; al-Khafājī, *Sharḥ al-Shifā'* iii, 233; al-Haythamī, *Majma' al-Zawā'id* i, 353; Ibn Ḥibbān, *Ṣaḥīḥ* viii, 152; al-Ḥākim, *al-Mustadrak* ii, 361.

286. This refers to the Ḥadīth Qudsi: "But for thee, but for thee, I would not have created the spheres."(Tr.)

287. Qāḍī Iyāḍ, *al-Shifā'* i, 353; al-Khafājī, *Sharḥ al-Shifā'* iii, 249; Bayhaqī, *Dalā'il al-Nubūwwa* v, 318.

Messenger. If I had come across my own father at that time, I would have struck him!"[288]

Also, on the day of the conquest of Makkah, a man called Fadala approached God's Messenger (Upon whom be blessings and peace) with the intention of striking him. The Messenger looked at him, and said, smiling: "*What have you told yourself?*", praying that he might be forgiven. Fadala became a believer, and said: "At that moment there was no one in the world I loved more."[289]

The Seventh Event: According to a sound narration, at the very moment some Jews, with the intention of assassinating him, were going drop down a large rock on God's Noble Messenger (Upon whom be blessings and peace), while he was sitting, he rose through Divine protection; so the plot came to nothing.[290]

There were many events similar to these seven. The scholars of Hadith, and foremost Imam Bukhari and Imam Muslim, relate from 'A'isha that after the verse, *And God will defend you from men* was revealed, God's Messenger told those who guarded him from time to time: "*O men, leave me, for God, the Great and Mighty, protects me!*"[291]

Thus, from the beginning up to here, this treatise shows that every species of being, every realm of creation in the universe, recognized the Noble Messenger (Upon whom be blessings and peace), and was connected with him. His miracles were manifested in every one of them. This means that the Prophet

---

288. Qāḍī Iyāḍ, *al-Shifā'* i, 353; al-Khafājī, *Sharḥ al-Shifā'* iii, 248; al-Haythamī, *Majma' al-Zawā'id* vi, 183-4; 'Alī al-Qārī, *Sharḥ al-Shifā'* i, 718; al-'Asqalānī, *al-Iṣāba* ii, 157.

289. Qāḍī Iyāḍ, *al-Shifā'* i, 353; al-Khafājī, *Sharḥ al-Shifā'* iii, 248; 'Alī al-Qārī, *Sharḥ al-Shifā'* i, 718.

290. Qāḍī Iyāḍ, *al-Shifā'* i, 353; al-Khafājī, *Sharḥ al-Shifā'* iii, 243; 'Alī al-Qārī, *Sharḥ al-Shifā'* i, 176; Abū Na'īm, *Dalā'il al-Nubūwwa* ii, 489-90.

291. *Tirmidhī*, v, 351 no: 3406; *Tirmidhī* (*Taḥqīq*: Aḥmad Shākir) no: 3049; Qāḍī Iyāḍ, *al-Shifā'* i, 352; al-Ḥākim, *al-Mustadrak* ii, 313.

Muhammad (PBUH) was the official and Messenger of God Almighty, but in regard to His titles of Creator of the Universe and Sustainer of all Creatures. For example, every office or department of government knows and recognizes a high-ranking official, an inspector, of the king, and whichever of them he enters, those in it show an interest in him, for he acts in the name of the king of all of them. If he is only an inspector in the judiciary, then only that department of government recognizes him; the other offices do not. And if he is an inspector in the army, the civil service does not recognize him. And so, it is understood that all the realms and spheres of Divine rule, every species and group from the angels to the flies and spiders, knew and recognized God's Messenger, or had been informed about him. That is to say, he was the Seal of the Prophets and the Messenger of the Sustainer of All the Worlds. And his prophethood was more comprehensive and all-embracing than those of all the preceding prophets.

■ SIXTEENTH SIGN

The wonders that took place before his prophetic mission, but which were related to it, are called *irhasat*, and these too were indications and proofs of his prophethood. They were of three kinds:

THE FIRST KIND

This kind of *irhasat* comprises the tidings of Muhammad's (PBUH) prophethood given by the Torah, the Bible, the Psalms of David, and the scriptures revealed to other prophets, as stated by the Qur'an. Indeed, since those Books are revealed scriptures and those who brought them were prophets, it is necessary and certain that they should have mentioned the one who would supersede their religions, change the shape of the universe, and illuminate half the earth with the light he brought. Is it possible that those Books, which foretold insignificant events, would not speak of the most important phenomenon of humanity, the prophethood of Muhammad (PBUH)? Yes, since they would certainly speak of it, they would either denounce it as a falsehood and so save their religions from destruction and their books from abrogation, or they would affirm it, and through that man of truth, save their religions from superstition and corruption. Now, both friend and foe agree that there is no sign of any such denouncement in the Books, in which case there must be affirmation. And since there is certain affirmation, and since there is a definite reason and fundamental cause for such affirmation, we too shall demonstrate through three categorical proofs the existence of this affirmation:

First Proof: God's Noble Messenger (Upon whom be blessings and peace) says to them through the tongue of the Qur'an: "Your scriptures describe and confirm me; they confirm me in the things I say." He challenges them with verses such as,

> *Say, "Bring the Torah and read it, if you are men of truth!"*[292] * *Say, "Come, let us gather together—our sons and your sons, our women and your women, ourselves and yourselves; then let us earnestly pray and invoke the curse of God on those who lie!"*[293]

Despite his continuously taunting them with verses such as these, no Jewish scholar or Christian priest was able to show he had made any error. If they had been able to, those very numerous and very obdurate and jealous unbelievers and dissembling Jews and the whole world of unbelief would have proclaimed it everywhere. The Prophet also said:

"Either you find any error of mine, or I shall fight you until I destroy you!" And they chose war and wretchedness. That means they could not find any error. For if they had, they would have been saved from all that.

---

292. Qur'ān, 3:93.
293. Qur'ān, 3:61.

Second Proof: The words of the Torah, the Bible, and the Psalms do not have the miraculousness of those of the Qur'an. They have also been translated again and again, and a great many alien words have become intermingled with them. Also, the words of commentators and their false interpretations have been confused with their verses. In addition, the distortions of the ignorant and the hostile have been incorporated into them. In these ways, the corruptions and alterations have multiplied in those Books. In fact, Shaykh Rahmatullah al-Hindi, the well-known scholar, proved to Jewish and Christian scholars and priests thousands of corruptions in them, and silenced them. Nevertheless, despite these corruptions, in our times the celebrated Husayn Jisri (May God have mercy on him) extracted one hundred and ten indications to the prophethood of Muhammad (PBUH), and included them in his *Risalat al-Hamidiya.* This was translated into Turkish by the late İsmail Hakkı of Manastır; whoever wishes may refer to it.

Also, many Jewish and Christian scholars acknowledged and admitted that the attributes of Muhammad the Arabian (Upon whom be blessings and peace) were written in their Books. The famous Roman Emperor Heraclius, who was a non-Muslim himself, said: "Jesus foretold Muhammad's coming." [294]

Also, another Roman ruler called Muqawqis, the Governor of Egypt, and celebrated Jewish scholars and leaders such as Ibn Suriya, Zubayr b. Batiya, Ibn Akhtab and his brother Ka'b b. Asad, although remaining non-Muslim, admitted: "He is described in our Books."[295]

Also, some of the well-known Jewish scholars and Christian priests gave up their obduracy on seeing Muhammad's (PBUH)

294. Ibn Sayyid al-Nās, *'Uyūn al-Āthār* ii, 26; Qāḍī Iyāḍ, *al-Shifā'* i, 364.

295. Suyūṭī, *al-Khaṣā'iṣ al-Kubrā* ii, 139; Qāḍī Iyāḍ, *al-Shifā'* i, 366; 'Alī al-Qārī, *Sharḥ al-Shifā'* i, 744-5; Ibn Kathīr, *al-Bidāya wa'l-Nihāya* iv, 80, 81, 272; Bayhaqī, *Dalā'il al-Nubūwwa* iii, 362; Wāqidi, *Kitāb al-Maghāzī* 403-4; Abū Na'īm, *Dalā'il al-Nubūwwa* i, 85.

attributes as described in the above-mentioned books, and believed in him. They then pointed out these references to other Jewish and Christian scholars, and convinced them. Among them were the famous 'Abd Allah b. Salam, Wahb b. Munabbih, Abu Yasir, the two sons of Sa'ya, Asid and Tha'laba, and Shamul.[296] The latter lived at the time of Tubba', the ruler of Yemen. Shamul became a believer before Muhammad's prophetic mission and without ever seeing him, just as Tubba did.[297] While the guest of the Bani Nadir before the prophetic mission, a gnostic called Ibn Hayban declared: "A prophet will soon appear, and this is the place to which he will emigrate." He died there. Later, when that tribe was at war with God's Messenger (Upon whom be blessings and peace), Asid and Tha'laba came forward and cried out to the tribe: "By God, he is the one Ibn Hayban promised would come."[298] But they did not heed him, and paid the penalty.

Also, many of the Jewish scholars like, Ibn Yasin, Mikhayriq, and Ka'b al-Ahbar, became believers on seeing the prophetic attributes in their Books, and silenced those who did not accept faith.[299]

Also, the famous Christian scholar and monk, Bahira, who was mentioned above:[300] God's Messenger (Upon whom be blessings and peace) was twelve years old when he went to

296. Qāḍī Iyāḍ, *al-Shifā'* i, 366; Alī al-Qārī, *Sharḥ al-Shifā'* i, 744-5; Ibn Kathīr, *al-Bidāya wa'l-Nihāya* iv, 80-1; Bayhaqī, *Dalā'il al-Nubūwwa* iii, 361-2; Wāqidi, *al-Maghāzī* 405-4; Ibn Jawzī, *Ṣifāt al-Ṣafwā* iii, 361-2; Abū Na'īm, *Dalā'il al-Nubūwwa* i, 79; ii, 492.

297. Bayhaqī, *Dalā'il al-Nubūwwa* i, 367; ii, 526; vi, 240-9; al-Hindī, *Kanz al-'Ummāl* xi, 401; xii, 390-408; Qāḍī Iyāḍ, *al-Shifā'* i, 364; 'Alī al-Qārī, *Sharḥ al-Shifā'* i, 739-43; al-Haythamī, *Majma' al-Zawā'id* viii, 240.

298. Bayhaqī, *Dalā'il al-Nubūwwa* ii, 80-1; iv, 31; 'Alī al-Qārī, *Sharḥ al-Shifā'* i, 744-5; Yūsuf Nabhānī, *Ḥujjat Allāh 'alā'l-'Ālamīn* 137; Abū Na'īm, *Dalā'il al-Nubūwwa* i, 82; Ibn al-Jawzī, *Ṣifāt al-Ṣafwā* i, 87.

299. Qāḍī Iyāḍ, *al-Shifā'* i, 364; 'Alī al-Qārī, *Sharḥ al-Shifā'* i, 739; Ibn al-Jawzī, *Ṣifāt al-Ṣafwā* i, 87; Yūsuf Nabhānī, *Ḥujjat Allāh 'alā'l-'Ālamīn* 87-8, 135; Bayhaqī, *Dalā'il al-Nubūwwa* 161-3; Abū Na'īm, *Dalā'il al-Nubūwwa* i, 78-9.

300. See, page 169 fn. 176. Also: Bayhaqī, *Dalā'il al-Nubūwwa* ii, 24; Yūsuf Nabhānī, *Ḥujjat Allāh 'alā'l-'Ālamīn* 158.

Damascus with his uncle, and it was for his sake that Bahira invited the Quraysh. For he had seen a cloud casting its shadow on the travelling caravan. When it continued to do so, he realized that the one he was seeking had remained with the caravan, and had sent someone to fetch him. He told Abu Talib: "Return to Makkah! The Jews are exceedingly jealous and will resort to treachery, for his attributes are described in the Torah."

Also, Nestor the Abyssinian, and the ruler of that country, the Negus, came to believe on seeing Muhammad's attributes written in their Books.[301]

Also, a well-known Christian scholar called Daghatr became a believer on seeing the description of the Prophet, and was martyred when he proclaimed this among the Byzantines.[302]

Also, from the Christian leaders, Harith b. Abi Shumar al-Ghasani and the prominent rulers and religious leaders of Damascus such as Sahib al-Ilya, Heraclius, Ibn Natur and al-Jarud, entered the fold of Islam, after seeing the Prophet's description in their Books. Of them, only Heraclius concealed his belief for the sake of worldly rule.[303]

Also, like these, Salman al-Farsi had also formerly been a Christian. He searched for the Noble Messenger (Upon whom be blessings and peace) after seeing his description.[304]

Also, a famous scholar called Tamim, and the well-known Abyssinian ruler, the Negus, and the Abyssinian Christians, and the priests of Najran, all unanimously declared that they had

---

301. Qāḍī Iyāḍ, *al-Shifā'* i, 364; 'Alī al-Qārī *Sharḥ al-Shifā'* i, 744.

302. See, page 202, fn. 297.

303. *Bukhārī*, Bad' al-Waḥy 6; Shahādāt 28; 'Alī al-Qārī, *Sharḥ al-Shifā'* i, 744; Yūsuf Nabhānī, *Ḥujjat Allāh 'alā'l-'Ālamīn* 121, 150-1; Qasṭalānī, *al-Mawāhib al-Ladunnīya* vi, 198; Ṭabarānī, *al-Mu'jam al-Kabīr* iii, 2108; *Ibn 'Adiyy, al-Kāmil fi'l-Ḍu'afā* iii, 1094; Abū Na'īm, *Dalā'il al-Nubūwwa* i, 101-2.

304. al-'Asqalānī, *Fatḥ al-Bārī*, vii, 222; Bayhaqī, *Dalā'il al-Nubūwwa* ii, 82; Ibn Kathīr, *al-Bidāya wa'l-Nihāya* ii, 310-6; *Musnad* v, 437; Ibn Ḥishām, *Sīrat al-Nabī* i, 233; Abū Na'īm, *Dalā'il al-Nubūwwa* no: 213; al-Ḥākim, *al-Mustadrak* iii, 604; Qāḍī Iyāḍ, *al-Shifā'* i, 364; 'Alī al-Qārī, *Sharḥ al-Shifā'* i, 670; Yūsuf Nabhānī, *Ḥujjat Allāh 'alā'l-'Ālamīn* 144; Abū Na'īm, *Dalā'il al-Nubūwwa* i, 258-64.

seen the Prophet's description in their Books, and had come to believe in him.[305]

The Third Proof: Here, as examples, we shall point out from the Gospel, the Torah, and the Psalms, a few instances of verses concerning our Prophet (Upon whom be blessings and peace).

First: In the Psalms, there is the following verse:

O God, send to us after the period between prophets one who will establish an exemplary model.[306]

Here, "One who will establish an exemplary model" refers to the Prophet Muhammad (PBUH).

A verse from the Gospels says:

The Messiah said: "I am leaving for my father and your father, so that He may send you the Paraclete,"[307]

that is, Ahmad Muhammad.

A second verse from the Gospels:

I ask from my Lord for the Paraclete that he may abide with you forever.[308]

Paraclete, meaning 'the distinguisher of good from evil,' is the name of our Prophet in those Books.

A verse from the Torah says:

Verily God told Abraham that Hagar —the mother of Isma'il— will bear children. There will emerge from her sons one whose hand will be above all, and the hands of all will be opened to him in reverence.[309]

---

305. *Musnad* i, 461; *Abū Dā'ūd* Janā'iz 58; Qāḍī Iyāḍ, *al-Shifā'* i, 364; 'Alī al-Qārī, *Sharḥ al-Shifā'* i, 744-6; Jisri, *Risale-i Hamidiye* (Turkish trans.) i, 240; Yūsuf Nabhānī, *Ḥujjat Allāh 'alā'l-'Ālamīn* 163.

306. Yūsuf Nabhānī, *Ḥujjat Allāh 'alā'l-'Ālamīn* 104, 115.

307. Ḥalabī, *al-Sīrat al-Ḥalabīya* i, 352; Jisri, *Risale-i Hamidiye* (Turkish trans.) i, 250; Qasṭalānī, *al-Mawāhib al-Ladunnīya* vi, 201.

308. 'Alī al-Qārī, *Sharḥ al-Shifā'* i, 743; Yūsuf Nabhānī, *Ḥujjat Allāh 'alā'l-'Ālamīn* 99; Jisri, *Risale-i Hamidiye* i, 255; Gospel of John, 14:16.

309. 'Alī al-Qārī, *Sharḥ al-Shifā'* i, 743; Yūsuf Nabhānī, *Ḥujjat Allāh 'alā'l-'Ālamīn* 105-6; Genesis, Chap. 17.

Another verse from the Torah:

And He said to Moses: "O Moses, verily I shall send them a prophet like you, from the sons of their brothers [the children of Isma'il]; I shall place My word in his mouth, and shall punish whoever does not accept the words of the one who will speak in My name."[310]

A third verse from the Torah:

Moses said: "O Lord! Verily I have found in the Torah the best of Communities that will emerge for the benefit of humanity, that will enjoin good and forbid wrong, and that will believe in God. Let it be my Community!" God said: "That is the Community of Muhammad."[311]

A REMINDER: In those books, the name of Muhammad is given in Syriac form, such as Mushaffah, Munhamanna, Himyata, and names meaning Muhammad in Hebrew. Otherwise the name of Muhammad is explicitly mentioned only in a few places, which were also altered by the jealous Jews.[312]

A verse from the Psalms of David states:

O David! A prophet will appear after you, named Ahmad Muhammad; he will be truthful, and he will be a chief, and his Community will be forgiven.[313]

One of the Seven 'Abd Allah's, 'Abd Allah b. 'Amr b. al-'As, who made extensive studies of the earlier scriptures, and 'Abd Allah b. Salam, who was the earliest to accept Islam from among the famous Jewish scholars, and the famous scholar Ka'b al-Ahbar from among the Children of Israel, all pointed

---

310. 'Alī al-Qārī, *Sharḥ al-Shifā'* i, 743; Yūsuf Nabhānī, *Ḥujjat Allāh 'alā'l-'Ālamīn* 86; Ḥalabī, *al-Sīrat al-Ḥalabīya* i, 347; Deuteronomy, Chap. 18.

311. 'Alī al-Qārī, *Sharḥ al-Shifā'* i, 746; Yūsuf Nabhānī, *Ḥujjat Allāh 'alā'l-'Ālamīn* 107-18; Isaiah, Chap. 42.

312. Yūsuf Nabhānī, *Ḥujjat Allāh 'alā'l-'Ālamīn* 112-3; Qasṭalānī, *al-Mawāhib al-Ladunnīya* vi, 189.

313. Ḥalabī, *al-Sīrat al-Ḥalabīya* i, 353; Kandahlawī, *Ḥayāt al-Ṣaḥāba* i, 18; Ibn Kathīr, *al-Bidāya wa'l-Nihāya* ii, 326; 'Alī al-Qārī, *Sharḥ al-Shifā'* i, 739; Yūsuf Nabhānī, *Ḥujjat Allāh 'alā'l-'Ālamīn* 122.

out in the Torah, which was not then corrupted to its present extent, the following verse, which after addressing Moses, then addresses the Prophet-yet-to-come:

O Prophet, verily We have sent you as a witness, a bearer of glad tidings, a warner and a protection for the unlettered. You are My bondsman, and I have named you 'the Reliant on God.' You shall not be harsh, stern, and clamorous in the market places, nor shall you requite evil with evil, but instead pardon and forgive. God shall not take you unto Himself until you straighten a crooked people by causing them to say, "No god but God."[314]

Another verse from the Torah:

Muhammad is God's Messenger, his birthplace is Makkah, he will emigrate to Tayba, his rule will be in Damascus, and his Community will constantly praise God.[315]

In this verse, a Syriac word meaning Muhammad is mentioned for the word Muhammad.

Here is another verse from the Torah:

You are My bondsman and messenger, and I have named you 'Reliant on God,'[316]

which is addressed to a prophet who is to come after Moses, and is from the progeny of Isma'il, the brother of Isaac.

In the following verse from the Torah,

My chosen bondsman is not harsh or stern,[317]

---

314. *Bukhārī*, Buyū' 5; Ḥalabī, *al-Sīrat al-Ḥalabīya* i, 346; *Dārimī*, Muqaddima 2; Kandahlawī, *Ḥayāt al-Ṣaḥāba* i, 17; Ibn Kathīr, *al-Bidāya wa'l-Nihāya* ii, 326; Yūsuf Nabhānī, *Ḥujjat Allāh 'alā'l-'Ālamīn* 105, 135; al-'Ajurrī, *al-Sharī'a* 444, 452; Qasṭalānī, *Mawāhib al-Ladunnīya* vi, 192.

315. *Dārimī*, Muqaddima 2; Ḥalabī, *al-Sīrat al-Ḥalabīya* i, 346-51; 'Alī al-Qārī, *Sharḥ al-Shifā'* i, 739; Yūsuf Nabhānī, *Ḥujjat Allāh 'alā'l-'Ālamīn* 116; Abū Na'īm, *Dalā'il al-Nubūwwa* i, 72.

316. See, fn. 314. (This is part of the same verse.)

317. *Dārimī*, Muqaddima 2; Yūsuf Nabhānī, *Ḥujjat Allāh 'alā'l-'Ālamīn* 105, 119; 'Alī al-Qārī, *Sharḥ al-Shifā'* i, 739.

The meaning of Mukhtar (chosen) is the same as 'Mustafa,' a name of Muhammad.

In several places in the Gospels, a prophet who will come after Jesus is referred to as "the Master of the World." He is described as:

> *He will have with him a staff of iron with which he will fight, as will his people.*[318]

This verse indicates that a prophet will come with a sword, charged with waging *jihad*. *Qadib min hadid* (literally, staff of iron) means sword. And so will be his community. In agreement with the Biblical verse mentioned above, and referring to it as well as some other verses, the folowing Qur'anic verse at the end of *Sura al-Fath* also states that his community, like him, will be commanded to wage *jihad*:

> *And their similitude in the Gospel is like a seed that sends forth its blade, then makes it strong; it then becomes thick, and it stands on its own stem, filling the sowers with wonder and delight. As a result, it fills the unbelievers with rage at them.*[319]

In the Thirty-Third Chapter[320] of the Fifth Book of the Torah, there is the following verse:

> *The Lord came from Sinai, rose up unto us from Sa'ir, and shined forth from Mount Paran.*[321]

In this verse, with the phrase "the Lord came from Sinai," the prophethood of Moses is mentioned; with the phrase "rose up unto us from Sa'ir" (Sa'ir being a mountain near Damascus), the prophethood of Jesus is indicated. And the phrase "He shined forth from Mount Paran (the Paran Mountains being the mountains of Hijaz), gives tidings of the prophethood of

318. Yūsuf Nabhānī, *Ḥujjat Allāh 'alā'l-'Ālamīn* 99, 114.
319. Qur'ān, 48:29
320. Deuteronomy, 33:1.
321. Ḥalabī, *al-Sīrat al-Ḥalabīya* i, 348; Yūsuf Nabhānī, *Ḥujjat Allāh 'alā'l-'Ālamīn* 113.

Muhammad (PBUH), all will agree. Moreover, confirming the sentence, "*This is their similitude in the Torah*,"[322] is the following verse of the Torah concerning the Companions of the Prophet who would shine forth from the Paran Mountains:

> *The flags of the blessed ones will be with him, and they will be on his right.*[323]

In this verse, the Companions are described as "the blessed ones," that is, his Companions are blessed, righteous men, the beloved ones of God.

In the Forty-Second Chapter of the Book of Isaiah, there are the following verses:

> *See My servant, whom I uphold; My Chosen One, in whom I delight. He will reveal justice to the nations of the world.... He will encourage the fainthearted, those tempted to despair. He will see full justice given to all who have been wronged. He will not be satisfied until truth and righteousness prevail throughout the earth, nor until even distant lands beyond the seas have put their trust in him.*[324]

Here, the verses explicitly describe Muhammad (Upon whom be blessings and peace), the prophet at the end of time.

In the Fourth Chapter of the Book of Micah, are the following verses:

> *But in the last days it shall come to pass that the mountain of the House of God will be the most renowned one of all the mountains of the world, praised by all nations; people from all over the world will make pilgrimage there. "Come," they will say to one another, "let us go up to the mountain of God and the House of God."*[325]

---

322. Qur'ān, 48:29.
323. Ḥalabī, *al-Sīrat al-Ḥalabīya* i, 348; Yūsuf Nabhānī, *Ḥujjat Allāh 'alā'l-'Ālamīn* 113.
324. Isaiah, 42:1-4, 9.
325. Micah, 4:1-2.

These verses obviously describe the most blessed mountain in the world, Mount 'Arafat, and the worship and proclamations of "God is Most Great!" of those making the Hajj, who will flock there from all climes, and the Community of Muhammad, famous for the Divine Mercy it will receive.

In the Seventy-Second Chapter of the Psalms, there are the following verses:

And he will reign from sea to sea,
And from the River to the ends of the earth.
The kings of Yemen and the Islands
All will bring their gifts.
And to him all the kings will prostrate themselves,
All the nations will serve him.
....
And he will live,
And on his behalf prayer will be made constantly,
All day long he will be praised.
....
His name will prove to be to time indefinite,
It will continue as long as the sun.
All will be blessed in him,
All nations will praise him.[326]

These verses describe the Glory of the World, the Prophet Muhammad (Upon be blessings and peace) in most clear fashion. Apart from Muhammad the Arabian, what prophet has come since David (Upon whom be peace) who has spread his religion from East to West, made kings pay tribute, and brought rulers to submission as though prostrating; to whom every day one fifth of mankind offer benedictions and prayers, and whose lights have irradiated from Madinah? Has there been any other?

Again, the Turkish translation of John's Gospel, Chapter

326. Yūsuf Nabhānī, *Ḥujjat Allāh 'alā'l-'Ālamīn* 91-104; Jisri, *Risale-i Hamidiye* (Turkish trans.) i, 410; Psalms, 72:8, 10, 11, 15-17.

Fourteen verse twenty,[327] says:

> *I shall not speak with you for much longer, for the ruler of the world is coming, and I am nothing compared with him.*

Thus, the title Ruler of the World means Glory of the World. And the title of Glory of the World is one of the most famous of Muhammad the Arabian's (Upon whom be blessings and peace) titles.

Again in John's Gospel, Chapter Sixteen verse seven, it says:

> *But I am telling you the truth. My departure is but for your benefit. For, unless I depart, the Comforter will not come.*[328]

Now see, who other than Muhammad the Arabian (Upon whom be blessings and peace) is the Ruler of the World and true consoler of men? Yes, the Glory of the World is he, and he is the one who will save transitory man from eternal extinction and thus comforts him.

Again, the eighth verse of Chapter Sixteen in John's Gospel:

> *When he comes, he will give the world convincing evidence concerning its sin, its righteousness, and its judgement.*[329]

Who other than Muhammad the Arabian (Upon whom be blessings and peace) has turned the world's wrongdoing into righteousness, saved men from sin and associating partners with God, and transformed politics and world rule?

Also from the Gospel of John, the eleventh verse of Chapter Sixteen:

> *There is deliverance from judgement, for the Ruler of this World has already been judged.*[330]

---

327. 14:30. (Tr.)
328. 'Alī al-Qārī, *Sharḥ al-Shifā'* i, 743; Yūsuf Nabhānī, *Ḥujjat Allāh 'alā'l-'Ālamīn* 99.
329. 'Alī al-Qārī, *Sharḥ al-Shifā'* i, 743; Yūsuf Nabhānī, *Ḥujjat Allāh 'alā'l-'Ālamīn* 99.
330. Yūsuf Nabhānī, *Ḥujjat Allāh 'alā'l-'Ālamīn* 95-7; *al-Anwār al-Muḥammadīyya*.

Here "the Ruler of the World" is certainly Ahmad Muhammad (Upon whom be blessings and peace), for he is known as the Master of Humanity.[331]

Also, in John's Gospel, the thirteenth verse of Chapter Twelve:[332]

> *But when he, the Spirit of Truth, comes, he will guide you all to the truth, for he will not be presenting his own ideas, but will be passing onto you what he has heard. He will tell you about the future.*[333]

This verse is explicit. Who apart from Muhammad the Arabian (Upon whom be blessings and peace) has called all men to the truth, whose every statement was based on Revelation, has spoken what he had heard from Gabriel, and informed man in detail about the resurrection of the dead and the hereafter? Who other than he could do this?

Also, the Books of other prophets include names in Syriac and Hebrew that correspond to the various names of the Prophet (PBUH), such as Muhammad, Ahmad, Mukhtar. For example, in the scriptures of the Prophet Shu'ayb, his name is *Mushaffah*,[334] and means 'Muhammad.' In the Torah, he is mentioned as *Munhamanna*, which again means 'Muhammad,' and as *Himyata*,[335] which means 'the Prophet of al-Haram.' In the Psalms, he is called *al-Mukhtar*.[336] Again in the Torah, the name is *al-Hātam al-Khātam*.[337] Both in the Torah and in the

---

331. Yes, he is such a lord and ruler that in most centuries for one thousand three hundred and fifty years he has had at least three hundred and fifty million followers and subjects, who have obeyed his commands in complete submission, and every day renew their allegiance to him by calling down God's blessings on him.

332. 16:13. (Tr.)

333. Ḥalabī, *al-Sīrat al-Ḥalabīya* i, 346; 'Alī al-Qārī, *Sharḥ al-Shifā'* i, 743.

334. Ḥalabī, *al-Sīrat al-Ḥalabīya* i, 353; Yūsuf Nabhānī, *Ḥujjat Allāh 'alā'l-'Ālamīn* 112; Qasṭalānī, *Mawāhib al-Ladunnīya* vi, 189.

335. Ḥalabī, *al-Sīrat al-Ḥalabīya* i, 346, 354; Yūsuf Nabhānī, *Ḥujjat Allāh 'alā'l-'Ālamīn* 112-3.

336. Ḥalabī, *al-Sīrat al-Ḥalabīya* i, 353; Yūsuf Nabhānī, *Ḥujjat Allāh 'alā'l-'Ālamīn* 112; Qasṭalānī, *al-Mawāhib al-Ladunnīya* vi, 189; 'Alī al-Qārī, *Sharḥ al-Shifā'* i, 739.

337. Yūsuf Nabhānī, *Ḥujjat Allāh 'alā'l-'Ālamīn* 114.

Psalms, it is *Muqim al-Sunna,*[338] in the scriptures of Abraham and in the Torah, he is mentioned as *Mazmaz,*[339] and again in the Torah, as *Ahyad*.

God's Most Noble Messenger (Upon whom be blessings and peace) himself said: "*In the Qur'an, my name is Muhammad, in the Bible, Ahmad, and in the Torah, Ahyad.*"[340] In fact, the Bible refers to him as "The one with the sword and the staff."[341] Indeed, the greatest of the prophets who wielded the sword, and was charged with fighting in God's way together with his community, was God's Messenger (Upon whom be blessings and peace). The Gospels also describe him as "wearing a crown."[342] Yes, this title is particular to God's Messenger, for "crown" means turban, for in former days, it was the Arabs who as a people, all wore the turban and headband. This definitely therefore refers to God's Messenger.

The term *Paraclete* in the Gospel, or *Faraqlit*, is defined in Biblical interpretation as "the one who distinguishes truth from falsehood."[343] It is therefore the name of one who in the future will lead people to the truth.

In one place in the Gospels, Jesus (Upon whom be peace) says: "I am going so that the Lord of the World may come."[344] Who other than the Noble Prophet (Upon whom be blessings and peace) has come after Jesus who will be the Ruler of the World, distinguish and separate truth from falsehood, and guide mmankind in place of Jesus? That is to say, Jesus (Upon whom

---

338. Yūsuf Nabhānī, *Ḥujjat Allāh 'alā'l-'Ālamīn* 115.

339. Yūsuf Nabhānī, *Ḥujjat Allāh 'alā'l-'Ālamīn* 113; Ḥalabī, *al-Sīrat al-Ḥalabīya* i, 353.

340. Yūsuf Nabhānī, *Ḥujjat Allāh 'alā'l-'Ālamīn* 108, 112; Ḥalabī, *al-Sīrat al-Ḥalabīya* i, 353.

341. Yūsuf Nabhānī, *Ḥujjat Allāh 'alā'l-'Ālamīn* 114; Ḥalabī, *al-Sīrat al-Ḥalabīya* i, 353.

342. Yūsuf Nabhānī, *Ḥujjat Allāh 'alā'l-'Ālamīn* 113, 114; 'Alī al-Qārī, *Sharḥ al-Shifā'* i, 739.

343. Yūsuf Nabhānī, *Ḥujjat Allāh 'alā'l-'Ālamīn* 112.

344. See, page 135, fn. 328.

be peace) was constantly giving his community the good news: Another will come; no need will remain for me. I am his forerunner and herald. Confirming this is the following verse of the Qur'an:

> *And remember, Jesus, the son of Mary, said: "O Children of Israel! I am the Messenger of God unto you, confirming that which was revealed before me in the Torah and bringing the good tidings of a Messenger to come after me, whose name is Ahmad [the Praised One]."*[345]

Yes, in the Gospels, Jesus gave the glad tidings many times, that the greatest leader of mankind would come. He is mentioned with various names, in, of course, Syriac and Hebrew—which scholars have seen, which bear the meaning of Ahmad, Muhammad, and the Distinguisher between Truth and Falsehood. That is to say, on many occasions Jesus (Upon whom be peace) told of the coming of Ahmad (Upon whom be blessings and peace).[346]

Question: Why is it that while the other prophets foretell the coming of Muhammad (PBUH), Jesus (PUH) does so more fully and in the form of good news?

The Answer: Because Ahmad (Upon whom be blessings and peace) defended Jesus (Upon whom be peace) against the fearsome denials and slander of the Jews, and saved his religion from corruption. Furthermore, in the face of the burdensome Shari'a of the Children of Israel, who did not recognize Jesus, he came with an elevated Shari'a which was easy, all-encompassing, and completed the deficiencies of Jesus'

345. Qur'ān, 61:6.

346. At the site of the tomb of Sham'ūn al-Ṣafā, the famous traveller Evliya Chelebi came across the following verses from the Gospels, written on gazelle hide: "A youth from the progeny of Abraham is to be a prophet. He will not be a liar; his birthplace will be Makkah; he will come with piety; his blessed name is Aḥmad Muḥammad;* those who obey him will prosper in this world and the next."

*The word, written as 'Mawamit,' was corrupted from 'Mamad,' itself a corruption of Muḥammad.

Shari'a. For these reasons, Jesus often gave the good news, the Ruler of the World will come!

Now it is clear that in the Torah, the Gospels, the Psalms of David, and in the scriptures of other prophets, there are numerous discussions of a prophet who is to come at a later time, many verses mentioning him. Just as we pointed out examples of these, showing that he is mentioned in these Books under various names. Who, other than Muhammad (Upon whom be blessings and peace), the Prophet of the end of time, could it be that these scriptures of the prophets speak of so repeatedly in their verses, and with such importance?

THE SECOND KIND

The signs of prophethood that were manifested by way of *irhasat* also include those tidings of his coming given before his prophetic mission in that time between prophets by the soothsayers and certain people known as saints and gnostics at that time; they published their claims and passed them down to subsequent generations in their poetry. These are numerous, and we shall mention some that are well-known, and have been accepted and narrated by the scholars of history and the Prophet's life.

First: One of the rulers of Yemen, called Tubba, saw descriptions of God's Messenger (Upon whom be blessings and peace) in former scriptures, and believed in him. He announced this by means of a poem, which went like this:

I bear witness to Ahmad, for he is a Messenger from God, the Creator of man;

Were I to live long enough to see him, I would be a minister and a cousin to him..[347]

That is, I would have been like 'Ali.

347. Ibn Kathīr, *al-Bidāya wa'l-Nihāya* ii, 166; Qāḍī Iyāḍ, *al-Shifā'* i, 363; 'Alī al-Qārī, *Sharḥ al-Shifā'* i, 740; al-Ḥākim, *al-Mustadrak* ii, 388; Yūsuf Nabhānī, *Ḥujjat Allāh 'alā'l-'Ālamīn* 138.

Second: Quss b. Sa'ida was the most renowned and most significant orator of the Arabs, a monotheist, and man of enlightened mind. Before Muhammad's prophetic mission, he announced his messengership with these lines:

Ahmad shall be sent forth amongst us, the best prophet ever sent;
God's blessings be upon him, whenever a riding party sets out amidst cries![348]

Third: Ka'b b. Lu'ayy, one of the forefathers of the Prophet, announced Muhammad's prophethood by way of inspiration as follows:

Suddenly, Muhammad the Prophet will appear,
Giving tidings most true.[349]

Fourth: Sayf b. Dhiyazan, one of the rulers of Yemen, read descriptions of God's Messenger (Upon whom be blessings and peace) in the old scriptures, and believing in him, longed to see him. When 'Abd al-Muttalib, Muhammad's grandfather, went to Yemen with some of the Quraysh, Sayf summoned them and said: "A child will be born in Hijaz, with a mark between his shoulders resembling a seal. He will be the leader of all humanity." Then, in private he told 'Abd al-Muttalib: "You are his grandfather,"[350] foretelling his prophethood in a wondrous way.

Fifth: Waraqa b. Nawfal was a cousin of Khadija. When the first Revelation came, the Noble Messenger (Upon whom be blessings and peace) was deeply shaken. Khadija described the event to the well-known Waraqa b. Nawfal, who told her to

---

348. Suyūṭī, *al-Fatḥ al-Kabīr* ii, 133; Ibn Kathīr, *al-Bidāya wa'l-Nihāya* ii, 230; Qāḍī Iyāḍ, *al-Shifā'* i, 363; 'Alī al-Qārī, *Sharḥ al-Shifā'* i, 740; Ṭabarānī, *al-Majmū' al-Kabīr* xii, 1254; Bayhaqī, *Dalā'il al-Nubūwwa* ii, 101; Abū Na'īm, *Dalā'il al-Nubūwwa* i, 105.

349. Ibn Kathīr, *al-Bidāya wa'l-Nihāya* ii, 244; Qāḍī Iyāḍ, *al-Shifā'* i, 364; 'Alī al-Qārī, *Sharḥ al-Shifā'* i, 740; Abū Na'īm, *Dalā'il al-Nubūwwa* i, 89-90.

350. Ibn Kathīr, *al-Bidāya wa'l-Nihāya* ii, 328; Qāḍī Iyāḍ, *al-Shifā'* i, 343; 'Alī al-Qārī, *Sharḥ al-Shifā'* i, 740; al-Ḥākim, *al-Mustadrak* ii, 388; Abū Na'īm, *Dalā'il al-Nubūwwa* i, 95-6; Ḥalabī, *al-Sīrat al-Ḥalabīya* i, 187.

send him to him. God's Messenger went to Waraqa and told him how the Revelation had come. Waraqa said: "Good news, O Muhammad! I testify that you are the awaited prophet who was foretold by Jesus."[351] That is, Do not worry! It was truly the coming of Revelation.

Sixth: Before the prophetic mission, a gnostic called Athkalan al-Himyari asked the Quraysh when he saw them: "Is there anyone among you who claims prophethood?" They replied in the negative. He again asked them at the start of his mission, and this time their reply was affirmative. Athkalan said: "The world is awaiting him!"[352]

Seventh: Ibn al-'Ala, a famous Christian scholar, told of God's Messenger (PBUH) before his mission, never having seen him. He later came, saw the Messenger, and said: "By the One Who sent you in truth, I found your description in the Gospels, and the Son of Mary gave glad tidings of your coming."[353]

Eighth: Mentioned above was the Negus of Abyssinia, who declared: "Would that I had been the servant of Muhammad the Arabian (Upon whom be blessings and peace), rather than a king. To serve him would have been far superior to this sovereignty."[354]

In addition to these tidings given by these learned men through Divine inspiration from the Unseen, soothsayers too gave news from the Unseen of the coming of God's Messenger (Upon whom be blessings and peace), and of his prophethood, by means of jinn and spirit beings. These are numerous also and

351. *Bukhārī*, Bad' al-Waḥy 3; Anbiyā' 21; Ta'bīr 1; *Musnad* (*Taḥqīq*: Aḥmad Shākir) iv, 304 no: 2846; Qāḍī Iyāḍ, *al-Shifā'* i, 363; 'Alī al-Qārī, *Sharḥ al-Shifā'* i, 743; 'Ajurrī, *al-Sharī'a* 443; Abū Na'īm, *Dalā'il al-Nubūwwa* i, 217.

352. Qāḍī Iyāḍ, *al-Shifā'* i, 363; 'Alī al-Qārī, *Sharḥ al-Shifā'* i, 742; Yūsuf Nabhānī, *Ḥujjat Allāh 'alā'l-'Ālamīn* 140.

353. 'Alī al-Qārī, *Sharḥ al-Shifā'* i, 744; Yūsuf Nabhānī, *Hujjat Allāh 'alā'l-'Ālamīn* 121, 208.

354. Qāḍī Iyāḍ, *al-Shifā'* i, 365; Yūsuf Nabhānī, *Ḥujjat Allāh 'alā'l-'Ālamīn* 115; Bayhaqī, *Dalā'il al-Nubūwwa* ii, 285.

we shall mention a few which are well-known, have reached the degree of 'consensus in meaning,' and are related in most of the books of history and the Prophet's biography. Referring the lengthy accounts of them to those books, we shall give only a summary of them.

The First is the famous soothsayer, Shiqq, who had only one eye, one arm, and one leg; he was quite simply half a man. His repeated predictions concerning the messengership of Muhammad (PBUH) have passed into the history books, with the certainty of 'consensus in meaning.'[355]

The Second is the famous soothsayer of Damascus, Satih, who was a monstrosity lacking bones, and even limbs, whose face was in his chest aand who lived a very long time. He was highly reputed at that time for the correct information he gave concerning the Unseen. The Persian king, Khusraw, even, sent a learned envoy called Mubezan to ask Satih to interpret a strange dream he had at the time of Muhammad's birth, in which the fourteen pinnacles of his palace collapsed. Satih said: "Fourteen men will rule over you, then your empire will be destroyed. Also someone will come who will announce a religion; he will abolish both your religion and your empire," sending news of this to Khusraw.[356] In this way, Satih explicitly foretold the coming of the Prophet of the end of time.

As written in detail in the books of history and the Prophet's biography, soothsayers like Sawad b. Qarib al-Dawsi, Khunafir, Af'a Najran, Jidhl b. Jidhl al-Kindi, Ibn Khalasat al-Dawsi, and Fatima bint al-Nu'man al-Najariyya, foretold the coming of the Prophet of the end of time, stating that that Prophet was

355. Qāḍī Iyāḍ, *al-Shifā'* i, 364; 'Alī al-Qārī, *Sharḥ al-Shifā'* i, 747; Yūsuf Nabhānī, *Ḥujjat Allāh 'alā'l-'Ālamīn* 168-72; Abū Na'īm, *Dalā'il al-Nubūwwa* i, 123, 125.

356. Ibn Kathīr, *al-Bidāya wa'l-Nihāya* ii, 355-69; Bayhaqī, *Dalā'il al-Nubūwwa* ii, 126, 129; Abū Na'īm, *Dalā'il al-Nubūwwa* i, 125; Qāḍī Iyāḍ, *al-Shifā'* i, 365; Alī al-Qārī, *Sharḥ al-Shifā'* i, 747; Suyūṭī, *al-Khaṣā'iṣ al-Kubrā* i, 128-30; al-Haythamī, *Majma' al-Zawā'id* viii, 848-9, 851.

Muhammad (Upon whom be blessings and peace).[357]

Also, one of 'Uthman's relations, Sa'd b. bint al-Kurayz, received knowledge from the Unseen by means of soothsaying about the prophethood of Muhammad (Upon whom be blessings and peace). In the early days of Islam, he told 'Uthman Dhi'l-Nurayn to go and accept faith. 'Uthman did so and entered the fold of Islam at the beginning. Sa'd expressed the event with a poem, which went like this:

Through my words, God has guided 'Uthman to the source
That yields righteousness; truly God guides to the truth.[358]

Like soothsayers, jinns who were invisible but whose voices were heard, called *hātif*, repeatedly foretold the coming of God's Noble Messenger (Upon whom be blessings and peace). For example:

An invisible jinn shouted out the following to Dhayab b. al-Harith, and was the reason of he and others accepting Islam: "O Dhayab! O Dhayab! Listen to the oddest thing: Muhammad has appeared with the Book. He is calling on Makkah, yet they do not respond to him!"[359]

Another unseen jinn called out to Sama' b. Qarrat al-Ghatafani, "The truth has come in manifest radiance, the false is destroyed and uprooted," and caused him and some others to believe.[360]

Such messages and good tidings of unseen jinns are extremely well-known and numerous.

Just as the voices of jinns and the soothsayers foretold him, so too idols and sacrifices slaughtered for the idols gave news

357. Ibn Kathīr, *al-Bidāya wa'l-Nihāya* ii, 335; Bayhaqī, *Dalā'il al-Nubūwwa* ii, 248; Abū Na'īm, *Dalā'il al-Nubūwwa* i, 125; Qāḍī Iyāḍ, *al-Shifā'* i, 365; 'Alī al-Qārī, *Sharḥ al-Shifā'* i, 747; Suyūṭī, *al-Khaṣā'iṣ al-Kubrā* i, 128-30; al-Haythamī, *Majma' al-Zawā'id* viii, 248-9, 251.

358. Suyūṭī, *al-Khaṣā'iṣ al-Kubrā* i, 258.

359. Ḥalabī, *al-Sīrat al-Ḥalabīya* i, 335-7; Suyūṭī, *al-Khaṣā'iṣ al-Kubrā* i, 358; Yūsuf Nabhānī, *Ḥujjat Allāh 'alā'l-'Ālamīn* 181.

360. 'Alī al-Qārī, *Sharḥ al-Shifā'* i, 748; Suyūṭī, *al-Khaṣā'iṣ al-Kubrā* i, 252.

of the prophethood of God's Messenger (Upon whom be blessings and peace). For example:

One is the famous story of the idol of the Mazan tribe, who shouted out: "This is the Prophet who has been sent; he comes with the revealed truth,"[361] telling of Muhammad's (PBUH) prophethood.

Another is the well-known incident which caused 'Abbas b. Mardas to accept Islam: there was an idol called Dimar, which one day called out: "Dimar was worshipped before the declaration of Muhammad; that misguidance can no longer continue."[362]

Before he accepted Islam, 'Umar heard an animal sacrificed to an idol exclaim: "O sacrificer, the means of success are at hand: an eloquent man proclaiming, No god but God!"[363]

There are very many more examples like these, which have been accepted as authentic and narrated in reliable books.

And just as soothsayers, gnostics, invisible jinns, and even idols and sacrifices told of Muhammad's (PBUH) messengership, and each instance was the cause of people coming to believe in him, so too inscriptions on stones over and in graves, and on gravestones, like "Muhammad, a worker of righteousness, the trustworthy," were the means of some people coming to believe.[364] Because, in the time shortly before Muhammad lived, there were only seven men bearing that name, and not one of them deserved the epithet of righteous and trustworthy.[365]

---

361. Bayhaqī, *Dalā'il al-Nubūwwa* ii, 255; Ḥalabī, *al-Sīrat al-Ḥalabīya* i, 325; Ibn Kathīr, *al-Bidāya wa'l-Nihāya* ii, 337; al-Haythamī, *Majma' al-Zawā'id* viii, 242; 'Alī al-Qārī, *Sharḥ al-Shifā'* i, 747; Suyūṭī, *al-Khaṣā'iṣ al-Kubrā* i, 252-71.

362. al-Haythamī, *Majma' al-Zawā'id* viii, 246; Ibn Kathīr, *al-Bidāya wa'l-Nihāya* ii, 341-2; Bayhaqī, *Dalā'il al-Nubūwwa* i, 118.

363. *Bukhārī*, Manāqib al-Anṣār 35; al-Sā'atī, *al-Fatḥ al-Rabbānī* xx, 2030.

364. Qāḍī Iyāḍ, *al-Shifā'* i, 467; 'Alī al-Qārī, *Sharḥ al-Shifā'* i, 467; 'Alī al-Qārī, *Sharḥ al-Shifā'* i, 749; Ḥalabī, *al-Sīrat al-Ḥalabīya* i, 354.

365. Ḥalabī, *al-Sīrat al-Ḥalabīya* i, 131-4.

THE THIRD KIND

These are *irhasat* including the wondrous events which occurred at the time of, and in conjunction with, the birth of God's Noble Messenger (Upon whom be blessings and peace). There were also events that occurred before his prophetic mission which were miracles. They were many, and we shall mention a few examples which became famous, have been accepted by the authorities on Hadiths, and whose authenticity have been established.

The First: On the night of the Prophet's birth, both his mother, and the mothers of 'Uthman b. al-'As and 'Abd al-Rahman b. 'Awf, who were with her, saw a brilliant, widely scattered light, about which they said: "At the time of his birth we saw such a light that it lit up the east and the west for us."[366]

The Second: That night most of the idols in the Ka'ba toppled over and fell to the ground.[367]

The Third: That night the famous *aywan* of Khusraw's palace shook and cracked apart, and its fourteen pinnacles collapsed.[368]

The Fourth: That night the small lake of Saveh which was considered to be holy, sank into the ground,[369] and at Istakhrabad the fire which, burning continuously for a thousand years, the Zoroastrians had worshipped, was extinguished.[370]

Thus, these four events indicated that the one had just been born would abolish fire-worship, destroy the palace of the Persian kings, and prevent those things being sanctified which God did not permit.

---

366. Qāḍī Iyāḍ, *al-Shifā'* i, 466; 'Alī al-Qārī, *Sharḥ al-Shifā'* i, 750; al-Khafājī, *Sharḥ al-Shifā'* iii, 311; al-Sā'atī, *al-Fatḥ al-Rabbānī* xx, 2030.

367. Suyūṭī, *al-Khaṣā'iṣ al-Kubrā* i, 119-31; ii, 272; Bayhaqī, *Dalā'il al-Nubūwwa* i, 19.

368. 'Alī al-Qārī, *Sharḥ al-Shifā'* i, 750; Bayhaqī, *Dalā'il al-Nubūwwa* i, 126; Suyūṭī, *al-Khaṣā'iṣ al-Kubrā* i, 128; ii, 272.

369. Qāḍī Iyāḍ, *al-Shifā'* i, 367; 'Alī al-Qārī, *Sharḥ al-Shifā'* i, 751; Bayhaqī, *Dalā'il al-Nubūwwa* i, 127; Suyūṭī, *al-Khaṣā'iṣ al-Kubrā* i, 128.

370. Qāḍī Iyāḍ, *al-Shifā'* i, 367; 'Alī al-Qārī, *Sharḥ al-Shifā* i, 751; 'Ali al-Qārī al-Makkī, *al-Masnū' fī Ma'rifat al-Ḥadīth al-Mawḍū' 'al-Mawḍū'āt al-Ṣughrā'* (*Taḥqīq*: Abū Ghuḍḍa) 18.

The Fifth: Although they did not coincide with the night of his birth, certain events that took place not long before it are also included in the *irhasat* of Muhammad (PBUH). One is the War of the Elephant, which is mentioned in the Qur'an in *Sura al-Fil*. Abraha, the king of Abyssinia came to destroy the Ka'ba, driving a huge elephant called Mahmudi before his forces. When they came close to Makkah, the elephant was unable to move. They could not make it move forward, and had to retreat. While retreating, a flock of birds attacked and routed them, and they fled. This extraordinary story is recorded in detail in the history books. The event was one of the proofs of the prophethood of Muhammad (Upon whom be blessings and peace), for it occurred close in time to his birth and saved the Holy Ka'ba, his *qibla*, birthplace, and native land from Abraha's destruction.

The Sixth: According to the testimony of Halima al-Sa'diya and her husband, when God's Messenger was with them in his childhood, they frequently saw a cloud above him shielding him from the sun. They told everyone this, and it was well-known and authenticated.[371]

Also, as testified to by the monk Bahira, when the Noble Messenger went to Damascus at the age of twelve, he saw a cloud casting a shadow over his head, and he pointed this out.[372]

Again before his prophetic mission, one time God's Messenger returned from a trading journey he made together with Khadija's servant, Maysara, when Khadija saw two angels shading him like clouds. She mentioned this to her servant Maysara, and he replied: "I observed the same thing throughout our journey."[373]

371. Qāḍī Iyāḍ, *al-Shifā'* i, 368; al-Khafājī, *Sharḥ al-Shifā'* iii, 318; 'Alī al-Qārī, *Sharḥ al-Shifā'* i, 753.

372. See, page 169, fn. 176.

373. Qāḍī Iyāḍ, *al-Shifā'* i, 368; al-Khafājī, *Sharḥ al-Shifā'* iii, 318; 'Alī al-Qārī, *Sharḥ al-Shifā'* i, 753; Bayhaqī, *Dalā'il al-Nubūwwa* ii, 65.

The Seventh: It is established in a sound narration that before his prophetic mission, God's Messenger (Upon whom be blessings and peace) sat down beneath a tree. Although the place was dried up, it suddenly grew green. The tree's branches inclined over his head, twisting back and shading him.[374]

The Eighth: When the Noble Messenger (Upon whom be blessings and peace) was small, he stayed in Abu Talib's house. Whenever he ate together with Abu Talib and his household, they would eat to repletion; whereas when he was not present, they were not satisfied.[375] This is both well-known and definite.

Also, Umm Ayman, who looked after and served the Prophet when he was small, said: "God's Messenger never complained about being hungry or thirsty, neither when small nor when he was older."[376]

The Ninth: It is both well-known and definite that unlike other members of her tribe, his wet-nurse Halima al-Sa'diya's goats and possessions were very productive and abundant.[377]

Also, flies did not bother him; they never alighted on his clothes or blessed body[378]—just as one of his progeny, Sayyid 'Abd al-Qadir Gilani, received this legacy from his forefather, for flies never alighted on him either.

The Tenth: After God's Noble Messenger (Upon whom be blessings and peace) was born, and especially on the night of his birth, there was a great increase in falling stars. As shown with decisive proofs in the Fifteenth Word, falling stars are a sign and indication of jinns and devils being barred from receiv-

---

374. Qāḍī Iyāḍ, *al-Shifā'* i, 368; al-Khafājī, *Sharḥ al-Shifā* iii, 318; 'Alī al-Qārī, *Sharḥ al-Shifā'* i, 753. See, Concordance.

375. Qāḍī Iyāḍ, *al-Shifā'* i, 367; al-Khafājī, *Sharḥ al-Shifā'* iii, 315; 'Alī al-Qārī, *Sharḥ al-Shifā'* i, 751; Abū Na'īm, *Dalā'il al-Nubūwwa* i, 166.

376. Qāḍī Iyāḍ, *al-Shifā'* i, 368; al-Khafājī, *Sharḥ al-Shifā'* iii, 325; 'Alī al-Qārī, *Sharḥ al-Shifā'* i, 752; Bayhaqī, *Dalā'il al-Nubūwwa* vi, 125.

377. See, page 210, fn. 239.

378. Qāḍī Iyāḍ, *al-Shifā'* i, 368; al-Khafājī, *Sharḥ al-Shifā* iii, 319; 'Alī al-Qārī, *Sharḥ al-Shifā'* i, 753; Sha'rānī, *al-Ṭabaqāt al-Kubrā* i, 109.

ing news of the Unseen. Thus, since God's Messenger had appeared in the world together with Revelation, it was necessary to prevent the knowledge about the Unseen being transmitted by soothsayers, diviners, and jinn, which was inaccurate and mixed with lies, so that their knowledge should not cause any doubts about Revelation, and should not resemble it. Before the prophetic mission, soothsaying was widespread. Then the Qur'an brought it to an end after it was revealed. Indeed, many soothsayers accepted Islam, for they could no longer find their informers, who were jinns. That is, the Qur'an had put an end to it. And these days a new type of soothsaying has appeared in the form of mediums among the spiritualists of the West. However, we shall not go into that now.

In Short: Very many events occurred and individuals appeared confirming and causing others to confirm the prophethood of the Noble Messenger (Upon whom be blessings and peace) before the commencement of his mission. For sure, before the appearance of the one who was going to be the ruler of the world[379] and would change the world's spiritual shape, and would make this world into the tillage for the next, and proclaim the high value of the creatures of the world, and show to man and jinn the way to eternal happiness and save them from everlasting extinction, and solve the obscure talisman of the world and riddle of the wisdom in its creation, and would know and make known the purposes of the universe's Creator, and recognize the Creator and acquaint Him to all men—before such a one appeared, surely everything, all species and realms of beings would be happy at his coming, would await him and welcome and applaud him, and if his coming was made known

379. Yes, the Sultan of *Lawlāk** was such a leader that his rule has been continuing for one thousand three hundred and fifty years. Every century after the first, he has had at least 350 million followers and subjects. With half the globe under his banner, every day his followers renew their allegiance to him in perfect submission by calling down on him peace and blessings, and obey his commands.

*'Alī al-Qārī, *Sharḥ al-Shifā'* i, 6. [See also, page122, fn. 286].

to them by their Creator, they in turn would announce it. Just as we saw in the above Signs and examples how each realm of creature displayed his miracles as if welcoming him, and confirmed his prophethood through the tongue of miracles.

SEVENTEENTH SIGN

After the Qur'an, the greatest miracle of God's Noble Messenger (Upon whom be blessings and peace) was his own self. That is, the elevated moral virtues brought together in his person which as friend and foe agreed, every aspect of which were of the very highest level. A hero of the greatest bravery, 'Ali, said again and again: "Whevever the fighting grew fierce, we would take refuge behind God's Messenger." Like this, his was the highest and unattainable degree in all praiseworthy qualities. For this greatest miracle, we refer readers to the *Shifa' al-Sharif* of Qadi Iyad, the learned scholar of the Maghrib, for he described and proved beautifully this miracle of praiseworthy moral qualities.

A further great miracle of Muhammad (PBUH) which is verified by friend and foe alike is his illustrious Shari'a, the like of which neither came before it nor will come after it. For a partial explanation of it, we refer readers to all the thirty-three Words, thirty-three Letters, thirty-one Flashes, and thirteen Rays which we have written.

Among his greatest miracles, a certain one, the many reports of which are unanimous, is the Splitting of the Moon. This miracle is related through many chains of transmission from many of the leading Companions like Ibn Mas'ud, Ibn 'Abbas, Ibn 'Umar, 'Ali, Anas, and Hudhayfa. In addition, the Qur'an announced this supreme miracle to the whole world with the verse:

The Hour is nigh, and the moon split.[380]

380. Qur'ān, 54:1.

The obdurate idolators of the Quraysh at that time could not deny what this verse states; they could only declare that it was "magic." That is to say, the unbelievers also confirmed the splitting of the moon as certain. For this supreme miracle, we refer readers to the Addendum of the Thirty-First Word.*

Furthermore, just as the Noble Messenger (Upon whom be blessings aand peace) showed the inhabitants of the earth the miracle of the Splitting of the Moon, so too he showed the inhabitants of the heavens his supreme miracle of the Ascension. Referring that greatest miracle to the Treatise on the Ascension, the Thirty-First Word, which demonstrates with decisive proofs —even to deniers— how luminous, exalted, and true a miracle it was, we shall mention here only his journey to Jerusalem, the preliminary part of the miracle of the Ascension. For it was a miracle too that when asked by the Quraysh the following morning, he provided them with a description of the *Masjid al-Aqsa*. It was as follows:

The morning after the night of the Ascension, he informed the Quraysh about the Ascension. They dismissed it as false, and said: "If you really went to the *Masjid al-Aqsa* in Jerusalem, then describe to us its doors, walls, and condition."

God's Noble Messenger later said: "I was annoyed by their question and denial in a way that I had never been annoyed before. Suddenly, God Almighty lifted the veil between me and the *Masjid al-Aqsa* and showed it to me; I looked at it, and saw and described it."[381] Then the Quraysh understood that he was giving the correct and complete description.

God's Messenger (Upon whom be blessings and peace) also told them: "During the journey, I saw one of your caravans. It will arrive here tomorrow at such-and-such a time." They waited for the caravan. It was delayed for an hour, so in order that the

381. *Bukhārī*, Manāqib al-Anṣār 41; Tafsīru Sūra 17; *Muslim*, Īmān 276, 278; Tafsīru Sūra 17; *Musnad* i, 309; iii, 377; Qāḍī Iyāḍ, *al-Shifā'* i, 191.

* See also, the Third Addendum of the present work. (Tr.)

Messenger's prediction should be right, the sun was arrested for an hour, as is confirmed by those who investigated the event. That is to say, in order to prove what he said to be right, the earth stopped its journeying, its duty, for an hour, and that immobility was shown as the sun being arrested in its motion.[382]

Thus, the mighty earth abandoned its duty in order to confirm a single statement of Muhammad the Arabian (Upon whom be blessings and peace), and the mighty sun witnessed it. And so you may understand how unfortunate are those who do not affirm him nor obey his commands, and how fortunate are those who affirm him and say: "We have heard and we obey!"; so offer praise and thanks to God for Islam and belief!

■ EIGHTEENTH SIGN

The greatest miracle of God's Noble Messenger (Upon whom be blessings and peace), an eternal one, is the All-Wise Qur'an, which comprises hundreds of evidences of his prophethood, and forty aspects of whose own miraculousness have been proven. The Twenty-Fifth Word has explained concisely and proved these forty aspects in its approximately one hundred and fifty pages. Therefore, referring that supreme miracle, a treasury of miracles, to that Word, here we shall explain only one or two points.

FIRST POINT

If it is asked: The miraculousness of the Qur'an lies in its eloquence. But all classes of men have the right to have a share of its understanding, and only one learned scholar out of a thousand can understand the miraculousness in its eloquence?

The Answer: The All-Wise Qur'an has a different kind of miraculousness corresponding to the understanding of each class; it indicates the existence of its miraculousness to each in

382. Qāḍī Iyāḍ, *al-Shifā'* i, 284; 'Alī al-Qārī, *Sharḥ al-Shifā'* i, 591-2; Suyūṭī, *al-Durar al-Muntathira* 193; al-Haythamī, *Majma' al-Zawā'id* viii, 296; al-Sā'atī, *al-Fatḥ al-Rabbānī* vi, 155; al-Albānī, *Silsilat al-Aḥādīth al-Ḍa'īfa* 972.

a different way. For example, to the scholars of rhetoric and eloquence, it exhibits the miraculousness of its extraordinary eloquence. And to the poets and orators, it shows its exalted, beautiful, and original style, which no one can imitate although it pleases everyone. The passage of time does not cause its style to age, it always remains fresh and new. Its prose and word-order are so well-ordered that it is both elevated and pleasant. And to soothsayers and other diviners of the Unseen, its displays its miraculousness in its extraordinary reports concerning the Unseen. And to historians, it demonstrates its miraculousness by giving information concerning events of past ages, as well as those of the future, and of the Intermediate Realm, and of the Hereafter. And to social and political scientists, it shows the miraculousness in its sacred principles. Yes, the Great Shari'a, which proceeds from the Qur'an, indicates that mystery of miraculousness. And to those occupied with knowledge of God and cosmic truths, it shows the miraculousness of the sacred Divine truths in the Qur'an, or else it indicates the existence of that miraculousness. And to the Sufis and saints, it shows the miraculousness in the hidden mysteries of its verses, which constantly rise and fall like waves in the sea of the Qur'an. And so on. To each of forty classes of men, it opens up a window and shows its miraculousness. The ordinary people even, who only listen to the Qur'an understanding a little of its meaning, confirm that it does not resemble any other book. Such people say: "The Qur'an is either inferior to the other books we have heard read, which not even an enemy could claim—just as it is impossible, or it is superior to all of them and is thus a miracle." Now, in order to help him, we shall explain further the miraculousness which the ordinary man understood by just listening. It is as follows:

When the Qur'an of Miraculous Exposition appeared challenging the whole world, it aroused passionate feelings of two kinds in people:

The First: In friends, the desire to imitate it; that is, the desire to resemble the style of their beloved Qur'an, and a wish to speak like it.

The Second: In enemies, the desire to criticize and dispute it; that is, the wish to invalidate its claim of miraculousness by competing with its style.

Thus, because of these two intense emotions, millions of books were written in Arabic, and are to be seen. Now, whoever listens to the most eloquent, the most brilliant, of these books being read together with the Qur'an is bound to say that the Qur'an does not resemble any of them. That means that the Qur'an is not of the same level as them. In which case, it must either be inferior to all of them, which together with being impossible a hundred times over, no one, not even Satan, could claim,[383] or the Qur'an of Miraculous Exposition is superior to all of them.

Furthermore, the All-Wise Qur'an demonstrates its miraculousness before the uneducated mass of people, who do not understand its meaning, by not wearying them. Indeed, they say: "If I hear the finest and best known poems two or three times, I become bored of them. But the Qur'an never wearies me; even, the more I listen to it, the more it pleases me. It cannot therefore be written by man."

And to children who try to memorize it, the All-Wise Qur'an shows its miraculousness by settling in their memories with the greatest of ease, despite their small, delicate, weak and simple heads being unable to retain for long a single page of other books, and many of the verses and phrases of that large Qur'an resembling one another, which should cause muddle and confusion.

And even to the sick and the dying, who are disturbed by the slightest sound and noise, the murmuring and sound of the

383. The important First Topic of the Twenty-Sixth Letter forms an explanation and elucidation of this sentence.

Qur'an makes felt a sort of its miraculousness, by being as sweet and agreeable for them as Zamzam water.

In Short: The All-Wise Qur'an demonstrates its miraculousness to forty different classes and groups of people, or it indicates to the existence of its miraculousness. It neglects no one. Even for those who can comprehend only what their eyes see and who have no ear to hear with, no heart to feel with, and no knowledge to judge with, the Qur'an alludes to its miraculousness in a fashion.[384] It is like this:

In the Qur'an of Miraculous Exposition handwritten by the calligrapher Hafiz Osman and later printed, many of the words look to one another. For example, if a needle is passed through the word "dog" in the phrase "they were seven, the dog being the eighth" in *Sura al-Kahf* (18:22) and through the underlying pages, with a slight deviation it will go through the word "Qitmir" in *Sura al-Fatir* (35:13), thus establishing the dog's name. In a similar way, the words "they will be all brought before us" (*muḥḍarūn/-īn*) occur twice in *Sura Ya Sin* (36:53 and 75), the first overlying the second. The same words are again repeated twice in *Sura al-Saffat* (37:57 and 127), and these look both to each other and to those in *Sura Ya Sin*. Also, the phrase "in pairs" (*mathnà*) occurs only three times in the Qur'an, and two of these corresponding cannot be mere coincidence.[385] There are numerous similar examples. One word even coincides with slight deviation on five or six underlying pages. And I have seen a copy of the Qur'an in which passages looking to one another

384. Here the mention of the aspect of its miraculousness directed to those without ear, heart and knowledge, and who see only with their eyes, is extremely concise, abbreviated, and even deficient. But it has been demonstrated most clearly and brilliantly in the Twenty-Ninth and Thirtieth Letters,* so that even the blind can see it. We have had written a copy of the Qur'ān which shows this aspect of miraculousness, which, God willing, will be published, then everyone will be able to see it.

*The Thirtieth Letter had been planned and intended, but it gave up its place to Signs of Miraculousness, while itself never materialized.

385. The phrase occuring towards the end of Sūra al-Sabā' (34:46) corresponds to the same phrase as the beginning of Sūra al-Fāṭir (35:1).

on facing pages were written in red ink. At that time I said that that too indicated another sort of miracle. Some time later I saw that many phrases looked to others on the reverse of pages, corresponding to one another in a meaningful way. Thus, since the arrangement of the Qur'an in the writing and script of printed copies of the Qur'an also is through the guidance of the Prophet and Divine inspiration, it contains the sign of a sort of miraculousness. For it is neither the work of chance, nor of the human mind. Sometimes there are deviations, but that is generally the fault of the printing, and if it had been absolutely in order, the words would have corresponded to one another exactly.

Furthermore, on every page of the Qur'an's Suras of long and medium length which were revealed in Madinah, the word "Allah" has been repeated in the most wondrous manner. In addition to being repeated mostly five, six, seven, eight, nine or eleven times on the same page, the repetitions of the two sides of the same page or on facing pages display beautiful and significant numerical relationships.[386, 387, 388, 389]

---

386. Also, for those who practise the recitation of the Divine Names and praises and supplicate God, the Qur'ān's adorned and rhymed words, and eloquent and artistic style, and the many virtues of its eloquence, which draw attention to itself, afford an elevated seriousness and sense of the Divine presence, and a collectedness of mind; they do not mar or spoil these. Whereas, rhetoric, artistic wording, rhyme and poetic composition of that sort usually weaken seriousness, make their elegance felt, disturb the sense of God's presence, and distract attention. In fact, I frequently used to recite Imām al-Shāfi'ī's famous supplication, which is the most subtle and serious of supplications, is composed in the most elevated versified form, and once caused the end of dearth and famine in Egypt. On reading it, I observed that since it was in verse and rhymed, it spoilt the elevated seriousness of the supplication. I recited it constantly for eight or nine years, and I was unable to reconcile the verse and rhyme with its serious nature. I understood from this that there is a sort of miraculousness in the rhyming and ordering and qualities of the Qur'ān's words, which are particular and natural and original to it, that preserves completely the seriousness and sense of the Divine presence, not spoiling them. Thus, even if those who recite supplications and the Divine Names and praises do not understand this sort of miraculousness with the mind, they perceive it with the heart.

387. Another aspect of the miraculousness of the Qur'ān of Miraculous Exposition is that it expresses the most elevated and brilliant degree of the Prophet's (PBUH) belief, who manifested the Greatest Name.

It also expresses and instructs in a natural manner the religion of truth, which, being most vast, extensive, and lofty, sets forth the elevated truths of the worlds of the hereafter and of dominicality like a sacred map. (***Cont. overleaf***) →

SECOND POINT

At the time of Moses (Upon whom be peace), it was magic that was prevalent, so his most important miracles resembled it. And at Jesus (Upon whom be peace)'s time, it was medicine that was prevalent and his miracles were mostly of that kind. Similarly, at the time of the Most Noble Prophet (Upon whom be blessings and peace), in the Arabian Peninsula four things were prevalent:

The First: Eloquence and rhetoric.

The Second: Poetry and oratory.

The Third: Soothsaying and divining matters of the Unseen.

The Fourth: Knowledge of past events and cosmology.

And so, when the Qur'an of Miraculous Exposition appeared, it challenged those with knowledge of these four fields.

Firstly, it made the men of rhetoric and eloquence bow before it; they all listened to it in astonishment.

Secondly, it filled the poets and orators with amazement, that is, those who spoke well and declaimed fine poetry, so that they bit their fingers in astonishment. It reduced to nothing the value of their finest poems written in gold, causing them to remove the famous 'Seven Hanging Poems', their pride and

---

(387 cont.) And it conveys in all His infinite glory and majesty, the address of the Creator of the Universe, in respect of His being the Sustainer of all beings. Certainly, in the face of the Qur'ān's exposition which is thus, if, in accordance with the verse,

> *Say: If the whole of mankind and the jinn were to gather together to produce the like of this Qur'ān, they could not produce its like* [17:88],

all the minds of mankind were to unite and become a single mind, they could not contest it or oppose it. How could they? They are as distant from the Qur'ān as the earth is from the Pleiades. For in view of the three above principles, it is certainly not possible to imitate the Qur'ān, nor to compose its like.

388. At the bottom of every page of the Qur'ān, the verses are complete, and they end rhyming in a fine way. The reason is this: When the verse called *Mudāyana* (2:292) provides the standard for the pages, and the Sūras Ikhlāṣ and Kawthar, the standard for the lines, this fine quality of the All-Wise Qur'ān and sign of its miraculousness becomes apparent.

389. Because of unfortunate haste, we had to content ourselves in this section with some slight indications and brief instances and small signs of a highly important ⟶

glory, from the walls of the Ka'ba.

And it silenced the soothsayers and sorcerers, who gave news of the Unseen, and made them forget the knowledge they had received. It drove away the jinns, and put an end to soothsaying.

And it saved those with knowledge of the past and cosmology from superstition and falsehood, and instructed them in true facts and luminous knowledge.

Thus, these four groups bowed before the Qur'an in perfect wonder and veneration, becoming its students. At no time could any of them attempt to contest it.

If it is asked: How do we know that no one could dispute or contest it?

The Answer: If it had been possible to dispute it, for sure someone would have attempted it. For their religion, their possessions, their lives, and their families had been put into peril. If they had disputed it, they would have been saved. If it had been possible, they were bound to contest it. And if they had done so, since the supporters, unbelievers, and dissemblers were many, and truly many, they were sure to have supported such a contest, and would have advertised it widely. Just as they spread everything that was against Islam. And if someone had disputed the Qur'an and they had made it known to everyone, it

and magnificent wonder, one which from the point of view of the Risale-i Nur's success is beautiful, illuminating, and encouraging. Now, that important truth and encouraging wonder —under the name of 'coincidence' (*tawāfuq*), and five or six sorts at that— forms a chain of wonders of the Risale-i Nur, and flashes of a visible sort of the Qur'ān's miraculousness, and a source of signs to the ciphers of the Unseen. Later, we had a copy of the Qur'ān written which showed in gilded letters a flash of its miraculousness which appeared from the 'coinciding' of the word 'Allāh.' And I wrote eight short pieces, called the Eight Symbols (*Rumûzat-ı Semaniye*), which explain the subtle relationships evident in the coinciding of the Qur'ān's letters, and their allusions concerning the Unseen. I also wrote five treatises, one about the wonders of 'Ghauth al-Gīlānī', three about those of 'Alī, and one called Indications of the Qur'ān (*İşârât-ı Kur'aniye*), which by means of *tawāfuq* or 'coincidences', confirm, commend, and applaud the Risale-i Nur. That is to say, that important truth was perceived and written in summary fashion in the writing of the Miracles of Muḥammad, but unfortunately the author saw and described only a tiny part of if he continued without further pursuing it.

would certainly have been recorded in the books of history in glittering terms. But all the histories and books are in evidence; apart from a few passages about Musaylima the Liar, there is nothing in any of them. Whereas for twenty-three years the All-Wise Qur'an continuously taunted and challenged them in a way that would increase their obduracy. It in effect said:

"Let someone unlettered like Muhammad the Trustworthy compose the like of the Qur'an. You can't do it, so, come on, not an unlettered person, but someone very learned and literary. You can't do that either. Rather than a single person, gather together all your scholars and men of eloquence, and let them assist one another, and the false gods on which you rely can also lend a hand. You won't be able to do this either, so use the literary works of the past, and even call on those of the future to help you, and then compose the like of the Qur'an. And if you can't do this, then do not compose all the Qur'an, but only ten Suras. Come on, you can't manage ten which are truly like the Qur'an's Suras, so put it together out of stories and fictitious tales; just produce the like of the word-order and eloquence. And don't write a long Sura, just a short one. And if you can't do this, your religion, lives, property, and families will all be in danger, both in this world and in the next!"

Thus, with these eight alternatives, the Wise Qur'an has challenged and silenced men and jinn, not for twenty-three years, but for one thousand three hundred. Nonetheless, in those early times, those unbelievers did not have recourse to the easiest way, dispute or contest, but chose the most fearsome way, that of war, putting their lives, possessions, and families into danger. That means, to dispute it was not possible.

And so, would not any intelligent person, particularly the people of Arabia at that time—and the Quraysh, who were very clever, have ensured that one of their literary men composed a Sura similar to one of the Qur'an's and so be saved from the

Qur'an's attacks; would they have abandoned the short and easy way, cast all they possessed into peril, and travelled the way most fraught with difficulties?

In Short: As the famous Jahiz put it: "Dispute with words was not possible, so they were compelled to fight with the sword."

If it is asked: Some learned scholars have said that not one of the Qur'an's Suras, but not a single of its verses can be disputed, nor even a single sentence, nor a word, nor have they been disputed. But this appears to be exaggerated and the reason cannot accept it, for many of men's words resemble those of the Qur'an. What is the reason for their saying this?

The Answer: There are two schools of thought concerning the miraculousness of the Qur'an.

The prevailing and preferred school states that the subtle qualities of eloquence and meaning in the Qur'an are beyond human power.

The second, and less preferred, school states that it is within human ability to dispute one of the Qur'an's Suras, but Almighty God has prevented this as a miracle of Muhammad (PBUH). Like a man may rise to his feet, but if a prophet tells him that he cannot and he is unable to, then it is a miracle. This opinion is called the Sarfa School. That is, Almighty God prevented men and jinn from successfully disputing a single of the Qur'an's Suras. According to this school, scholars who state that a single of its words cannot be disputed, are correct. Because since on account of its miraculousness Almighty God prevented them, they could not so much as open their mouths to dispute it. And even if they had done so, they could not have uttered a word.

However, according to the first-mentioned prevalent and preferred school of thought, that statement of scholars has the following subtle aspect: the All-Wise Qur'an's phrases and words look to one another. It sometimes happens that a single word looks to ten places; in it are ten relationships and ten fine points of eloquence. We have pointed out examples of some of these in the commentary called *Isharat al-I'jaz* (Signs of Miraculousness,) in the phrases of *Sura al-Fatiha* and those of,

> *Alif. Lam. Mim. * This is the Book; in it is guidance sure, without doubt.*[390]

For example, take a highly decorated palace; to situate in relation to all the decorations a stone which is like the central point of numerous, various decorations, is dependent on knowing the entire wall together with all its decorations. And to situate the pupil of the eye in a human head is dependent on knowing its relations with the whole body and all the body's wondrous functions, together with the eye's position before those duties. In just the same way, the most advanced of the people of truth, have demonstrated numerous relationships in the Qur'an's words and their aspects and connections with other verses and phrases. Scholars of the Hurufi School in particular, have gone further, explaining and demonstrating to their followers a page of hidden meanings in a single of the Qur'an's letters.

Furthermore, since it is the speech of the Creator of all things, each of its words may be like a heart or seed. That is, a heart contained in an immaterial body formed of mysteries, or the seed of an immaterial tree.

Thus, words like those of the Qur'an, and even phrases or verses, may occur in man's speech, but an all-encompassing knowledge is necessary to situate them exactly as they are in the Qur'an, taking into account the many relationships.

THIRD POINT

A brief but true reflection on the essential nature of the Qur'an of Miraculous Exposition was once inspired in my heart

390. Qur'ān, 2:1-2.

as a Divine bounty. Now I will give below a translation of that Arabic piece.

The six aspects of the Qur'an of Miraculous Exposition are brilliant and luminous; neither doubt nor misgiving can penetrate it. For its back leans on God's Throne; there is the light of Revelation in that aspect. Before it and its goal is the happiness of both worlds; it has laid its hand on post-eternity and the Hereafter, and contains the light of happiness and Paradise. Above it shines the seal of miraculousness. Beneath it lie the pillars of proof and evidence. Its inner face is pure guidance, while its right causes the mind to affirm it with phrases like "Will they not think?" Providing spiritual sustenance to hearts, its left causes the conscience to testify to God's blessings. So from what side, what corner, can the thieves of doubt and misgiving enter the Qur'an of Miraculous Exposition?

Yes, the Qur'an of Miraculous Exposition contains the meaning of the consensus of the books of the prophets, the saints, and those who affirm Divine Unity, whose centuries, ways, and temperaments were all different. That is, those who sought the truth through either the intellect or heart mentioned in their books the All-Wise Qur'an's concise decrees and principles, in such a way as to confirm them. Thus, they are like the roots of the heavenly tree of the Qur'an.

The All-Wise Qur'an is also based on Revelation and is Revelation. For the Glorious One Who revealed it, demonstrated and proved it was Revelation through the miracles of Muhammad (PBUH). And the Qur'an too, which reveals, shows through the miraculousness on it that it comes from the Divine Throne. And the alarm of the Most Noble Prophet (Upon whom be blessings and peace) to whom it was revealed, when it was first revealed and his unconscious state during its revelation and his sincerity and veneration towards the Qur'an, which were greater than everyone's, all demonstrate that it was Revelation coming from pre-eternity; it was his guest.

Moreover, the Qur'an is self-evidently pure guidance, for observedly its opposite is the misguidance of unbelief. It is also of necessity the source of the lights of belief, and the reverse of this is of course, darkness. We have proved this decisively in many of the Words.

Furthermore, the Qur'an is of a certainty the assembly of truths; illusion and superstition cannot intrude on it. The elevated perfections which the World of Islam, to which it gave form, and the Shari'a, which it manifested, display testify and prove that it is pure truth and contains no contradictions. Its discussions concerning the World of the Unseen testify to this too, like those concerning the Manifest World.

Without doubt, the Qur'an also leads to the happiness of both worlds, and urges man to it. If anyone doubts this, let him read the Qur'an once and heed what it says. Moreover, the fruits the Qur'an produces are both perfect and living. In which case, the roots of the tree of the Qur'an are founded in reality and are living. For the life of the fruit points to the life of the tree. See, how many perfect, living, luminous fruits it has produced each century, like the saints and purified scholars!

Also, with a conviction arising from innumerable various signs, it may be said the Qur'an is accepted and sought after by both men, and jinn, and angels, for when it is recited, they gather round it, drawn like moths.

And together with being Revelation, the Qur'an has been strengthened and fortified with rational proofs; the unanimity of the wise and intelligent testifies to this. The great scholars of theology, and the geniuses of philosophy like Ibn-i Sina and Ibn Rushd unanimously demonstrated the Qur'anic principles, in accordance with their own methods and proofs.

The Qur'an is also affirmed by all sound natures. So long as it is not corrupted in any way, human nature confirms it. For an easy conscience and peace of mind are to be found through its lights. That is to say, unspoilt human nature affirms it through the testimony of a tranquil conscience, and says to the Qur'an through the tongue of disposition: "Our natures cannot be perfected without you!" We have proved this truth in many places.

The Qur'an is also observedly and self-evidently an eternal and perpetual miracle; it always displays its miraculousness. It never dies away like other miracles, its time never comes to an end; it is everlasting.

Furthermore, there is such breadth in the Qur'an's guidance that the Angel Gabriel and a young child may listen to its same lesson side by side, and both receive their share. And a brilliant philosopher like Ibn Sina may study the same of its lessons side by side with an ordinary reciter, and they both receive their instruction. It may even happen that due to the strength and purity of his belief, the common man may benefit more than Ibn Sina.

Also, there is in the Qur'an such an eye that it sees and encompasses the whole universe, and holds it before it like the pages of a book, describing its levels and worlds. Like a watchmaker turns, opens, shows, and describes his clock, so too does the Qur'an, as though it was holding the universe in its hand. Thus, it is such a Qur'an of Mighty Stature that it declares: "Know that there is no god but God," and proclaims the Divine Unity.

> *O God! Make the Qur'an our companion in this world, and a friend for us in the grave, and at the resurrection an intercessor, and on the Bridge a light, and from the Fire a shield and screen, and in Paradise a companion, and in all good works, a guide and leader. O God! Illuminate our hearts and graves with the light of belief and the Qur'an; and illumine the proof of the Qur'an for the sake of and in veneration of the one to whom the Qur'an was revealed, and grant blessings and peace to him and his Family from the Most Merciful One, the Gentle One. Amen.*

NINETEENTH SIGN

It has been proved in the previous Signs most decisively and indubitably that the Most Noble Prophet (Upon whom be blessings and peace) was God Almighty's Messenger. His messengership being thus established through thousands of certain evidences, Muhammad the Arabian (Upon whom be blessings and peace) was the most brilliant and conclusive proof of Divine Unity and eternal happiness. In this Sign, we shall offer a concise and summary definition of that shining evidence, that articulate proof. For since he is the proof and his conclusion is knowledge of God, we must surely recognize the proof and learn the manner of his evidence. And so, with an extremely brief summary, we shall describe in what ways he is a proof of it, and its correctness. It is as follows:

Just as, like all the beings in the universe, God's Noble Messenger (Upon whom be blessings and peace) pointed through his own self to the Creator of the Universe's existence and Unity, so too he proclaimed with his tongue that evidence of his self, together with the evidence offered by all beings. Since he was the evidence, we shall point in fifteen Principles to the proof and integrity, the truthfulness and veracity of that evidence.

First Principle: This proof, who indicated to the universe's Maker with both his self, and his tongue, and his conduct, and his speech, was both verified by the reality of the universe, and was veracious. For the evidence to Divine Unity made by all beings is surely confirmation of the one who proclaims that Unity. That is to say, the cause he proclaims is verified by the whole universe. Also, since the perfection of Divine Unity and absolute good of eternal happiness he expounded is in agreement and conformity with the beauty and perfection of all the truths of the world, he is certainly veracious in his cause. That is to say, the Noble Messenger (Upon whom be blessings and peace) was an articulate proof of Divine Unity and eternal happiness who was both veracious and verified.

Second Principle: Also, since that veracious and verified proof performed thousands of miracles greater than all the previous prophets, came with a Shari'a that will never be abrogated, and his call was to all men and jinn, he was surely the chief of all the prophets, and therefore gathered together in himself the essence and unanimity of all their miracles. That means the strength of the consensus of the prophets and the testimony of their miracles forms a support for his truthfulness and veracity. He is also the master and leader of all the saints and purified scholars who attain to perfection through his training and guidance and the light of his Shari'a. In which case, gathered together in him were the mystery of their wonders, their unanimous affirmation, and the strength of their verifications. For they travelled the way their master opened up and left open, and they found the truth. In which case, all their wonder-working and verifications and consensus forms a support for their sacred master's truthfulness and veracity. Also, as was seen in the previous Signs, this proof of Divine Unity was equipped with such certain, evident, and definite miracles and wondrous *irhasat*, and his prophethood was proved by such irrefutable evidences that their affirmation could not be disputed, even if the whole universe were to unite against him.

Third Principle: And in that herald of Divine Unity and giver of the tidings of eternal happiness who was himself a clear miracle were such elevated moral qualities, and in the duties of his messengership, such sublime attributes, and in the Shari'a he propagated, such high virtues, that even his most bitter enemy had to confirm them, being unable to deny them. Since the highest and best moral qualities, the most elevated and perfect attributes, and the most precious and acceptable virtues were present in his self, his duties, and his religion, for sure, that being was the exemplar, model, personification, and master of the perfections and elevated moral qualities in beings. In which case, these perfections in his self, his duty, and his religion form a support for his veracity and truthfulness so powerful that it can in no way be shaken.

Fourth Principle: And this herald of Divine Unity and happiness, who was the source of perfections and teacher of elevated virtues, did not speak of himself; he was made to speak. Yes, he was made to speak by the Creator of the Universe. He received instruction from his Pre-Eternal Master, then he taught. For the Creator of the Universe showed through the thousands of proofs of his prophethood, in part described in the above Signs, through all those miracles He created through his hand, that he was not speaking on his own account, but conveying His speech. Furthermore, the Qur'an that came to him shows through its forty aspects of miraculousness, outer and inner, that he was Almighty God's interpreter. Also, through all his sincerity, fear of God, seriousness, reliability, and all his other qualities and conduct, he showed that he was not speaking his own ideas in his own name, but was rather speaking in the name of his Creator. In addition, all those who penetrate to reality who heed him have affirmed him with the truths they have investigated and laid open; they have believed with 'knowledge of certainty' that he was not speaking on his own behalf, but that the Creator of the Universe was causing him to speak and teaching, teaching by means of him. In which case, his veracity and truthfulness are supported by the consensus of these four powerful principles.

Fifth Principle: And this Interpreter of Pre-Eternal Speech saw spirit beings, conversed with angels, and offered guidance to men and jinn. He received knowledge surpassing the world of men and jinn, and even the worlds of spirits and the angels; he had access to, and relationships with the realms that lie beyond theirs. The miracles mentioned previously and the story of his life which has the authenticity of 'consensus' all prove this fact. In which case, unlike soothsayers and others who give news of the Unseen, no jinn, no spirit being, no angel, and apart from Gabriel, not even the highest angels in attendance on God Almighty, could interfere in the tidings he gave. And on some occasions, he even left Gabriel, his companion, behind.

Sixth Principle: And this being, the lord of the angels, jinn, and men, was the most illumined and perfect fruit of the tree of the universe, and the personification of Divine Mercy, and the exemplar of dominical love, and the most luminous proof of the Truth, and the most radiant lamp of reality, and the key to the talisman of the universe, and the solver of the riddle of creation, and the expounder of the wisdom of the world, and the herald of Divine sovereignty, and the describer of the beauties of dominical art, and in regard to the comprehensiveness of his disposition, he was the most complete example of the perfections of beings. In which case, these attributes of his and his spiritual personality indicate, indeed, show that this being was the ultimate cause of the universe's existence; that is to say, the universe's Creator looked to this being and created the universe. It may be said that if He had not created him, He would not have created the universe. Yes, the truths of the Qur'an and lights of belief he brought to men and jinn, and the elevated virtues and exalted perfections apparent in his being are a decisive witness to this fact.

Seventh Principle: And this proof of the Truth and lamp of reality demonstrated such a religion and Shari'a that it comprises principles ensuring the happiness of both worlds. And in addition to being comprehensive, it explains with complete correctness the universe's truths and duties, and the Creator of the Universe's Names and attributes. Thus, Islam and the Shari'a are so comprehensive and perfect, and describe the universe and Himself in such a way, that anyone who studies its nature carefully is bound to understand that that religion is a declaration, a manifesto, describing both the One Who made this beautiful universe, and the universe itself. Just as a palace's builder writes an instruction sheet suitable to the palace, in order to describe himself through His attributes, so too such an elevatedness, comprehensiveness, and truth are apparent in the religion and Shari'a of Muhammad (PBUH) that they demonstrate that his religion proceeded from the pen of the One Who creates and regulates the universe. And whoever ordered the universe so well, is the One Who ordered this religion equally well. Yes, the perfect order of the one requires the perfect order of the other.

Eighth Principle: Thus qualified by the abovementioned attributes and sustained by totally unshakeable, powerful supports, Muhammad the Arabian (Upon whom be blessings and peace) proclaimed his message over the heads of men and jinn in the name of the World of the Unseen, turned to the Manifest World; he addressed the peoples and nations waiting beyond the centuries of the future; he called out to all jinn and men; he made all places and all times hear. Yes, we too hear!

Ninth Principle: And his address is so elevated and powerful that all the centuries heed it. Yes, all the centuries hear the echo of his voice.

Tenth Principle: And it is apparent from that being's manner that he saw, and spoke accordingly. For at times of greatest peril, he spoke unhesitatingly, fearlessly, with utter steadfastness. On occasion he challenged the whole world on his own.

Eleventh Principle: And with all his strength he made so powerful a call and summons that he caused half the earth and a fifth of mankind to respond to his voice, declaring: "Yes, we have heard and we obey!"

Twelfth Principle: And he called with such seriousness and instructed so fundamentally that he inscribed his principles on the face of the centuries and on the very stones of all corners of the world; he engraved them on the face of time.

Thirteenth Principle: And he proclaimed the soundness of the injunctions he conveyed with such confidence and sureness, that should the whole world have gathered, they could not have made him revoke or abjure a single of those precepts. Witness to this are all his life and his illustrious biography.

Fourteenth Principle: And he called and summoned with such confidence and trust that he became obliged to no one and no difficulty upset him; with complete sincerity and honesty, he accepted before anyone the precepts he had brought, and acted accordingly, and proclaimed them. And witness to this was his famous asceticism and independence, and his never stooping to the ephemeral glitter of this world, which were well-known by everyone, friend and foe.

Fifteenth Principle: And his obedience to the religion he brought, and his worship of his Maker, and his abstaining from whatever was forbidden, all of which he performed to a greater degree than everyone else, demonstrate conclusively that he was the envoy and herald of the Monarch of Pre-Eternity and Post-Eternity; he was the most sincere servant of the One Who is worshipped by right, and the interpreter of His pre-eternal word.

The conclusion of these Fifteen Principles is this: the one qualified by the above-mentioned attributes proclaimed Divine Unity with all his strength repeatedly and constantly throughout his life, saying: "So know that there is no god but God."

O God, grant him blessings and peace to the number of good deeds of his community, and to his Family.

Glory be unto You! We have no knowledge save that which You have taught us; indeed You are All-Knowing, All-Wise!

* * *

A DIVINE GIFT AND A MARK OF DOMINICAL FAVOUR

In the hope of complying with the meaning of the verse,

But the favour of your Sustainer, rehearse and proclaim,

I shall mention a mark of Almighty God's favour and mercy which was apparent in the writing of this treatise, so that those who read it may understand its importance.

I had no intention of writing this treatise, for the Nineteenth and Thirty-First Words about the messengership of Muhammad (PBUH) had been written. Then suddenly I felt a compelling impulse to write it. Also my power of memory had been extinguished due to the calamities I had suffered. Moreover, in accordance with my way, I had not taken the path of narrative, that is, "he said that," "it was said that," in the works I had written. Furthermore, I had no books of Hadith or the Prophet's biography available to me. Nevertheless, saying: "I place my trust in God," I began. It was extremely successful, and my memory assisted me in a way that surpassed even that of the Old Said. Thirty to forty pages were written at speed every two or three hours. Once fifteen pages were written in a single hour. It was mostly narrated from such books as Bukhari, Muslim, Bayhaqi, Tirmidhi, *Shifa' al-Sharif,* Abu Na'im, and Tabari. My heart was trembling, because if there had been any error in relating them —since they are Hadiths— it would have been a sin. But it was clear that Divine favour was with us and there was need for the treatise. God willing, what has been written is sound. If perhaps there are any errors in the wording of some of the Hadiths or in the names of the narrators, I request that my brothers will look on them tolerantly and correct them.

Said Nursi

Ustad Said Nursi, our master, dictated and we wrote the first draft. He had no books with him, nor did he refer to any. He would suddenly dictate at great speed, and we wrote. We would write thirty, forty, and sometimes more, pages in two or three hours. We formed the conviction that this success was itself a wonder proceeding from the miracles of the Prophet Muhammad (PBUH).

Abdullah Çavuş	*Süleyman Sami*	*Hâfız Halid*	*Hâfız Tevfik*
His student in permanent attendance on him.	His scribe of rough drafts in permanent attendance on him.	His scribe of rough drafts in permanent attendance on him.	His scribe of rough and final drafts.

The First Addendum
to the Miracles of Muhammad (PBUH)

[The Nineteenth Word about the Messengership of Muhammad (PBUH) and the Miracle of the Splitting of the Moon have been included here due to their 'station.']

In the Name of God, the Merciful, the Compassionate.

Also being the Fourteenth Flash, this Word consists of fourteen 'Droplets.'

FIRST DROPLET

There are three great and universal things which make known to us our Sustainer. One is the book of the universe, a jot of whose testimony we have heard from the thirteen Flashes together with the Thirteenth Word of the Risale-i Nur. Another is the Seal of the Prophets (Peace and blessings be upon him), the supreme sign of the book of the universe. The other is the Qur'an of Mighty Stature. Now we must become acquainted with the Seal of the Prophets (PBUH), who is the second and articulate proof, and must listen to him.

Yes, consider the collective personality of this proof: the face of the earth has become his mosque, Mecca, his *mihrab*, and Medina, his pulpit. Our Prophet (Peace and blessings be upon him), this clear proof, is leader of all the believers, preacher to all mankind, the chief of all the prophets, lord of all the saints, the leader of a circle for the remembrance of God comprising all the prophets and saints. He is a luminous tree whose living roots are all the prophets, and fresh fruits are all the saints; whose claims all the prophets relying on their miracles and all the saints relying on their wonder-working confirm and corroborate. For he declares and claims: "There is no god but God!" And all on left and right, that is, those luminous reciters of God's Names lined up in the past and the future, repeat the same words, and through their consensus in effect declare: "You speak the truth and what you say is right!" What false idea has the power to meddle in a claim which is thus affirmed and corroborated by thousands?

SECOND DROPLET

Just as that luminous proof of Divine unity is affirmed by the unanimity and consensus of those two wings, so do hundreds of indications in the revealed scriptures, like the Torah and Bible,[1] and the thousands of signs that appeared before the beginning of his mission, and the well-known news given by the voices from the Unseen and the unanimous testimony of the soothsayers, the indications of the thousands of his miracles like the Splitting of the Moon, and the justice of Shari'a all confirm and corroborate him. So too, in his person, his laudable morals, which were at the summit of perfection; and in his duties, his complete confidence and elevated qualities, which were of the highest excellence, and his extraordinary fear of God, worship, seriousness, and fortitude, which demonstrated the strength of

1. In his *Risale-i Hamidiye*, Ḥusayn Jisrī extracted one hundred and fourteen indications from those scriptures. If this many have remained after the texts have become corrupted, there were surely many explicit mentions before.

his belief, and his total certainty and his complete steadfastness, — these all show as clearly as the sun how utterly faithful he was to his cause.

THIRD DROPLET

If you wish, come! Let us go to Arabian Peninsula, to theEra of Bliss! In our imaginations we shall see him at his duties and visit him. Look! We see a person distinguished by his fine character and beautiful form. In his hand is a miraculous book and on his tongue, a truthful address; he is delivering a pre-eternal sermon to all mankind, indeed, to man, jinn, and the angels, and to all beings. He solves and expounds the strange riddle of the world's creation; he discovers and solves the abstruse talisman which is the mystery of the universe; and he provides convincing and satisfying answers to the three awesome and difficult questions that are asked of all beings and have always bewildered and occupied minds: "Where do you come from? What are you doing here? What is your destination?"

FOURTH DROPLET

See! He spreads such a Light of truth that if you look at the universe as being outside the luminous sphere of his truth and guidance, you see it to be like a place of general mourning, and beings strangers to one another and hostile, and inanimate beings to be like ghastly corpses and living creatures like orphans weeping at the blows of death and separation. Now look! Through the Light he spreads, that place of universal mourning has been transformed into a place where God's Names and praises are recited in joy and ecstasy. The foreign, hostile beings have become friends and brothers. While the dumb, dead inanimate creatures have all become familiar officials and docile servants. And the weeping, complaining orphans are seen to be either reciting God's Names and praises or offering thanks at being released from their duties.

FIFTH DROPLET

Also, through his Light, the motion and movement of the universe, and its variations, changes and transformations cease being meaningless, futile, and the playthings of chance; they rise to being dominical missives, pages inscribed with the signs of creation, mirrors to the Divine Names, and the world itself becomes a book of the Eternally Besought One's wisdom. Man's boundless weakness and impotence make him inferior to all other animals and his intelligence, an instrument for conveying grief, sorrow, and sadness, makes him more wretched, yet when he is illumined with that Light, he rises above all animals and all creatures. Through entreaty, his illuminated impotence, poverty, and intelligence make him a petted monarch; due to his complaints, he becomes a spoiled vicegerent of the earth. That is to say, if it was not for his Light, the universe and man, and all things, would be nothing. Yes, certainly such a person is necessary in such a wondrous universe; otherwise the universe and firmaments would not be in existence.

SIXTH DROPLET

Thus, that Being brings and announces the good news of eternal happiness; he is the discoverer and proclaimer of an infinite mercy, the herald and observer of the beauties of the sovereignty of dominicality, and the discloser and displayer of the treasures of the Divine Names. If you regard him in that way, that is in regard to his being a worshipful servant of God, you will see him to be the model of love, the exemplar of mercy, the glory of mankind, and the most luminous fruit of the tree of creation. While if you look in this way, that is, in regard to his Messengership, you see him to be the proof of God, the lamp of truth, the sun of guidance, and the means to happiness. And look! His Light has lighted up from east to west like dazzling lightning, and half the earth and a fifth of mankind has accepted the gift of his guidance and preserved it like life itself. So how is it that our evil-commanding souls and satans do not accept with all its degrees, the basis of all such a Being claimed, that is, *There is no god but God*?

SEVENTH DROPLET

Now, consider how, eradicating in no time at all their evil, savage customs and habits to which they were fanatically attached, he decked out the various wild, unyielding peoples of that broad peninsula with all the finest virtues, and made them teachers of all the world and masters to the civilized nations. See, it was not an outward domination, he conquered and subjugated their minds, spirits, hearts, and souls. He became the beloved of hearts, the teacher of minds, the trainer of souls, the ruler of spirits.

EIGHTH DROPLET

You know that a small habit like cigarette smoking among a small nation can be removed permanently only by a powerful ruler with great effort. But look! This Being removed numerous ingrained habits from intractable, fanatical large nations with slight outward power and little effort in a short period of time, and in their place he so established exalted qualities that they became as firm as if they had mingled with their very blood. He achieved very many extraordinary feats like this. Thus, we present the Arabian Peninsula as a challenge to those who refuse to see the testimony of the blessed age of the Prophet. Let them each take a hundred philosophers, go there, and strive for a hundred years; would they be able to carry out in that time one hundredth of what he achieved in a year?

NINTH DROPLET

Also, you know that an insignificant man of small standing among a small community in a disputed matter of small importance cannot tell a small but shameful lie brazen-faced and without fear without displaying anxiety or disquiet enough to inform the enemies at his side of his deception. Now look at that Being; although he undertook a tremendous task which required an official of great authority and great standing and a situation of great security, can any contradiction at all be found in the words he uttered among a community of great size in the face of great hostility concerning a great cause and matters of great significance, with great ease and freedom, without fear, hesitation, diffidence, or anxiety, with pure sincerity, great seriousness, and in an intense, elevated manner that angered his enemies? Is it at all possible that any trickery should have been involved? God forbid! *It is naught but Revelation inspired.*[2] The truth does not deceive, and one who perceives the truth is not deceived. His way, which is truth, is free of deception. How could a fancy appear to one who sees the truth to be the truth, and deceive him?

TENTH DROPLET

Now, look! What curiosity-arousing, attractive, necessary, and awesome truths he shows, what matters he proves!

You know that what impels man most is curiosity. Even, if it was to be said to you: "If you give half of your life and property, someone will come from the Moon and Jupiter and tell you all about them. He will also tell you the truth about your future and what will happen to you," you would be bound to give them if you have any curiosity at all. Whereas that Being tells of a Monarch Who is such that in His realm, the Moon flies round a moth like a fly, and the moth, the earth, flutters round a lamp, and the lamp, the sun, is merely one lamp among thousands in one guest-house out of thousands of that Monarch.

Also, he speaks truly of a world so wondrous and a revolution so momentous that if the earth was a bomb and exploded, it would not be all that strange. Look! Listen to Suras like, *When*

2. Qur'ān, 53:4.

the sun is folded up;[3] * *When the sky is cleft asunder;*[4] * *[The Day] of Noise and Clamour;*[5] which he recites.

Also, he speaks truly about a future in comparison with which the future in this world is like a tiny mirage. And he tells most seriously of a happiness in comparison with which all worldly happiness is but a fleeting flash of lightning in relation to an eternal sun.

ELEVENTH DROPLET

For sure, wonders await us under the apparent veil of the universe which is thus strange and perplexing. So one thus wonderful and extraordinary, a displayer of marvels, is necessary to tell of its wonders. It is apparent from that Being's conduct that he has seen them, and sees them, and says that he has seen them. And he instructs us most soundly concerning what the God of the heavens and the earth, Who nurtures us with His bounties, wants and desires of us. Everyone should therefore leave everything and run to and heed this Being who teaches numerous other necessary and curiosity-arousing truths like these, so how is it that most people are deaf and blind, and mad even, so that they do not see this truth, and they do not listen to it and understand it?

TWELFTH DROPLET

Thus, just as this Being is an articulate proof and true evidence at the degree of the veracity of the unity of the Creator of beings, so is he a decisive proof and clear evidence for the resurrection of the dead and eternal happiness. Yes, with his guidance he is the reason for eternal happiness coming about and is the means of attaining it; so too through his prayers and supplications, he is the cause of its existence and reason for its

3. Qur'ān, 81:1.
4. Qur'ān, 82:1.
5. Qur'ān, 101:1.

creation. We repeat here this mystery, which is mentioned in the Tenth Word, due to its 'station'.

See! This Being prays with a prayer so supreme that it is as if the Arabian Peninsula and the earth itself performs the prayers through his sublime prayer, and offers entreaties. See, he also entreats in a congregation so vast that it is as if all the luminous and perfected members of mankind from the time of Adam till our age and until the end of time, are following him and saying "Amen" to his supplications. And see! He is beseeching for a need so universal that not only the dwellers of the earth, but also those of the heavens, and all beings, join in his prayer, declaring: "Yes! O our Sustainer! Grant it to us! We too want it!" And he supplicates with such want, so sorrowfully, in such a loving, yearning, and beseeching fashion that he brings the whole cosmos to tears, leading them to join in his prayer.

And see! The purpose and aim of his prayer is such it raises man and the world, and all creatures, from the lowest of the low, from inferiority, worthlessness, and uselessness to the highest of the high; that is to having value, permanence, and exalted duties. And see! He seeks and pleads for help and mercy in a manner so elevated and sweet, it is as if he makes all beings and the heavens and the earth hear, and bringing them to ecstasy, to exclaim: "Amen, O our God! Amen!" And see! He seeks his needs from One so Powerful, Hearing, and Munificent, One so Knowing, Seeing, and Compassionate, that He sees and hears the most secret need of the most hidden living being and its entreaties, accepts them, and has mercy on it. For He gives what is asked for, if only through the tongue of disposition. And He gives it in so Wise, Seeing, and Compassionate a form that it leaves no doubt that that nurturing and regulation is particular to the All-Hearing and All-Seeing One, the Most Generous and Most Compassionate One.

THIRTEENTH DROPLET

What does he want, this pride of the human race, who taking behind him all the eminent of mankind, stands on top of the world, and raising up his hand, is praying? What is this unique being, who is truly the glory of the cosmos, seeking? Listen! He is seeking eternal happiness. He is asking for eternal life, and to meet with God. He wants Paradise. And he wants all the Sacred Divine Names, which display their beauty and decrees in the mirrors of beings. Even, if it were not for reasons for the fulfilment of those countless requests, like mercy, grace, wisdom, and justice, a single of that Being's prayers would have been sufficient for the construction of Paradise, the creation of which is as easy for Divine power as the creation of the spring. Yes, just as his Messengership was the reason for the opening of this place of examination and trial, so too his worship and servitude to God were the reason for the opening of the next world.

Would the perfect order observed in the universe, which has caused scholars and the intelligent to pronounce: "It is not possible for there to be anything better than what exists;" and the faultless beauty of art within mercy, the incomparable beauty of dominicality, — would these permit the ugliness, the cruelty, the lack of order of its hearing and responding to the least significant, the least important desires and voices, and its considering unimportant the most important, the most necessary wishes, and its not hearing them or understanding them, and not carrying them out? God forbid! A hundred thousand times, God forbid! Such a beauty would not permit such an ugliness; it would not become ugly.

And so, my imaginary friend! That is enough for now, we must return. For if we remain a hundred years in this age in the Arabian Peninsula, we still would only completely comprehend one hundredth of the marvels of that Being's duties and the wonders he carried out, and we would never tire of watching him.

Now, come! We shall look at the centuries, which will turn above us. See how each has opened like a flower through the effulgence it has received from that Sun of Guidance! They have produced millions of enlightened fruits like Abu Hanifa, Shafi'i, Abu Bayazid Bistami, Shah Geylani, Shah Naqshband, Imam Ghazzali, and Imam Rabbani. But postponing the details of our observations to another time, we must recite some benedictions for that displayer of miracles and bringer of guidance, which mention a number of his certain miracles:

Endless peace and blessings be upon our master Muhammad, to the number of the good deeds of his community, to whom was revealed the All-Wise Criterion of Truth and Falsehood, from One Most Merciful, Most Compassionate, from the Sublime Throne; whose Messengership was foretold by the Torah and Bible, and told of by wondrous signs, the voices of jinn, saints of man, and soothsayers; at whose indication the moon split; our master Muhammad! Peace and blessings be upon him thousands and thousands of times, to the number of the breaths of his community; at whose beckoning came the tree, on whose prayer rain swiftly fell; and whom the cloud shaded from the heat; who satisfied a hundred men with his food; from between whose fingers three times flowed water like the Spring of Kawthar; and to whom God made speak the lizard, the gazelle, the wolf, the torso, the arm, the camel, the mountain, the rock, and the clod; the one who made the Ascension and whose eye did not waver; our master and intercessor, Muhammad! Peace and blessings be upon him thousands and thousands of times, to the number of the letters of the Qur'an formed in the words, represented with the permission of the Most Merciful in the mirrors of the airwaves, at the reciting of all the Qur'an's words by all reciters from when it was first revealed to the end of time.

And grant us forgiveness and have mercy on us, O God, for each of those blessings. Amen.

[I have described the Evidences for the Prophethood of Muhammad (PBUH) which I have here indicated briefly in a Turkish treatise called *Şuaât-ı Mârifeti'n-Nebi* and in the Nineteenth Letter (The Miracles of Muhammad). And there too aspects of the All-Wise Qur'an's miraculousness have been mentioned briefly. Again, in a Turkish treatise called *Lemeât* (Gleams) and in the Twenty-Fifth Word (The Miraculousness of the Qur'an) I have explained concisely forty ways in which the Qur'an is a miracle, and indicated forty aspects of its miraculousness. And of those forty aspects, only the eloquence in the word-order, I have written in forty pages in an Arabic commentary called, *Isharat al-I'jaz*. If you have the need, you may refer to those three works.]

FOURTEENTH DROPLET

The All-Wise Qur'an, the treasury of miracles and supreme miracle, proves the Prophethood of Muhammad (PBUH) together with Divine unity so decisively that it leaves no need for further proof. And we shall give its definition and indicate one or two flashes of its miraculousness which have been the cause of criticism.

The All-Wise Qur'an, which makes known to us our Sustainer, is thus: it is the pre-eternal translator of the great book of the universe; the discloser of the treasures of the Divine Names concealed in the pages of the earth and the heavens; the key to the truths hidden beneath these lines of events; the treasury of the favours of the Most Merciful and pre-eternal addresses, which come forth from the World of the Unseen beyond the veil of this Manifest World; the sun, foundation, and plan of the spiritual world of Islam, and the map of the worlds of the hereafter; the distinct expounder, lucid exposition, articulate proof, and clear translator of the Divine Essence, attributes, and deeds; the instructor, true wisdom, guide, and leader of the world of humanity; it is both a book of wisdom and law, and a book of prayer and worship, and a book of command and summons, and a book of invocation and Divine knowledge — it is book for all spiritual needs; and it is a sacred library offering books appropriate to the ways of all the saints and veracious, the purified and the scholars, whose ways and paths are all different.

Consider the flashes of miraculousness in its repetitions, which are imagined to be a fault: since the Qur'an is both a book of invocation, and a book of prayer, and a book of summons, the repetition in it is desirable, indeed, it is essential and most eloquent. It is not as the faulty imagine. For the mark of invocation is illumination through repetition. The mark of prayer is strengthening through repetition. The mark of command and summons is confirmation through repetition. Moreover, everyone is not capable of always reading the whole Qur'an, but is mostly able to read one Sura. Therefore, since the most important purposes of the Qur'an are included in most of the longer Suras, each is like a small Qur'an. That is to say, so that no one should be deprived, certain of its aims like Divine unity, the resurrection of the dead, and the story of Moses, have been repeated. Also, like bodily needs, spiritual needs are various. Man is need of some of them every breath; like the body needs air, the spirit needs the word *Hū* (He). Some he is in need of every hour, like "In the Name of God." And so on. That means the repetition of verses arises from the repetition of need. It makes the repetition in order to point out the need and awaken and incite it, and to arouse desire and appetite.

Also, the Qur'an is a founder; it is the basis of the Clear Religion, and the foundation of the world of Islam. It changed human social life, and is the answer to the repeated questions of its various classes. Repetition is necessary for a founder in order to establish things. Repetition is necessary to corroborate them. Confirmation and repetition are necessary to strengthen them.

Also, it speaks of such mighty matters and minute truths that numerous repetitions are necessary in different forms in order to establish them in everyone's hearts. Nevertheless, they are apparently repetitions, but in reality every verse has numerous meanings, numerous benefits, and many aspects and levels. In each place they are mentioned with a different meaning, for different benefits and purposes.

Also, the Qur'an's being unspecific and concise in certain matters to do with cosmos is a flash of miraculousness for the purpose of guidance. It cannot be the target of criticism and is not a fault, like some atheists imagine.

If you ask: "Why does the All-Wise Qur'an not speak of beings in the same way as philosophy and science? It leaves some matters in brief form, and some it speaks of in a simple and superficial way that is easy in the general view, does not wound general feelings, and does not weary or tax the minds of ordinary people. Why is this?"

By way of answer we say: Philosophy has strayed from the path of truth, that's why. Also, of course you have understood from past Words and what they teach that the All-Wise Qur'an speaks of the universe in order to make known the Divine Essence, attributes, and Names. That is, it explains the meanings of the book of the universe to make known its Creator. That means it looks at beings, not for themselves, but for their Creator. Also, it addresses everyone. But philosophy and science look at beings for themselves, and address scientists in particular. In which case, since the All-Wise Qur'an makes beings evidences and proofs, the evidence has to be superficial so that it will be quickly understood in the general view. And since the Qur'an of Guidance addresses all classes of men, the ordinary people, which form the most numerous class, want guidance which is concise with unnecessary things beings vague, and which brings subtle things close with comparisons, and which does not change things which in their superficial view are obvious into an unnecessary or even harmful form, lest it causes them to fall into error.

For example, it says about the sun: "The sun is a revolving lamp or lantern." For it does not speak of the sun for itself and its nature, but because it is a sort of mainspring of an order and centre of a system, and order and system are mirrors of the Maker's skill. It says:

The sun runs its course.[6]

that is, the sun revolves. Through calling to mind the orderly disposals of Divine power in the revolutions of winter and summer, and day and night with the phrase, *The sun revolves,* it makes understood the Maker's tremendousness. Thus, whatever the reality of this revolving, it does not affect the order, which is woven and observed, and which is the purpose. It also says,

And set the sun as a lamp.[7]

Through depicting through the word *lamp* the world in the form of a palace, and the things within it as decorations, necessities, and provisions prepared for man and living beings, and inferring that the sun is also a subjugated candleholder, it makes known the mercy and bestowal of the Creator. Now look and see what this foolish and prattling philosophy says:

"The sun is a vast burning liquid mass. It causes the planets which have been flung off from it to revolve around it. Its mass is such-and-such. It is this, it is that." It does not afford the spirit the satisfaction and fulfilment of true knowledge, just a terrible dread and fearful wonder. It does not speak of it as the Qur'an does. You may understand from this the value of the matters of philosophy, whose inside is hollow and outside,

6. Qur'ān, 36:38.
7. Qur'ān, 71:16.

ostentatious. So do not be deceived by its glittering exterior and be disrespectful towards the most miraculous expositions of the Qur'an!

O God! Make the Qur'an healing for us, the writer of this and his peers, from all ills, and a companion to us and to them in our lives and after our deaths, and in this world, and in the grave, and at the Last Judgement an intercessor, and on the Bridge a light, and from the Fire a screen and shield, and in Paradise a friend, and in all good deeds a guide and leader, through Your grace and munificence and beneficence and mercy, O Most Munificent of the Munificent and Most Merciful of the Merciful! Amen.

O God! Grant blessings and peace to the one to whom the All-Wise Qur'an, the Distinguisher between Truth and Falsehood, was revealed, and to all his Family and Companions. Amen. Amen.

[**NOTE:** The Six Drops of the Fourteenth Droplet in the Arabic Risale-i Nur, and especially the Six Points of the Fourth Drop, explain fifteen of the approximately forty sorts of the All-Wise Qur'an's miraculousness. Deeming those to be sufficient, we have limited the discussion here. If you wish, refer to them, and you will find a treasury of miracles...]

* * *

About the Miracle of the Splitting of the Moon

[Addendum to the Nineteenth Letter and Thirty-First Word]

In the Name of God, the Merciful, the Compassionate.
*The Hour is nigh, and the moon is split. * But if they see a sign, they turn away, and say: "This is evident magic."*[1]

Philosophers and their unreasoning imitators, who want to eclipse with their vicious delusions the Splitting of the Moon, which is a miracle of Muhammad (PBUH) that shines like the moon, say: "If the Splitting of the Moon had occurred, it would have been known to the whole world and would have been related throughout the subsequent history of man."

The Answer: Since the Splitting of the Moon was demonstrated as an evidence of prophethood, and happened instantaneously, at night when people were asleep, and before a gathering who, although they witnessed such an evidence, denied it; and since there were obstacles hindering the sighting of it such as mist, clouds, and time-differences between different parts of the world; and since at that time science and civilization were

1. Qur'ān, 54:1-2.

not widespread, and observation of the skies was very limited, and the event itself was exceptional, there was, therefore, nothing to necessitate that it should have been seen all over the world and passed into the general histories. For now, listen to Five Points out of many that will scatter those clouds of delusion concerning the Splitting of the Moon.

FIRST POINT

The extreme stubbornness of the unbelievers there at that time is well-known and is recorded in history. And yet, when the All-Wise Qur'an announced this event to the whole world through saying:

And the moon is split,

not one of those unbelievers, who denied the Qur'an, spoke up to give the lie to this verse; that is, not one of them denied the event it was announcing. If the event had not been considered as a definite fact by the unbelievers at that time, they would have taken the verse as a pretext, denied it in a most fearsome manner, and tried to attack and overthrow Muhammad's (PBUH) claim to prophethood. However, the biographies of the Prophet and histories mentioning the event relate nothing to suggest that the unbelievers denied it. The only thing that history relates is, as the verse:

And [they] say, "This is evident magic,"

points out, the unbelievers who saw the event declared it to be magic, and said that if the caravans in other places had seen it, it was true, otherwise he had bewitched them. The caravans arriving the following morning from the Yemen and other places announced that they had seen such a happening. So the unbelievers then said of the Pride of All the Worlds (PBUH) that, God forbid, the magic of Abu Talib's orphan had affected the heavens.[2]

2. Ibn Ḥajar, *Fatḥ al-Bārī*, vii, 145; Bayhaqī, *Dalā'il al-Nubūwwa*, ii, 266, 268.

SECOND POINT

The majority of the most illustrious scholars, like Sa'd al-Din Taftazani, declared that like the Prophet had satisfied the thirst of a whole army with water flowing from his fingers, and the whole congregation had heard a dry wooden post against which Muhammad (PBUH) had leant while delivering the sermon weep on being separated from him, the Splitting of the Moon, too, was *mutawatir*,[3] that is, had been transmitted by numerous authorities. That is to say, these events had been passed down from group to group forming such a vast congregation that a conspiracy to lie would have been impossible. Like the appearance of the famous Haley's Comet a thousand years ago had been unanimously reported, and the existence of the island of Ceylon was certain due to unanimous reports, although we had not seen it.

And so, it is unreasonable to foster baseless doubts in such certain, witnessed matters. It is enough that they are not impossible. And as for the Splitting of the Moon, it is quite as possible as a mountain's splitting with a volcanic eruption.

THIRD POINT

Miracles are for proving claims to prophethood and for convincing those who deny those claims, they are not for compelling people to believe. Therefore, miracles have to be manifested to those who hear claims to prophethood at a degree that will persuade them. Just as it would be contrary to the All-Wise and Glorious One's wisdom to display them all over the world or in so self-evident a manner that all would be compelled to believe, so would it also be contrary to the mystery of man's accountability. For this accountability requires "opening the door to the reason and not removing the power of choice." If the All-Wise Creator had left the moon split for one or two

3. *Bukhārī*, ii, 251; v, 62; vi, 178; al-Ḥākim, *al-Mustadrak*, ii, 472; Suyūṭī, *Naẓm al-Mutanāthir fi'l-Ḥadīth al-Mutawātir*, 135; Bayhaqī, *Dalā'il*, i, 279-81.

ours in order to show it to the whole world as the philosophers wished, and it had been recorded in all the general histories of man, then it would have been like all other occurrences in the heavens and would not have been an evidence to Muhammad's (PBUH) claim to prophethood nor been special to his messengership. Or else it would have been such a self-evident miracle that it would have negated the power of choice, a part of man's reason, compelling it to accept it; willy-nilly, it would have had to assent to his prophethood. Someone with a coal-like spirit like Abu Jahl would have remained at the same level as someone with a diamond-like spirit like Abu Bakr the Veracious; the mystery of man's accountability would have been lost. It was due to this mystery that, being both instantaneous, and at nighttime, and at a time of sleep, and time differences, mist, and cloud and other obstacles concealing it, it was not shown to the whole world and did not pass into the histories.

FOURTH POINT

Since this event occurred instantaneously at night while everyone was sleeping, of course it was not seen all over the world. Even if some people had seen it, they would not have believed their eyes. And even if it had made them believe, such a significant event would not have become a permanent source for future histories through isolated individual reports.

In some books it is written that after the moon split into two halves, it fell to earth, but veracious scholars have rejected such additions, saying that they were perhaps added by dissemblers with the intention of reducing to nothing the value of this evident miracle.

And, for example, just as the same time in England and Spain, which were then enveloped in mists of ignorance, would have been just after sunset, in America daytime, and in China and Japan morning, so too in other places there would have been other obstacles preventing it being seen. Now consider these unreasoning objectors who say that the histories of peoples like the English, Chinese, Japanese, and Americans do not mention it, and that therefore it did not occur. A thousand curses be on the heads of those who toady to Europe and repeat such things.

FIFTH POINT

The Splitting of the Moon happened neither of its own accord in consequence of certain causes, nor as a result of chance, nor was it a natural event that occurred through the ordinary laws of nature. Rather, the All-Wise Creator of the Sun and the Moon caused it to happen as something out of the ordinary in order to confirm His Messenger's messengership and to illuminate his claim.

As the mystery of guidance, the mystery of human accountability, and the wisdom of messengership required, it was demonstrated as a convincing proof to certain people specified by dominical wisdom. The mystery of wisdom required that it was not shown to people in every region of the world, who had not yet heard of Muhammad's (PBUH) claim to prophethood. Numerous obstacles prevented them, therefore, such as mist, cloud, and time-differences, and the fact that in some countries the moon had not risen, and in others the sun had risen, while in others it was morning, and in yet others the sun had just set.

If it had been shown to all and sundry, it would have been shown as a result of the Sign of Muhammad (PBUH), and a miracle of prophethood, in which case his messengership would have been so manifest that everyone would have been compelled to affirm it. No choice would have remained for the reason. *And belief is attained through man's power of choice and his reason.* The mystery of human accountability would have gone for nothing. And if it had been shown merely as an occurrence in the heavens, its connection with Muhammad's (PBUH) messengership would have been severed, and it would have retained no peculiarity to him.

To Conclude: There is no longer any doubt concerning the possibility that the Splitting of the Moon occurred; it has been proved decisively. And now we shall mention six[4] of the many evidences pointing to its occurrence.

The concurrence of the Companions of the Prophet, who were all men of justice, on its occurrence.

Their agreement in expounding the verse, *And the moon is split* of all exacting commentators on the Qur'an.

The fact that, relying on numerous different chains of authorities and lines of transmission, all the scholars of the Prophetic Hadiths and transmitters of the sound narrations narrated the event.[5]

The testimony of all the saints and the veracious, those who receive inspiration, and uncover the mysteries of the creation.

The confirmation of learned scholars and theologians, whose ways differ greatly from one another.

The fact that the Community of Muhammad (PBUH) accepted its occurrence, which, on an established principle, never agrees upon error.[6]

These six evidences prove the Splitting of the Moon as clearly as the sun.

CONCLUSION

Up to here this Addendum has been in the name of establishing the truth, and for the sake of silencing those enemies who deny it. Its concluding sentences will now be in the name of the truth and for the sake of belief. Indeed, establishing the truth spoke as above, now the truth speaks.

---

4. That is to say, there are six proofs concerning the event in the form of a sixfold consensus. Unfortunately, the explanation of them is brief, although they deserve more.

5. *Musnad* i, 377, 413, 447, 456; iii, 207, 220, 275, 278; iv, 81; *Tafsīr Ibn Kathīr* vi, 469.

6. Suyūṭī, *Naẓm al-Mutanāthir fi'l-Ḥadīth al-Mutawātir*, 180; Ṭabarānī, *al-Mu'jam al-Kabīr*, xii, 13623-4; xvii, 666-7; Ibn 'Adī, *al-Kāmil fi'l-Ḍu'afā'*, iii, 1307.

The Seal of the Office of Prophethood, who was the luminous moon of its heaven, proved his sainthood through his Ascension. This was the greatest wonder and supreme miracle of sainthood, achieved through his worship, which was so elevated as to make him God's beloved. That is to say, by travelling with his earthly body through the heavens, his superiority and his being God's beloved were demonstrated to the dwellers of the heavens and inhabitants of the lofty worlds. So too, through the moon, which is bound to the earth and suspended in the heavens, being split into two halves at the sign of an inhabitant of the earth, a miracle indicating to that earth-dweller's messengership was displayed to the other inhabitants of the earth. Thus, the person of Muhammad (PBUH) flew to the very summit of perfections on the two luminous wings of messengership and sainthood — like the two luminous unfolded wings of the moon; he ascended to the *distance of two bow-lengths*; he became the cause of pride of both the inhabitants of the heavens and the inhabitants of the earth....

> *Upon him and upon his Family be blessings and peace such as will fill the earth and the heavens.*
>
> *Glory be unto You! we have no knowledge save that which You have taught us; indeed, You are All-Knowing, All-Wise.*

* * *

The Third Addendum
to the Miracles of Muhammad (PBUH)

[This concerns the Messengership of Muhammad (PBUH) and is the answer, in concise index-like form, to the first of the three questions and difficulties in the Third Principle of the Thirty-First Word, about the Ascension of Muhammad.]

Question: Why is this mighty Ascension special to Muhammad the Arabian (Peace and blessings be upon him)?

The Answer to your first difficulty: It has been analysed in detail in the first thirty Words, so here we shall set out a concise list briefly indicating the perfections of Muhammad (PBUH), the signs of his prophethood, and the fact that he was the most worthy to make the Ascension. It is as follows.

Firstly: Despite numerous corruptions in the texts of Holy Scriptures like the Torah, Gospels, and Psalms, in recent times even, an exacting scholar like Husayn Jisri extracted one hundred and fourteen good tidings of Muhammad's prophethood (PBUH), which he set forth in his *Risale-i Hamidiye*.[1]

12. Ḥusayn al-Jisrī, *al-Risālat al-Ḥamīdiya* [Turk. trans. Manastırlı İsmail Hakkı], Istanbul 1308, 4 vols.; Suyūṭī, *al-Khaṣā'is al-Kubrā*, i, 26, 73.

Secondly: It has been proved historically that there were many predictions accurately forecasting the prophethood of Muhammad (PBUH), like those of the two soothsayers Shiqq and Satih, which, a while previously to his prophethood, gave news of it and the fact that he was to be the final prophet.[2]

Thirdly: There were hundreds of extraordinary happenings, famous in history, called *irhasat*, that is, signs forewarning men of a coming prophet, like, for example, on the night of Muhammad's (PBUH) birth, the idols in the Ka'ba fell from their places and the famous palace of Khosroes the Persian was rent asunder.[3]

Fourthly: History and the Prophet's biographies show that he satisfied the thirst of an army with water flowing from his fingers, that in the presence of a large congregation in the mosque, the dry wooden support against which Muhammad (PBUH) was leaning moaned like a camel and wept on being separated from him when he ascended the pulpit, and that he was distinguished by close on a thousand miracles attested to by the verses of the Qur'an, such as,

And the moon split,[4]

referring to the splitting of the moon, and verified by those who investigated them.

Fifthly: Anyone who considers the facts and is fair and just cannot hesitate to agree that, as is unanimously agreed by friend and foe alike, good moral qualities were to be found at the highest degree in his personality, and that, in accordance with the testimony of all his dealings and actions, attributes and character of the greatest excellence were apparent in the way he performed his duties and proclaimed Islam, and, in accordance with the fine qualities and conduct enjoined by the religion of

2. Ibn Sayyid al-Nās, *'Uyūn al-Āthār*, i, 29; Qāḍī Iyāḍ, *al-Shifā'*, i, 364-6.
3. Qāḍī Iyāḍ, *al-Shifā'*, i, 366-8; Bayhaqī, *Dalā'il al-Nubūwwa*, i, 126.
4. Qur'ān, 54:1.

slam, laudable virtues of the highest order were to be found in the law he brought.

Sixthly: As is alluded to in the Second Indication of the Tenth Word, it is a requirement of wisdom that Divinity be manifested. And this desire of Divinity to be manifested is met at the highest level and most brilliantly by the comprehensive worship performed by Muhammad (PBUH) in the practice of his religion. Also, wisdom and truth require that the Creator of the world displays His beauty in its utter perfection through some means. And the one who met that wish, and displayed and described His beauty most perfectly was self-evidently the person of Muhammad (PBUH).

It was also clearly Muhammad (PBUH) who, in response to the desire of the world's Maker to exhibit and attract attentive gazes towards His perfect art within infinite beauty, heralded that art with the loudest voice.

Again it was necessarily Muhammad (PBUH) who, in response to the desire of the Sustainer of All the Worlds to proclaim His unity in the levels of multiplicity, announced all the degrees of unity, each at the greatest level of unity.

And, as is indicated by the utter beauty in beings and as is required by truth and wisdom, the world's Owner desires to see and display in mirrors, His infinite essential beauty and the subtleties and qualities of His exquisiteness. And again it was self-evidently Muhammad (PBUH) who, in response to that desire, acted as a mirror and displayed His beauty in the most radiant fashion, and loved it and made others love it.

Also, in response to the desire of the Maker of the palace of this world to exhibit His hidden treasuries, which are filled with the most wonderful miracles and priceless jewels, and through them to describe and make known His perfections, it was again self-evidently Muhammad (PBUH) who exhibited, described, and displayed them in the most comprehensive fashion.

Also, since the Maker of the universe has made it in such a way that He adorns it with different varieties of wonders and embellishments and has included conscious creatures in it so that they might make tours and excursions and ponder over it and take lessons, wisdom requires that He should desire to make known the meanings and value of the works of art to those who observe and ponder over them. And it was again self-evidently Muhammad (PBUH) who, in response to this desire of the universe's Maker, by means of the All-Wise Qur'an, acted as guide in the most comprehensive fashion to jinn and man, indeed, to spirit beings and angels.

Also, the All-Wise Ruler of the universe wishes, by means of an envoy, to cause all conscious beings to unravel the obscure talisman containing the aims and purposes of the change and transformations in the universe and to solve the riddle of the three perplexing questions: "Where do beings come form?", "What is their destination?", and, "What are they?" And again it was self-evidently Muhammad (PBUH) who, in response to this wish of the All-Wise Ruler, by means of the truths of the Qur'an, unravelled the talisman and solved the riddle in the clearest and most comprehensive fashion.

Also, the All-Glorious Maker of the universe desires to make Himself known to conscious beings by means of all His fine artefacts and to make them love Him through all His precious bounties, and, most certainly, to make known to them by means of an envoy His wishes and what will please Him in return for those bounties. And again it was self-evidently Muhammad (PBUH) who, in response to this desire of the All-Glorious Maker, by means of the Qur'an, expounded those wishes and things that please Him in the most exalted and perfect fashion.

Also, since the Sustainer of All the Worlds has given to man, who is the fruit of the universe, a comprehensive disposition which encompasses the universe and has prepared him for universal worship, and since, because of his faculties and senses, multiplicity and the world afflict man, the Sustainer desires to turn man's face from multiplicity to unity, from transience to permanence. And again it was self-evidently Muhammad (PBUH) who, in response to this desire, by means of the Qur'an, acted as guide in the most comprehensive and complete fashion, and in the best way, and carried out the duty of prophethood in the most perfect manner.

Among beings the most superior are animate beings, and among animate beings the most superior are conscious beings, and among conscious beings the most superior are true human beings. So the one among true human beings who carried out the above-mentioned duties at the most comprehensive level and in the most perfect manner would rise through an all-embracing Ascension to *the distance of two bow-lengths*, knock at the door of eternal happiness, open the treasury of Mercy, and see the hidden truths of belief. Again it would be him.

Seventhly: As is plain to see, beings are made beautiful with the utmost degree of fine embellishment and adornment. Such an embellishment and adornment clearly demonstrate that their Maker possesses an extremely strong will to make beautiful and intention to adorn. The will to make beautiful and adorn demonstrates that the Maker necessarily possesses a strong desire for and holy love towards His art. And among beings the one who displayed altogether in himself the most comprehensive and subtle wonders of art, and knew them and made them known and himself loved, and who appreciated the beauties to be found in other beings, declaring: "What wonders God has willed!", and was most beloved in the sight of his Maker, Who nurtures and loves His art, would most certainly be him.

Thus, the one who, declaring: "Glory be to God! What wonders God has willed! God is most Great!" in the face of the exquisiteness that gilds beings and the subtle perfections that illuminate them, causes the heavens to ring out, and who, through the strains of the Qur'an, causes the universe to reverberate, and through his admiration and appreciation, his contemplation and display, and his mentioning of the Divine Names and affirmation of Divine unity, brings land and sea to ecstasy, is again self-evidently that one (PBUH).

And so, according to the meaning of 'the cause is like the doer,' it is pure truth and sheer wisdom that the one in whose scales shall be found the equivalent of all the good deeds performed by his community, and whose spiritual perfections draw strength from the benedictions of all his community, and who, as a result of the duties he discharged in his messengership, received immaterial recompense and boundless emanations of Divine mercy and love, should advance by the stairway of the Ascension as far as Paradise, *the Lote-tree of the farthest limit*, the Divine Throne, and *the distance of two bow-lengths.*[5]

* * *

5. See, Qur'ān, 53:1-18.

The Fourth Addendum
to the Miracles of Muhammad (PBUH)

[The Sixteenth Degree, on the Messengership of Muhammad (PBUH), from the Supreme Sign.]

Then that traveller through the world addressed his own intellect saying: "Since I am seeking my Master and Creator by means of the creatures of the cosmos, I ought before all else to visit the most celebrated of all these creatures, the greatest and most accomplished commander among them, according to the testimony even of his enemies, the most renowned ruler, the most exalted in speech and the most brilliant an intellect, who has illuminated fourteen centuries with his excellence and with his Qur'an, Muhammad the Arabian Prophet (May God's peace and blessings be upon him)." In order thus to visit him and seek from him the answer to his quest, he entered the blessed age of the Prophet in his mind, and saw that age to be one of true felicity, thanks to that being. For through the light he had brought, he had turned the most primitive and illiterate of peoples into the masters and teachers of the world.

He said too to his own intellect, "Before asking him concerning our Creator, we should first learn the value of this extraordinary being, the veracity of his words and the truthfulness of his warnings." Thus he began investigating, and of the numerous conclusive proofs that he found we will briefly indicate here only nine of the most general ones.

THE FIRST

All excellent qualities and characteristics were to be found in that extraordinary being, according to the testimony even of his enemies. Hundreds of miracles were made manifest at his hands, according to explicit Qur'anic verses or traditions enjoying the status of *tawatur.*[1] Examples of these miracles are his splitting of the moon —*And the moon split*[2]— with a single indication of his finger; his casting of a handful of dust into the eyes of his enemies, causing them to flee —*It was not your act when you threw, but God's*[3]— and his giving his thirsting army to drink from the water that flowed forth from his five fingers like the Spring of Kawthar. Since some of those miracles, numbering more than three hundred, have been set forth with decisive proofs in the remarkable and wondrous work known as The Miracles of Muhammad (the Nineteenth Letter), we leave discussion of the miracles to that book, and permit the traveller to continue speaking:

"A being who in addition to noble characteristics and perfections has all these luminous miracles to demonstrate, must certainly be the most truthful in speech of all men. It is inconceivable that he would stoop to trickery, lies and error, the deeds of the vile."

1. *Tawātur* is the kind of report that is transmitted by numerous authorities, about which there is consensus, and no room for doubt. (Tr.)

2. Qur'ān, 54:1.

3. Qur'ān, 8:17.

THE SECOND

He holds in his hand a decree from the Lord of the universe, a decree accepted and affirmed in each century by more than three hundred million people. This decree, the Qur'an of Mighty Stature, is wondrous in seven different ways. The fact that the Qur'an has forty different aspects of miraculousnes and that it is the word of the Creator of all beings has been set forth in detail with strong proofs in the Twenty-Fifth Word, The Miraculousness of the Qur'an, a celebrated treatise that is like the sun of the Risale-i Nur. We therefore leave such matters to that work and listen to the traveller as he says, "There can never be any possibility of lying on the part of the being who is the conveyor and proclaimer of this decree, for that would be a violation of the decree and treachery toward the One Who issued it."

THE THIRD

Such a Sacred Law, an Islam, a code of worship, a cause, a summons, and a faith did that being bring forth that the like of them does not exist, nor could it exist. Nor does a more perfect form of them exist, nor could it exist. For the Law appearing with that unlettered being has no rival in its administration of one fifth of humanity for fourteen centuries, in a just and precise manner through its numerous injuctions. Moreover the Islam that emerged from the deeds, sayings, and inward states of that unlettered being has no peer, nor can it have, for in each century it has been for three hundred million men a guide and a refuge, the teacher and educator of their intellects and the illuminator and purifier of their hearts, the cause for the refinement and training of their souls, and the source of progress and advancement of their spirits.

The Prophet is similarly unparalleled in the way in which he was the foremost in practising all the forms of worship found in his religion, and the first in piety and the fear of God; in his observing the duties of worship fully and with attention to their profoundest dimensions, even while engaged in constant struggle and activity; in his practice of worship combining in perfect fashion the beginning and end of worship and servitude to God without imitation of anyone.

With the *Jawshan al-Kabir,* from among his thousands of supplicatory prayers and invocations, he describes his Sustainer with such a degree of gnosis that all the gnostics and saints who have come after him have been unable, with their joint efforts, to attain a similar degree of gnosis and accurate description. This shows that in prayer too he is without peer. Whoever looks at the section at the beginning of the Treatise on Supplicatory Prayer, which sets forth some part of the meaning of one of the ninety-nine sections of the *Jawshan al-Kabir,* will say that the *Jawshan* too has no peer.

In his conveying of the message and his summoning men to the truth, he displayed such steadfastness, firmness and courage that although great states and religions, and even his own people, tribe and uncle opposed him in the most hostile fashion, he exhibited not the slightest trace of hesitation anxiety or fear. The fact that he successfully challenged the whole world and made Islam the master of the world likewise proves that there is not and cannot be anyone like him in his conveying of the message and summons.

In his faith, he had so extraordinary a strength, so marvellous a certainty, so miraculous a breadth, and so exalted a conviction, illumining the whole world, that none of the ideas and beliefs then dominating the world, and none of the philosophies of the sages and teachings of the religious leaders, was able, despite extreme hostility and denial, to induce in his certainty, conviction, trust and assurance, the slightest doubt, hesitation, weakness or anxiety. Moreover, the saintly of all ages, headed by the Companions, the foremost in the degrees of belief, have all drawn on his fountain of belief and regarded him as representing the highest degree of faith. This proves that his faith too is matchless. Our traveller therefore concluded, and affirmed with his intellect, that lying and duplicity have no place in the one who has brought such a unique sacred law, such an unparalleled Islam, such a wondrous devotion to worship, such an extraordinary excellence in supplicatory prayer, such a universally acclaimed summons to the truth and such a miraculous faith.

THE FOURTH

In the same way that the consensus of the prophets is a strong proof for the existence and Unity of God, so too it is a firm testimony to the truthfulness and messengerhood of this being. For all the sacred attributes, miracles and functions that indicate the truthfulness and messengerhood of the prophets (Upon whom be peace) existed in full measure in that being according to the testimony of history. The prophets have verbally predicted the coming of that being and given good tidings thereof in the Torah, the Gospels, the Psalms, and the pages; more than twenty of the most conclusive examples of these glad tidings, drawn from the scriptures, have been set forth and proven in the Nineteenth Letter. Similarly, through all the deeds and miracles associated with their prophethood they have affirmed and —as it were— put their signature to the mission of that being which is the foremost and most perfect in the tasks and functions of prophethood. Just as through verbal consensus they indicate the Divine Unity, through the unanimity of their deeds they bear witness to the truthfulness of that being. This too was understood by our traveller.

THE FIFTH

Similarly, the thousands of saints who have attained truth, reality, perfection, wondrous deeds, unveiling and witnessing through the instruction of this being and following him, bear unanimous witness not only to the Divine Unity but also to the truthfulness and messengerhood of this being. Again, the fact that they witness, through the light of sainthood, some of the truths he proclaimed concerning the World of the Unseen, and that they believe in and affirm all of those truths through the light of belief, either with 'knowledge of certainty,' or with the 'vision of certainty,' or with 'absolute certainty.' He saw that this too demonstates like the sun the degree of truthfulness and rectitude of that great being, their master.

THE SIXTH

The millions of purified, sincere, and punctilious scholars and faithful sages, who have reached the highest station of learning through the teaching and instruction contained in the sacred truths brought by that being, despite his unlettered nature, the exalted sciences he invented and Divine knowledge he discovered—they not only prove and affirm, unanimously and with the strongest proofs, the Divine Unity which is the foundation of his mission, but also bear unanimous witness to the truthfulness of this supreme teacher and great master, and to the veracity of his words. This is a proof as clear as daylight. The Risale-i Nur too with its one hundred parts is but a single proof of his truthfulness.

THE SEVENTH

The Family and Companions of the Prophet —who with their insight, knowledge, and spiritual accomplishment are the most renowned, the most respected, the most celebrated, the most pious and the most keensighted of men after the prophets—examined and scrutinized, with the utmost attention, seriousness and exactitude, all the states, thoughts and conditions of this being, whether hidden or open. They came to the unanimous conclusion that he was the most truthful, exalted, and honest being in the world, and this, their unshakeable affirmation and firm belief, is a proof like the daylight attesting the reality of the sun.

THE EIGHTH

The cosmos indicates its Maker, Inscriber, and Designer, Who creates, administers, and arranges it, and through determining its measure and form and regulating it, has disposal over it as though it was a palace, a book, an exhibition, a spectacle. And so too it indicates that it requires and necessitates an elevated herald, a truthful unveiler, a learned master, and a truthful teacher who will know and make known the Divine purposes in the universe's creation, teach the dominical instances of wisdom in its changes and transformations, give instruction in the results of its dutiful motions, proclaim its essential value and the perfections of the beings within it, and express the meanings of that mighty book; it indicates that he is certain to exist. Thus, the traveller knew that it testified to the truthfulness of this being, who performed these functions better than anyone, and to his being a most elevated and loyal official of the universe's Creator.

THE NINTH

There is behind the veil One Who wishes to demonstrate with these ingenious and wise artefacts the perfection of His talent and art; to make Himself known and loved by means of these countless adorned and decorated creations; to evoke praise and thanks through the unnumbered pleasurable and valuable bounties that he bestows; to cause men to worship Him with gratitude and appreciation in the face of His dominicality, through His solicitous and protective sustenance of life, and His provision of nurture and bounty in such manner as to satisfy the most delicate of tastes and appetites; to manifest His Divinity through the change of seasons, the alternation of night and day, and through all His magnificent and majestic deeds, all His awe-inspiring and wise acts and creativity, and thereby to cause men to believe in his Divinity, in submission, humility and obedience; and to demonstrate His justice and truthfulness by at all times protecting virtue and the virtuous and destroying evil and the evil, by annihilating with blows from heaven the oppressor and the liar. There will of a certainty be at the side of this Unseen Being His most beloved creature and most devoted bondsman, who, serving the purposes that have just been mentioned, discovers and unravels the talisman and riddle of the creation of the universe, who acts always in the name of that Creator, who seeks aid and success from Him, and who receives them from Him—Muhammad of Quraysh (Peace and blessings be upon him!)

The traveller further said, addressing his own intellect: "Since these nine truths bear witness to the truthfulness of this being, he must be the source of glory of mankind and the source of honour for the world. If we therefore call him the Pride of the World and Glory of the Sons of Adam, it will be fitting. The fact that the awesome sovereignty of that decree of the Compassionate One, the Qur'an of Miraculous Exposition that he holds in his hand, has conquered half the world, together with his individual perfections and exalted virtues, shows that he is the most important personage in the world. The most important word concerning our Creator is that which he utters."

Now see: the foundation of the summons of this extraordinary being and the aim of all his life, based on the strength furnished by his hundreds of decisive and evident and manifest miracles, and the thousands of exalted, fundamental truths contained in his religion, was to prove and bear witness to the existence of the Necessary Existent, His Unity, attributes and Names, to affirm, proclaim and announce Him. He is therefore like a sun in the cosmos, the most brilliant proof of our Creator, this being whom we call the Beloved of God. There are three forms of great and infallible consensus each of which affirms, confirms, and puts its signature to the witness he bears.

The First: the unanimous affirmation made by that luminous assembly known and celebrated throughout the world as the Family of Muhammad (Peace and blessings be upon him) including thousands of poles and supreme saints of penetrating gaze and ability to perceive the Unseen, such Imam Ali (May God be pleased with him), who said, "Were the veil to be lifted, my certainty would not increase," and Abd al-Qadir al-Gilani, the Ghauth al-A'zam (May his mystery be sanctified), who saw the Supreme Throne and the awesome form of Israfil while yet on the earth.

The Second: the confirmation made with a strong faith that permitted men to sacrifice their lives and their property, their fathers and tribes, by the renowned assembly known as the Companions, who found themselves among a primitive people and in an unlettered environment, devoid of all social life and political thought, without any scripture and lost in the darkness of a period between prophets; and who in a very brief time came to be the masters, guides, and just rulers of the most civilized and politically and socially advanced peoples and states, and to rule the world from east to west in universally approved fashion.

The Third: the confirmation provided with unanimous and certain knowledge by that lofty group of punctilious and profound scholars of whom in each age thousands spring forth, who advance in wondrous fashion in every science and work in different fields.

Thus, the testimony brought by this being to the Divine Unity is not particular and individual, but general and universal and unshakeable. If all the demons that exist were to unite, they could not challenge it. Such was the conclusion reached by the traveller.

In reference to the lesson learned in the School of Light by that traveller from the world, that wayfarer in life, when he visited in his mind the blessed age of the Prophet, we said at the end of the Sixteenth Degree of the First Station:

There is no god but God, the Necessary Existent, the One, the Unique, the Necessity of Whose Existence in Unity is indicated by the Pride of the World and the Glory of the Sons of Adam, through the majesty of the sovereignty of his Qur'an, the splendour of the expanse of his religion, the multiplicity of his perfections, and the exaltedness of his characteristics, as confirmed even by the testimony of his enemies. He bears witness and brings proof through the strength of his hundreds of manifest and evident miracles, that both testify to truth and are themselves the object of true testimony; and through the strength of the thousands of luminous and conclusive truths contained in his religion, according to the consensus of all the possessors of light, the agreement of his illumined Companions, and the unanimity of the scholars of his community, the possessors of proofs and luminous insight.

The Enduring One, He is the Enduring One!

Said Nursi

* * *

A Passage Worthy of Being Written in Gold and Diamonds

Yes, it was mentioned above: small stones glorifying and praising God in his hand; and in accordance with the verse, **"When you threw, it was not you who threw,"** *earth and small stones in the same hand becoming missiles and projectiles against the enemy, routing them; and according to the verse,* **"And the moon split,"** *the moon splitting at a sign of the fingers of the same hand; and water flowing like a spring from the ten fingers of the same hand, and their providing a whole army with water; and the same hand being healing to the sick and wounded —all this shows what a wondrous miracle of Divine Power that blessed hand was. It was as if for friends its palm was a small place for the remembrance of God, for as soon as small stones entered it, they glorified God and recited His Names; while in the face of enemies, it was a small dominical ammunitions store which when pebbles and earth entered it, they were transformed into missiles and projectiles. And for the sick and the wounded it was a small pharmacy of the Most Merciful One which was a cure for whatever ills it touched. When it rose with Glory, it split the moon, giving it the shape of two bows, while when it was lowered with Beauty, it became like a spring of mercy with ten spigots pouring forth the water of Kawthar. If the single hand of such a one is the means of those wondrous miracles, is it not then to be understood clearly how acceptable he is before the Creator of the Universe, and how loyal he is to his cause, and how fortunate are those who declare their allegiance to him?*

Books from the Risale-i Nur, and about the Risale-i Nur and its author, published in English:

THE SUPREME SIGN❖ (Revised edn.)
RESURRECTION AND THE HEREAFTER❖
NATURE: CAUSE OR EFFECT?* (Revised edn.)
BELIEF AND MAN* (Revised edn.)
FRUITS FROM THE TREE OF LIGHT* (Revised edn.)
THE MIRACLES OF MUHAMMAD* (Revised edn.)
THE KEY TO BELIEF*
MAN AND THE UNIVERSE* (Revised edn.)
SINCERITY AND BROTHERHOOD*
THE TONGUES OF REALITY*
THE IMMORTALITY OF MAN'S SPIRIT*
A GUIDE FOR YOUTH*
THIRTY-THREE WINDOWS*
THE SHORT WORDS*
MESSAGE FOR THE SICK*
ON RAMADAN, THANKS, AND FRUGALITY*
THE DAMASCUS SERMON❖ (Revised and enlarged edn.)
THE HIGHWAY OF THE PRACTICES OF THE PROPHET❖
THE MIRACLES OF MUHAMMAD (With notes and sources)❖
DIVINE DETERMINING (FATE AND DESTINY) AND MAN'S WILL IN ISLAM❖
ISLAM, THE WEST, AND THE RISALE-I NUR*
THE WORDS (1st Volume of Risale-i Nur—Hard Cover, Indexes)
BEDIUZZAMAN SAID NURSI—LETTERS 1928-1932 (2nd Vol. of Risale-i Nur—Hard Cover, Indexes)
THE FLASHES COLLECTION (3rd. Vol. of Risale-i Nur—Hard Cover, Indexes)
THE RAYS COLLECTION (4th. Vol. of Risale-i Nur—Hard Cover, Indexes)
THE AUTHOR OF THE RISALE-I NUR, BEDIUZZAMAN SAID NURSI (Hard Cover, Illustrated, Indexes)
SYMPOSIUM, BEDIUZZAMAN SAID NURSI 2, 1993
SYMPOSIUM, BEDIUZZAMAN SAID NURSI 3, 1995 (2 vols.)
SYMPOSIUM, BEDIUZZAMAN SAID NURSI 4, 1998
PANEL, BEDIUZZAMAN SAID NURSI❖

* Pocket size (16.5x10.5cm.)
❖ Paperback (19.5x13.5cm.)